Contents

Introduction

12. Game Maker's Language (GML)..270

13. Triggers................................341

14. Particles..................................345

15. Registry and File Management.......368

16. Creating Action Libraries and Extension Packages using ExtMaker...377

17. Multiplayer Gaming...................404

18. Adjusting Views , Advanced Technique and Error Management....................418

19. 3D Game Programming...............429

20. Creating the Executable and Selling your Game..................................450

Introduction

Before beginning go through these questions/Answers as most of the FAQ's are included in it

1) What is a game?

A game is something which contains rules and nobody knows who would be the winner.

2) What is a computer game?

A computer game is a software which simultaneously deals with   graphics ,   sounds , animations , scores and players.

3) What is 2D and 3D.

'D' stands for dimension,   we all are aware that the world in which we live is 3 Dimensional. Creating 3D games is not possible (Using the present technology) the games which you feel are 3D are not 3 Dimensional in reality , The programmer just gives it 3 Dimensional effect , we would learn about giving 3D effect later in this book.

Points to remember

1)You should not expect creating your own 'Age of Empires' or 'Gta' These games are made by professional designers and sound artists . Creating games like these is not impossible but would require a lot of patience, resources and hardware.

2)Never use copyright protected resources   (sprites, sounds, backgrounds, tilesets, images etc)without permission

3)Never forget to provide documentation for your games

4)Give credits if you are using resources made by others.

5)Use tiles for better looks

6)All the speed's have common unit 'pixels per step'

Introduction to Game Maker 8

1)What is Game Maker ?
Game Maker is a software written by Mark Overmars, it offers essential tools for game development.

2)Reason for choosing Game Maker
Game Maker allows you to make games without writing a single line of program code. Game Maker is drag-n-drop based so it is possible to create games in just half an hour.

3)Where will I find Game Maker?
Game Maker is available on the Internet check the website 'http://www.yoyogames.com' and download the latest version
(This book uses Game Maker 8 so it is recommended to download this version , this book can also be used for later versions too as   majority of the functions remain the same ,   just the User Interface may change.)

4)Cost Information
The following table will give you detailed information about the types of Game Maker and the limitations of functionality.

Lite	Pro
1)Free of cost.	1)20 Euros or US $ 25 (Subject to change)
2)Limited in functionality	2)Not limited in functionality
3)Logo shown	3)Doesn't show logos
4)Shows pop-ups	4)Doesn't show pop-ups
5)Can be used for commercial purposes	5)Can be used for commercial purposes

Chapter 1 Installing Game Maker .

Before installing don't forget to check whether your system meets the minimum system requirements as listed below;

1)OS:- Windows 2000 or later.
(Game Maker is even available for Apple MAC. However, In this version we are going to use Game Maker which is compatible with   Microsoft Windows)

2)Graphics Card:- At least 32 mega bytes of memory , Compatible with DirectX 8.0

3)Sound Card:-Compatible with DirectX 8.0

4)Physical Memory(RAM):- 128 mb or more
*   (Depending on Operating System)*

5)DirectX 8.0 or later

Note:-If DirectX is not installed ,   download and install it from Microsoft's website

'http://www.microsoft.com/windows/directx/'

Just double click on the gamemaker80.exe file

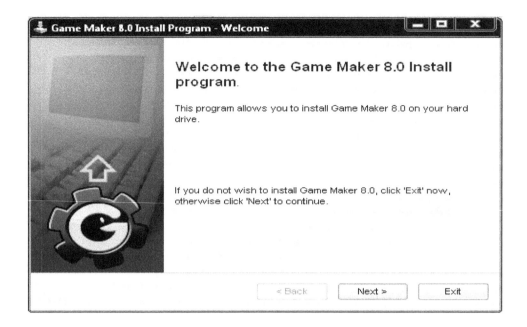

(Fig 000)

This is the starting window(Fig000) click on 'Next >' button.
The second window would appear(Fig001).

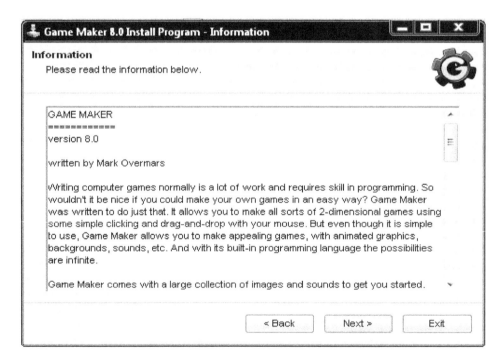

(Fig 001)
The second window shows general information again press 'Next >'

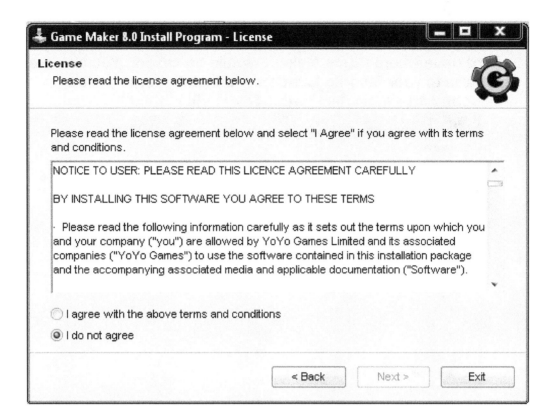

(Fig002)

Here if you observe the 'Next >' button is disabled. Check the "I agree" radio button the next button would be enabled press it.

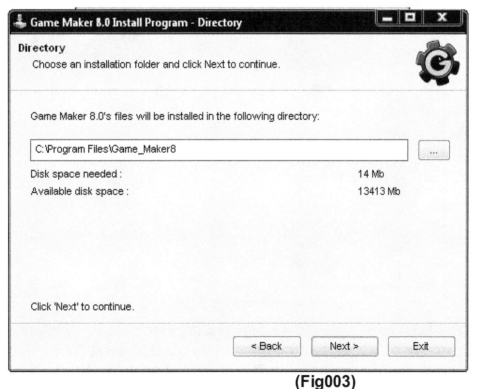

(Fig003)

Here you have to select the destination folder the default folder is 'C:\ProgramFiles\Game_Maker8' these is the location on your hard drive where Game Maker 8 would be saved . You can even browse to your favorite location and install there ,   After selecting a suitable destination folder click 'Next >'

(Fig004)

Fig004 shows the confirmation window if you want to change the path go back and change it else press 'Next >'

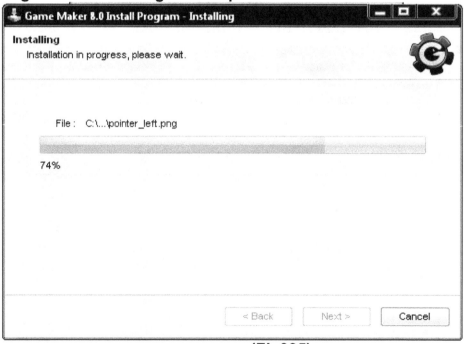

(Fig005)

The final screen would appear like (Fig006)
You can view the readme file . If you want to start Game maker.
Check the ' Launch Game Maker 8.0 ' checkbox . Press 'Exit'.

The figure shown abelow displays the simple mode of Game Maker,

the list to the extreme left is known as the resource list (all the objects , sounds , backgrounds are opened by double clicking(left mouse button) on this list , If your internet connection is active Game Maker communicates to their server and news appears on the screen , the news contains information about updates, competitions etc . The file menu contains 5 items

1)File
2)Edit
3)Resources
4)Window
5)Help.
Toolbox contains various tools for compiling , uploading etc , Every software has an about window , the about window gives certain info about copyright , ownership etc , About window of Game Maker is shown besides.

The PRO version is good to use , it is instantly updated the moment you purchase it from the internet , it unlocks many features like the Game Maker logo would not appear , you can even extend the functionality of your games by using DLL'S etc , the screen shot provided on the previous page was taken before updating to the PRO version

Before proceeding let us learn about the different elements of a window

Buttons are commonly used controls in Programming (Buttons cannot be used in console applications , Buttons generated by Game Maker in your game may appear different than the one shown above , the code associating the button is executed when the user presses the button.

The button shown above is disabled which means that the button cannot be pressed unless it is enabled , such types of buttons are used in setup programs , the button for proceeding is not enabled unless the user accepts the conditions regarding usage.

☐ CheckBox1

The element shown above is known as a checkbox , the code associated with a checkbox is executed when the user checks the checkbox (clicks the box) a checked box looks like the one shown below.

☑ CheckBox1

A radio button is similar to a Checkbox the only difference being instead of the box there is a circle,   Suppose there are 3 checkboxes you can check all of them but if there are 3 radio buttons you cannot check them all you must select one out of them .

Note :- There must at least be two radio buttons .

○ RadioButton2   ◉ RadioButton1

unchecked
checked

Next comes the progress bar ,   the progress bar is a very important tool as it shows the user that it's still processing otherwise one may feel that the program has frozen.

Note :- Progress bar shows the progress in percentage (0 to 100)

Progress bar (When Percentage = 0)

Progress bar (When Percentage = 25)

Progress bar (When Percentage = 50)

Progress bar (When Percentage = 75)

Progress bar (When Percentage = 100)

Chapter 2 Getting Started

Let us learn some terms which are frequently used in Game Maker.

1)<u>Sprites:-</u> Sprites are files containing pictures, characters etc.

2)<u>Sounds:-</u> Beeps and music files required by your game.

3)<u>Backgrounds:-</u> These are files which can be set as backgrounds(They must contain pictures only)

4)<u>Scripts:-</u> These are files which contain program code.(They are optional)

5)<u>Fonts:-</u> Fonts are files which contain information about how the letters would look on the screen.

6)<u>Timelines:-</u> Timeline help your game to perform actions after specific interval of time

7)<u>Objects:-</u> Object contain information about events they are very important part of a game . It is not possible to make a game in game maker without them

8)<u>Rooms:-</u> Rooms in other words mean levels.

9)<u>Game Information:-</u> It is the documentation which you provide for your games.

10)<u>Global Game Settings:-</u> They are the most important settings for your games

these settings deal with save/load options , screen-modes(Full screen or windowed), resolution, copyright, error handling etc

11)<u>Extension Packages:-</u> These are used to add more functionality to your games (They can only be used in the PRO edition only

12)<u>Paths:-</u> Paths contain information about the movement of an object in a room.

Note:- Game Maker comes preloaded with sprites, sounds, backgrounds which you can use royalty free in your games.

File Extensions

Maximum files contain extensions (example .doc, .xls, .odt etc). Extensions are used for recognizing type of file and the pattern in which it is coded. When you click on a file the file is opened by some software . '.exe', '.com', '.bat' extensions mean that they are software themselves . A text file cannot be opened by MS Paint in the same way a Picture file cannot be opened by a text editor . Windows knows which file should be opened by which software by their extensions . In same cases there are even files which contain no extension , some even contain more than one extensions . Game Maker has it's own set of extensions , to master Game Maker it is very important to know these extensions. Some extensions are used only by Game

Maker while others are used even by software other than Game maker

The following is a list of extensions used by Game Maker

Extension	Description
.gmk	Game Maker file
.gmspr	Game Maker sprite files
.wav	Sound files
.gmbck	Background files
.txt	Text Files (For scripts)
.rtf	Rich Text (For Game information)

Note:- 1).wav, .txt and .rtf extensions are even used by softwares other than Game maker. Script files and Game information files can be edited even by Wordpad but it is not recommended to do so.
2).gmk may differ depending on the version of Game Maker

Tip:- Game Maker 6 uses .gm6 extension

Game maker can be run in two modes
1)Simple
2)Advanced

Presently, it is recommended to use simple mode. One can use the advanced mode later.

Note:- 1)'.lib' files contain intermediate code .Don't move or modify these files as these files seriously affect the performance of Game Maker . The end user will not require these files.

Tip:- There are many companies all over the world for whom gaming is a serious business . Usually there are two teams the "Art team" and the "Technical team" The art team takes care of the characters maps, backgrounds, textures etc whereas the technical team is responsible for coding everything , they have to take care of resolution, platform for the game (PC , Xbox , Play station, PSP, mobiles etc), they even decide about downloading, installation etc.

Game development takes place in three stages

1)Alpha
2)Beta
3)Testing

When the coding(coding is optional when using game maker) is done and all the characters and maps are ready we get the alpha build of the games(Sounds are not integrated in the alpha build). The alpha build is sent to the clients . According to the feedback by the clients necessary changes are made , sounds are added and we get the beta build of the game.

Testing is the final and the most important stage in game development.
Testing should never be done by a single person,   at least four to five people must test a single game and on different computers. This is done to avoid any software and compatibility issues with different computer systems.

Now you are ready to start your first game,   before that it is very important to be clear with the central idea of your game . As this is our first game let's write down a very simple and basic central idea .Let us name our game as 'Space'
Here is the central idea of our game.

Space is a very basic entry level game ,   the player controls a spacecraft which has to fight with UFO's for survival. The difficulty in this game remains the same. The more you destroy the more you score is the basic principal of this game. We can add much more to it but as this is the first game I am limiting myself to this aspect only ,   in the succeeding chapters we would go on increasing the features.

After the central idea is written down it is recommended to write the Game Design Document (Hereafter Game Design document would be referred as GDD)
Here is the GDD for our game

Name

The name of our game is 'Space'

Tip :- It is very important to select a unique name for your game , you cannot use a copyright protected name.

Objects

Space will have 22 objects . Of these 22 objects 14 are just for decorating the room with no other functionality ,   however , even they are important as they provide the aesthetics.

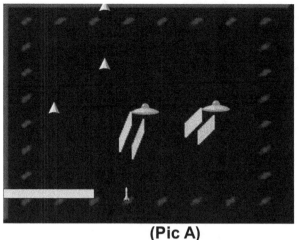

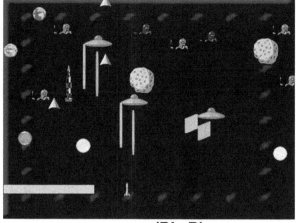

(Pic A)   (Pic B)

Compare 'Pic A' and 'Pic B' don't you feel 'Pic B' is better ?It is because
In 'Pic B' there are aliens,   meteorites,   rocket,   planets using these objects you get a better effect at the same time you create an impression on the one playing the game but one most not forget that too many objects spoil the room.

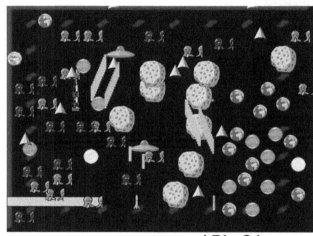

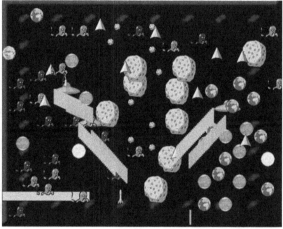

(Pic C)   (Pic D)

Just compare 'Pic C' or 'Pic D' with 'Pic B'.'Pic C' and 'Pic D' contain many objects ,   the player may get confused. In a game each and every thing must be balanced .The player would control the rocket and his goal is to shoot the UFO's. The triangle rockets cannot be fired we have to dodge them.

UFO   Rocket   Triangle
(These files are present in the Game Maker's sprite directory)

You (Player) would fire red and yellow laser's whereas the UFO's would fire green and blue laser's . Out of 22 objects 14 would be used for mere decoration this means that 8 objects would actually work. Out of these 8 object one would work in the background whereas others would really work. This means that the object is without any sprite. Such an object is used for adding background music. Background music is a very important element of a game. You can add background music even by the UFO object or even by the Triangle object , but it is not at all recommended because if such an object is eliminated the background music will stop. The balance seven objects are as follows

Object	Function
1)Space	The main spacecraft which you would control.
2)UFO	The spacecraft's which are to eliminated for gaining points
3)Triangle	These are obstacles , they simply reduce health
4)Laser red	Fired by the spacecraft for eliminating UFO's
5)Laser yellow	Fired by the spacecraft for eliminating UFO's
6)Laser blue	Fired by the UFO's for eliminating spacecraft
7)Laser green	Fired by the UFO's for eliminating spacecraft

Sounds

In this version we would use only 2 sounds
1)Background music
2)Explosion

Controls

The player can move the spacecraft by the arrow keys and fire by using the space bar.

Levels

In this version we would use only 1 level

After the GDD is written down it is recommended to write down the Technical design document (Hereafter Technical Design document would be referred as TDD)

Note:- In the TDD platform always remains Microsoft Windows as we will program games for windows only.

Here is the TDD for our game
Platform
Windows XP or later

Resolution
1600x1200

Screensavers and power options
Disabled

Note:-This was very basic TDD, complicated TDD's contain file handling,   save load options, screenshot settings, complicated error handlers, game process information etc.

2)Some game developers merge GDD and TDD and refer it as Design document.
You can even follow them there is absolutely no compulsion, There are more ways of representing information , they are explained in the chapter no 11. You can even make games without design documents but it is not recommended.
3)If you want to download the source file of this game you may mail me as n160165@yahoo.com
4)Information about controls can be entered in any of the Design Documents
          Now you are ready to start with your first game. So execute game maker

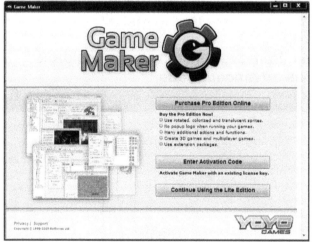

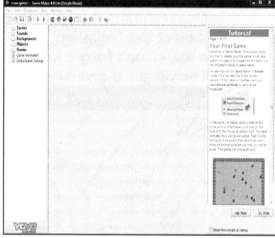

(Fig 007)   (Fig008)

If you are using the Lite edition   the window showed in (fig 007) would appear then a   window would ask whether you want to start with simple or advanced mode ,   choose simple mode we would use advanced mode later in this book.

Adding Sprites

As mentioned earlier sprites are files containing pictures, characters etc. To add sprites perform the following task
1)From the resources menu select 'Create Sprite'
 A window would appear as shown in (Fig 009)

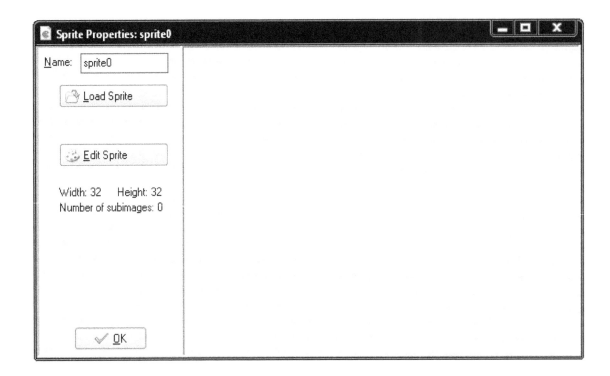

(Fig 009 , Simple Mode)

Then browse to the folder 'Game Maker/Sprites/Space' (Game Maker means the path where your game maker is installed) .Select the file 'alien_green_strip8'.
Note:- Don't forget to check the 'Remove Background' checkbox.
The diagram given below shows advanced mode.

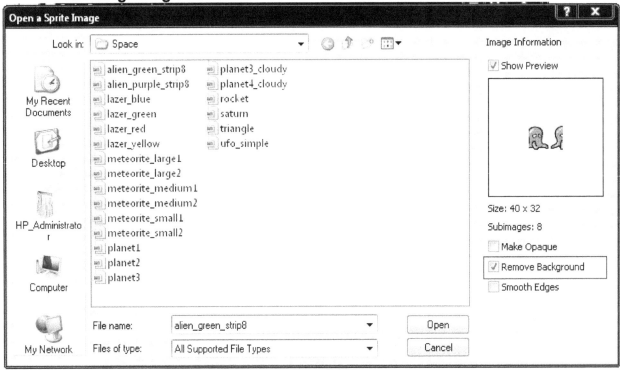

(Fig 010)

Click on open. Game Maker will load your sprite. Let the subimage be zero

Show:　0

(Fig 011)

If you are confused between images and subimages   see the picture given below , it has 8 subimages , the whole strip is an image whereas the different pictures depicting various action are the subimages.

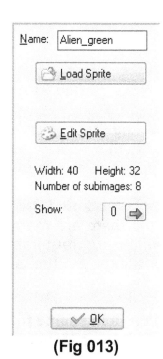

(Fig 012)

Note:- 0 stands for the first image, 1 stands for the second image and so on.
Name the sprite 'Alien_green'

Name: Alien_green

Load Sprite

Edit Sprite

Width: 40   Height: 32
Number of subimages: 8

Show: 0

OK

(Fig 013)

Click Ok . Using the some procedure load the other sprites(excluding the lazer sprites) and name them according to the name of the file. After loading all the sprites load the 'lazer_blue' sprite.

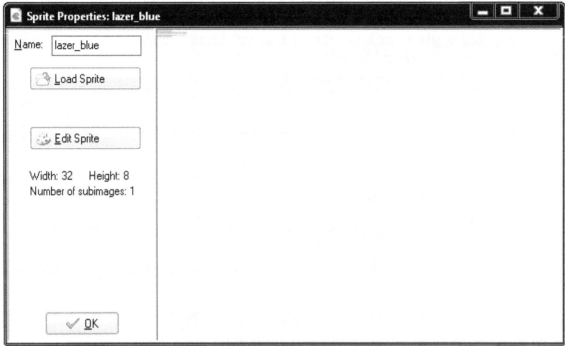

(Fig 014)

The reason for loading this particular sprite after the others is that we have to modify this sprite a bit. Press 'Edit Sprite' button .A window would appear as shown in Fig 015.

The sprite editing mentioned here is just basic , editing sprites is a vast topic there are many effects. The sprite editing in this example fulfills our requirements for only this game , you can do many things by the settings provided by Game Maker.

Tip :- The image editor is the same for Simple Mode as well as the Advanced mode of Game Maker.

Tip:- If the sprite files are stored in the format .bmp , .tiff , .png format they can be easily edited using third party tools like Gimp (Gimp can be installed using the disc supplied with this book)

(Fig 015)

Edit the sprite
1)From the Transform menu select 'Rotate'
2)Press 90 degrees or 270 degrees
3)Press OK

(Initial Image)   (Edited image)

Note:- In this case 90 or 270 degrees , clockwise or anti-clockwise doesn't make any difference , but it is not applicable to all the sprites.

Editing sprite is not over we have to resize the canvas or the sprite would appear like (Fig 016)

(Fig 016)

The reason being the canvas doesn't adapt itself to the changes made to the sprite ,   so we have to instruct Game Maker .To instruct Game Maker perform the following task
1)From the Transform menu select 'Resize Canvas'
2)Enter different values and select the appropriate one (The

**edited sprite should
look similar to the one given below)**

Game Maker would prompt a message box for confirmation press 'Yes'. Load the other lazer sprites and edit them using the same procedure mentioned above.

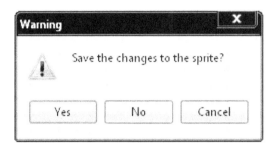

Adding Sounds

Sounds are the second basic elements of a game .Would you like to watch a film without sounds ?,   you would obviously not. Same principle applies to computer games ,   no one would love playing a game without sounds. It doesn't   matter whether your game is entry level or advanced . Sounds are a must.

Follow the given procedure to add sounds
1)From the Resources menu select 'Create Sound'

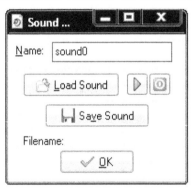

(Fig 017)

Press 'Load Sound'.Using the browse window locate the folder where sounds are saved. Load the music.midi file located in the folder named 'Tutorial1'. Rename the sound as 'back_music' . Note:- If you want to listen to the sound file press the play button

(Fig 018 Play button)

Using the same procedure load the file explosion.wav which is located in the same folder ('Tutorial1') and name the sound as 'Explosion'

Note:- Explosion would be played when a lazer would collide with the UFO
2)back_music would be played in the background

We still require a sound file which would be played when the rocket fires lazers. As mentioned earlier everything must be balanced in a game (Too many sounds would create the same problem as too many objects)
So Let us load the last sound file
1)Load the sound lazergun1 located in the sounds folder.
2)Name the file lazergun

Adding Background

We have successfully loaded the required sound files , now let us load backgrounds.(This is a basic game so here we would use only one background).To add a background select 'Create Background' from the 'Resources' menu.

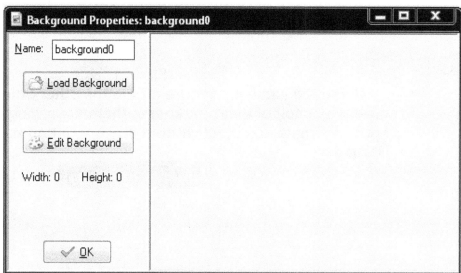

(Fig 019)

2)Set the name property to 'space'
3)Press 'Load Background'
4)Using the browse window browse to the 'backgrounds' folder of your game   maker installation and choose 'stars'
Note:- Addon(provided on the disc)must be installed.

Adding Objects

1)From the 'Resources' menu select 'Create Object'

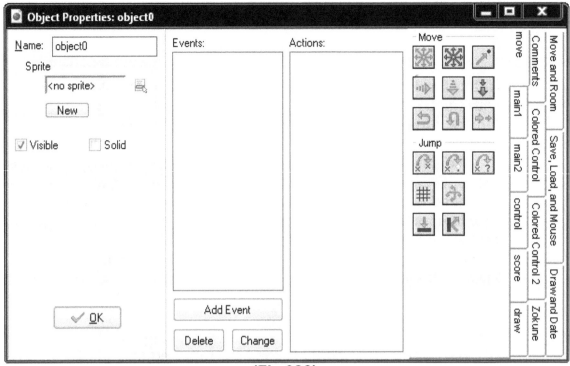
(Fig 020)

2)Set the name property to alien_green
3)Set the sprite property to alien_green

(Fig 021)

Using the same procedure create the other objects , add sprites to each of them , rename them according to their sprites. Create an object without any sprite and name it 'Manager'

(Fig 022)

Creating objects without any events is like a bird without wings. Events are the most essential parts of an object , they are the ones who make game maker understand the functions(how the object moves , what should be the result if it collides with other object, scoring etc) of an object in a game . It is possible to create objects without any event , the objects which are used just for decoration will not have even a single event , every event has a corresponding action , the action is executed when that particular event takes place.

Events

There are various types of available events in Game Maker.

(Fig 023)

Let's study each of them in detail

1)Create :- The actions associated with this event are executed just after the object is created.

2)Destroy :- The actions associated with this event are executed just after the object is destroyed.(Actually the associated actions are executed just before the object is destroyed.)

3)Alarm:- The actions associated with this event are executed just after the specified interval of time is elapsed.

4)Step:- This event is of 3 types
   a)Step
   b)Begin step
   c)End step

a)Step :- This event occurs at each and every step of the game. This event is used for action which should occur repeatedly. In this game we would use this event for the UFO's , the UFO's would fire using this event

b)Begin step :- This event occurs at the beginning of every step.

c)End step :- This event occurs at the end of each step.

Note:-The 'Begin' and the 'End' step events are rarely used whereas the 'Step' event is frequently used.

5)Collision :- The actions associated with this event are executed after there is a collision(the sprites come in contact with each other) between instances of two objects.

Note:- Collision can never take place even if one of the object is without sprite.

The solid property plays a very important role here. Game maker also detects secondary collisions , secondary collision means that object collide repeatedly till they completely pass through each other , this would not happen if any one of them or both of them are solid. If actions are not specified nothing happens even if the one of them or both of them are solid. Suppose there is a collision between a green ball and a red ball where the green ball goes and collides with the red ball , the actions associated with the green ball are executed before the actions associated with the red ball and vice versa (The solid property does not come into picture here)

6)Keyboard :- The actions associated with this event are executed just after the specified key is pressed on the keyboard.

7)Mouse :- The actions associated with this event are executed just after the specified key is pressed on the mouse. There are even more complicated events associated with mouse. There are many possibilities , you can program the actions to be executed when a specific key is pressed or released , this event can also be used for the scroll function.
Note:- Mouse event can also be used to deal with 2 joysticks.

8)Other :- The other event is explained using the table provided below

Event	Description
1)Outside room	Occurs when the instance is outside the room.(It will not occur if the instance is partially outside.)
2)Intersect boundary	Occurs when the object is partially out side the room.
3)Views	There are a number of events which can be used if you are using views in your game.
4)Game start	This event happens for all the object in the game, this event can be used for adding background music to our games.(Though it happens to all the instances only one instance defines this event)
5)Game end	This event is same as the one mentioned above , the only difference is that this event takes place at the end.

6)Room start	This event happens for all the instances in a room just after all the instances are created in the room.
7)Room end	This event happens to all the existing events when the room ends.
8)No more lives	This event is triggered when the number of lives becomes <= 0
9)No more health	This event is triggered when the health becomes <= 0
10)Animation ends	An animation is a set of pictures (coupled with sound) which are imaged one after the other in a series. The sprite shown in Fig 012 can be called as an animation, the event occurs after the last sprite is shown. Note:- It is not recommended to use this event for a sprite (like the rocket sprite)
11)End of path	This event takes place when the instance of an object follows a particular path and the end of that path has been reached. Note:- This event can be used for moving an object to a suitable position on the screen or to destroy it after the path is over.
12)Close button	This event occurs when the close button of the window is pressed. Note:-This event can only occur if the option of treating the close button as escape key is disabled.
13)User defined	There are 16 such events but to use them you must possess knowledge about the GML language. (GML is explained in the succeeding chapters.

9)Draw :- Game maker is programmed in such a way that each and every instance of a sprite is drawn at each step , the associated actions are executed before the sprite is drawn , this event can also be used for specifying parameters for your sprites.

Usage

a)Health can be drawn using this event
b)Lives can be drawn using this event
c)Script or a piece of code which deals with drawing arrow, rectangles etc can be executed

10)Key Press :- This event takes place when a specific key is

pressed

Note:- 1)The time period for which the key is pressed doesn't matter.

2)The action will occur just after the key is pressed.

11)Key Release :- This event occurs when a particular key is released.

Note:- Releasing the key means that the event will not occur after the key is pressed , This event can be used instead of Key Press event but it is not recommended ,   because the action will not be executed until the key is released , this is a common mistake. Therefore both   these events should be properly used .
2)This event is only for keys on the keyboard ,   this event can not be used for mouse keys or joystick keys.
For usage of this event go through the examples given below.

Usage

a)Racing games can be made using this event ,   you can use this event to stop a moving car if the arrow key is released.
b)Same way in a platform game the character can be stopped if an arrow key is released.
c)A gunman may stop firing if space bar(you can replace space bar with any other key) is released

12)Triggers :- Triggers are explained in detail in the 13th chapter , they are available only in the pro edition of Game Maker

There is a comparison given below between the event window of the Lite and the Pro edition respectively

(Lite)

(Pro)

Logic should be used everywhere in the field of programming ,   there are 2 or 3 events which are very similar to each other for Example a) Keyboard , b)Key Press , c)Key Release , you must decide which one is the suitable for your needs and think over it twice as a small bug can eventually ruin your enter game.Tracing the root cause of the problem is very difficult, irritating as well as time consuming so it is recommended to make a decision having valid logical reasoning.

The events are useless unless actions are associated with them, so let us learn the basic actions which are included in Game Maker.(The functionality of Game Maker can be increased by adding extra actions , you can even create them , they are taught in detail in the succeeding chapter's , in this chapter we would learn the utility of the basic ones).

Game Maker has organized all the actions under seven tabs. To add actions just drag them Actions field , to know the name of any action just hover your mouse on the icon.
a)Move
b)Main1
c)Main2
d)Control
e)Score
f)Extra
g)Draw

For your easy understanding refer the Flowchart form.

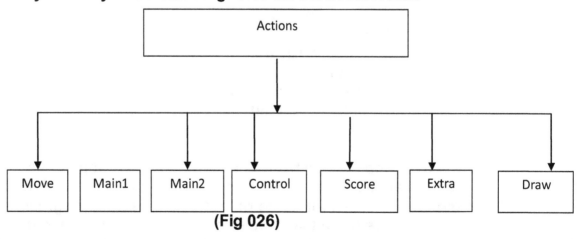

(Fig 026)

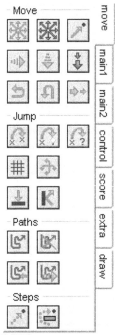

(Fig 027)

The move tab is divided unevenly in 4 parts let's study them briefly

1. Move
2. Jump
3. Paths
4. Steps

Tip:- a) Contains 9 actions , for a short description about each action just hover your mouse over the icon of the action.
b) You can use the delete button to delete an action but remember Game Maker would not prompt for confirmation.

1)Move :- Move part consists of 9 actions.

    a. Move fixed
    b. Move free
    c. Move towards
    d. Speed horizontal
    e. Speed vertical
    f. Set gravity
    g. Reverse horizontal
    h. Reverse vertical
    i. Set Friction

a)Move fixed :- Move fixed is used to move an object in a particular direction , There are overall 9 direction , The middle direction indicates that the object would stop moving. You can even choose more than one direction , in such a case the direction of the object would be selected randomly. You can even make other objects to move in a direction (The other object would be moved in there is an collision event) , you can even specify a particular object but all the instances of that object would move in that same direction.

Note:- 1)There is no use if the speed is zero.
2)If the speed is negative , the instance would move in the opposite direction
You may be wondering about the reason for including the middle direction, the reason is quite simple you can use it as brakes for stopping a car or an object which is in motion.
3)The relative property plays a very important role.
If relatively is not set then the new speed would be the value you enter and if relatively is checked then the new speed would be old speed + the new value.
4)You just have to enter values(numbers) in the text_boxes entering characters
(except the commands) and symbols would lead to errors

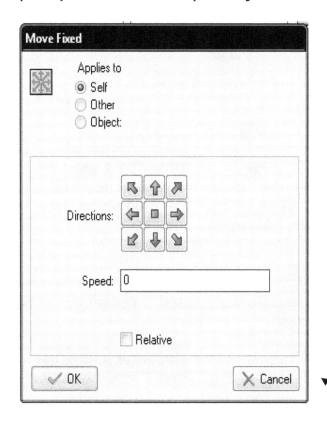

(Fig 028)

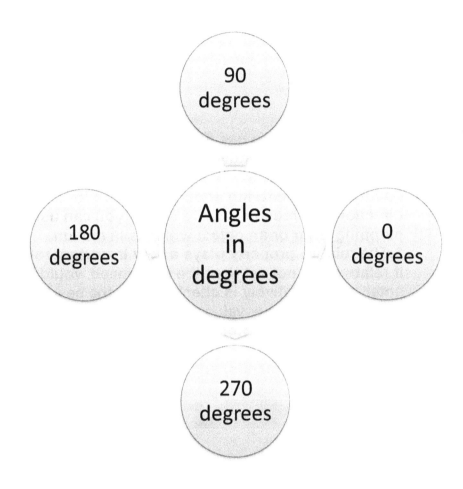

(Fig 029)

b)The move free action is same as the move fixed action the only difference being that you don't choose any direction but you set the value for direction , Game Maker can only understand the values entered in degrees.(0 degrees and 360 degrees mean the same)The Move random window would appear like
(Fig 030)

Note :- Game maker doesn't accept values in radians or any other units except degrees.

2)Suppose you enter 90 degrees but if you enter a negative speed the instance would travel 270 degrees to his position.

3) Game Maker doesn't understand whether your character is facing to the left or to the right.

4) If for example you specify 45 degrees, your instance would move in a direction between 0 and 90.

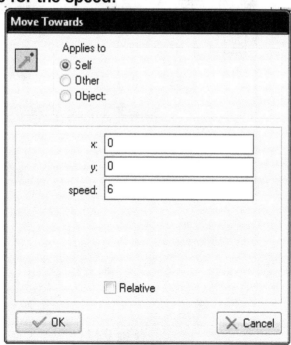

(Fig 030)

c)The move towards action is another type of movement , For example you can use this action for missiles to move towards the enemy by selecting the co-ordinates as enemy.x and enemy.y respectively. In this case relative means the relative direction it is not applicable for the speed.

(Fig 031)

Note:-There are 2 types of speeds namely a)Horizontal, b)Vertical
It is important to learn the sign conventions used by Game Maker so refer the (Fig 032) given below.

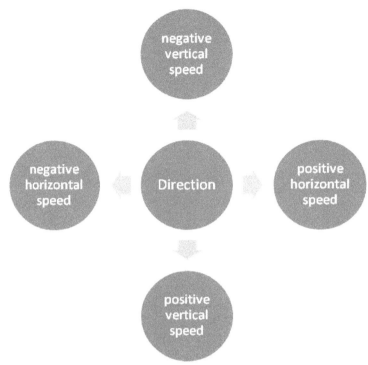

(Fig 032)

d)Speed Horizontal :- Let us you set the horizontal speed of an object.

(Fig 031)

e)Speed Vertical :- Let us you set the vertical speed of an object.

Speed Vertical

Applies to
- ⦿ Self
- ○ Other
- ○ Object:

vert. speed: [   ]

☐ Relative

✓ OK   ✗ Cancel

(Fig 032)

Note:-These speeds apply to all the instances of that particular object.

2)These speeds should not be used if you want your object to move randomly.

(If you want to set direction randomly use Move Fixed and select the directions of your wish)

3)These speeds are not substitutes for the Move Fixed   or the Move Free actions each one has it's own pros and cons.

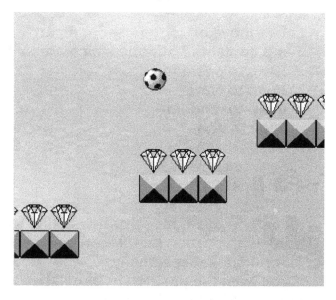

(Fig 033)

f)Set Gravity :- This action can be used in platform games.

In the picture (Fig 033)   It can be clearly seen that the ball

is in the air.
This is a right place for using the Gravity action for information about directions refer (Fig 028) . Relatively is used for speed. Game Maker allows to set Gravity in any angle you desire.

But remember Gravity would act upon the object even if the user tries to change the direction. If you set the gravity to negative you would be dragged in the opposite direction.

So it's better to use the right direction and a positive speed because if you open your save file after a month or two even you may get confused.

g)Reverse Horizontal :- With this action the horizontal motion of an instance is changed.(This action can be used for an object which collides with another vertical object)

h)Reverse Vertical :- With this action the vertical motion of an instance is changed.(This action can be used for an object which collides with another   horizontal object)

I)Set Friction :- This action can be used for reducing the speed of an object ,   in each step the amount of friction is subtracted from the speed
Note:- You can specify negative value for Friction ,   this would increase the speed of an instance.

Let us move on to the   second part 'Jump'
Jump contains 7 actions which are as follows
a)Jump to position
b)Jump to start
c)Jump to random
d)Align to grid
e)Wrap screen
f)Move to contact
g)Bounce

a)Jump to position :- Use this action to place the instance on a particular location on the screen by specifying the 'x' and the 'y' co-ordinates respectively.
If you want the position to be relative to the current position check the 'Relative' checkbox ,   even this action allows you to set the application of this property for the current instance or any other instance.

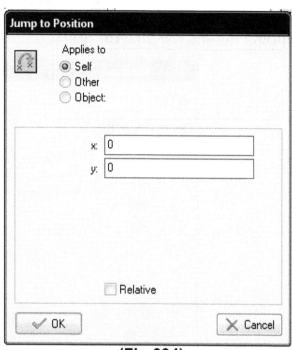

(Fig 034)

b) Jump to start :- This action takes the instance back to the place where it was created.(This event can be used when an object is destroyed. Reduce one life and then use this action)

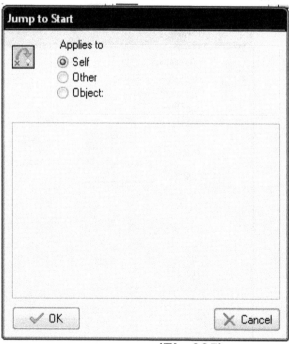

(Fig 035)

As you can see in fig 035 , there are very few parameters for this action.

c)Jump to Random :- Using this action you can make your instance to randomly appear in any part of the room (level) , you can even specify snapping (horizontally, vertically or both) Note:-Snapping means the size for grids.

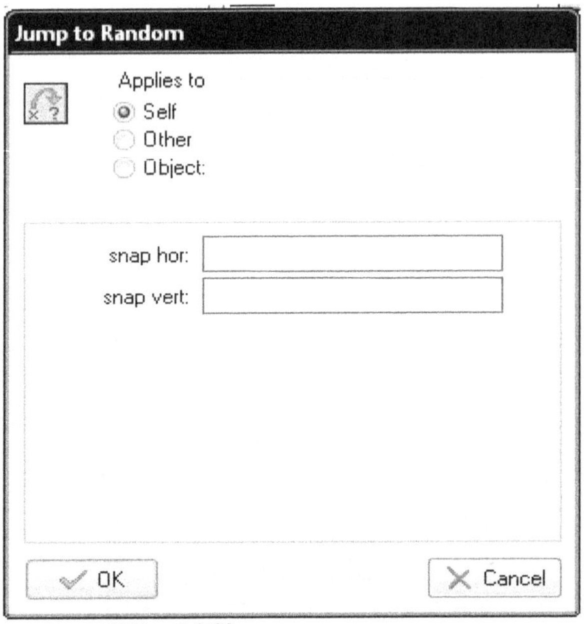

(Fig 036)

d)Align to Grid :- This action is used for aligning the object with the grid , this action too allows you to enter the snapping values , this action is used to make sure that the action stays on the boundaries of the GRID

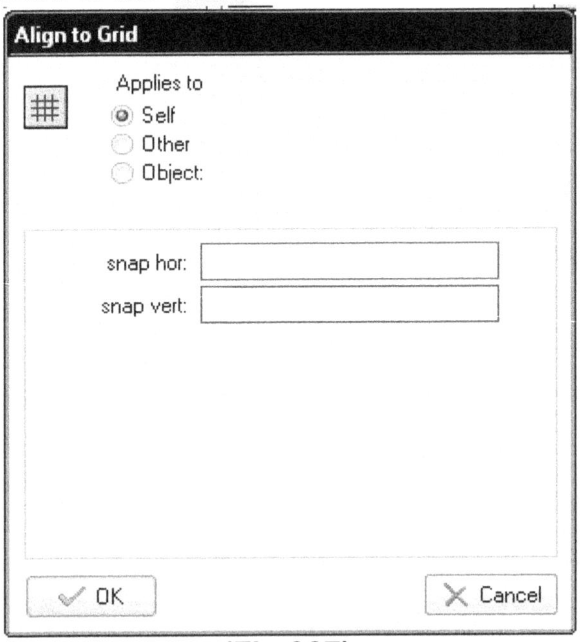

(Fig 037)

e)Wrap Screen :- This action can be used to make an instance reappear on the other side of the room when it leaves the first side , follow the given example , view the pictures given below.

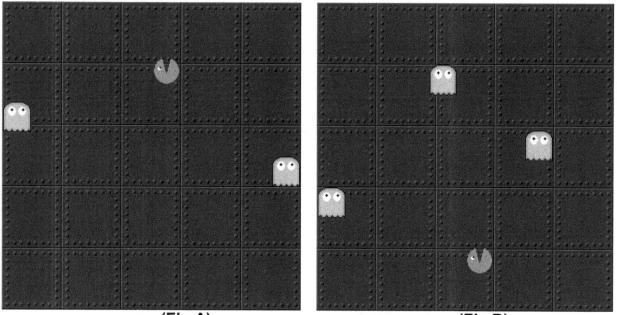

(Fig A)   (Fig B)

In the (Fig A) the pac man would just go out of the room but if the Wrap Screen action is used it would return from the other side as shown if (Fig B).
You can even choose a direction ,   the available directions are
a)Horizontal
b)Vertical
c)Both

f)Move to contact :-With this action you can move the instance in any way(direction) till the contact gets over or any other object(example wall) is obstructing it's path. You can even specify the maximal distance and the direction in which the instance must follow the contact ,   there is one more option available to consider solid objects or not.

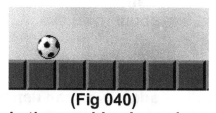
(Fig 040)

(Fig 041)

In the graphic given above (Fig 040) it can be clearly seen that the ball is following the road but if there is a collision (Fig 041) the ball (it can be any other object moving to contact) stops it's path.

g)Bounce :- The bounce action can be used in games like 'pinball' where the ball has to bounce back if collision takes place. If precisely is set false only the horizontal and vertical walls are taken into consideration but if precisely is set true the instance will bounce back even after a collision with a curved or an unevenly shaped object ,   you can even specify whether the instance should bounce back only against solid objects or against all objects.

Bounce

Applies to
- ⦿ Self
- ◯ Other
- ◯ Object:

precise: | not precisely |
against: | solid objects |

✓ OK   ✕ Cancel

(Fig 042)

The third type of part deals only with paths.
4 types of actions are available
a)Set path
b)End path
c)Path position
d)Path speed

Let us understand each of them in detail
a)Set path :- Path contains information about the movement of
an instance in a room ,   some feel that set path means that they
can create path (define movement) using this action but those
who feel so are thinking on the wrong line. This action can only
be used for path's which are actually made ,   you can define
directions but we will learn more about it in Chapter 8 .

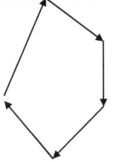

The figure given besides is a sample path

(Fig 043)

You cannot enter anything using your keyboard in the field besides path , for specifying the path you have to press the adjoining button. A list of available paths would appear(Fig 044).

(Fig 044)

The move, collide, escape are just examples , these names depend upon the you,
you can give any name of your desire but all the paths must have an unique name .

b)End Path :- The end path action is used to stop the instance from following a predefined path.(Fig 045)

c)Path position:- Path position is used to place the instance on a specified position on a path 0 indicates stating point whereas 1

indicates the ending point.(Fig 046)

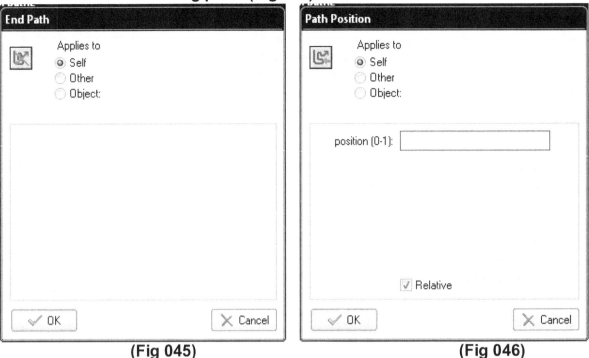

(Fig 045)   (Fig 046)

d)Path speed:- This action would just change the speed of the
instance following a path nothing else.(Fig 048)

(Fig 048)

d)Step:- Contains 2 actions
1)Step towards
2)Step avoiding

1)Step towards :- Would perform a step towards the position you
specify.
(Fig 049)

2)Step avoiding :- Performs a step towards a position(which you specify) avoiding solid instances or all instances.(Fig 050)

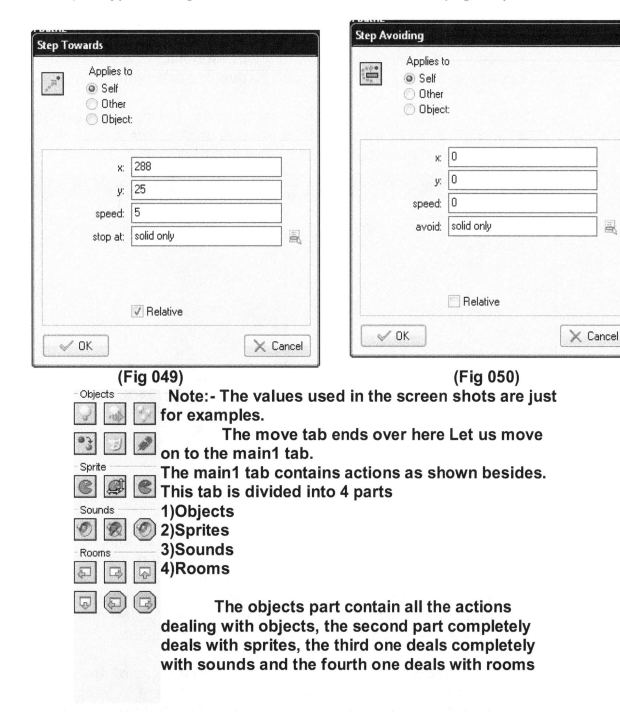

(Fig 049)   **(Fig 050)**

Note:- The values used in the screen shots are just for examples.

The move tab ends over here Let us move on to the main1 tab.

The main1 tab contains actions as shown besides. This tab is divided into 4 parts

1)Objects
2)Sprites
3)Sounds
4)Rooms

The objects part contain all the actions dealing with objects, the second part completely deals with sprites, the third one deals completely with sounds and the fourth one deals with rooms

Let us now gain some more knowledge about the objects part.

The objects part contains 6 actions , they are as follows
a)Create instance
b)Create moving
c)Create random
d)Change instance
e)Destroy instance
f)destroy at position

a)Create instance:- Creates instance of an object at a specified location in a room which may be relative or absolute(Fig 051)

b)Create moving:- Creates an instance of an object at a specified location in a room which may be relative or absolute and set's it in motion in a specified direction and speed.(Fig 052)

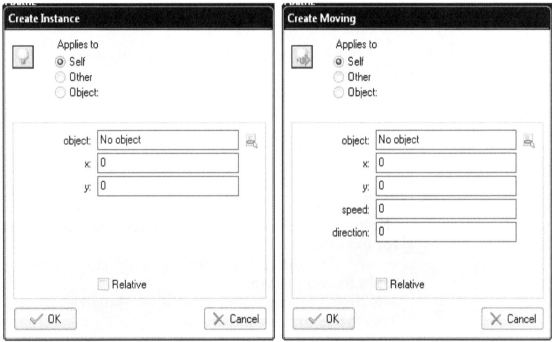

(Fig 051)   (Fig 052)

In the first field you have to select any of the available objects by pressing the adjoining button ,   in the remaining two you have to enter the position for your instance ,   the create moving action contains two more parameters speed and direction ,   Relative stands only for the position ,   the relatively property would not affect the speed and the direction.

c)Create random:- Create random creates instances of any one out of the four specified. Suppose if you don't want to specify four object then you can specify less than four but there is no point in specifying only one object , at least two should be used but you cannot specify more than four at the same time.
Tip:- Suppose you want to specify two objects but you want the probability of the first one to be more than the second you may enter the first object in more   than one field and the second only in one field ,   doing so would increase the chances of the first one (This is practically possible).

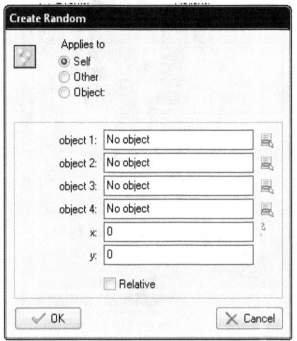

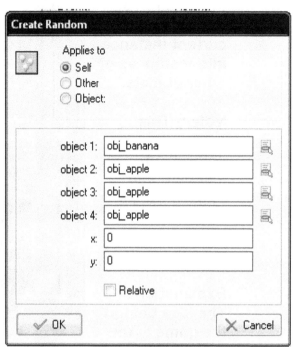

(Fig 053)   **(Fig 054)**

The default window for this action would appear like (Fig 053) , If you want to set probability observe (Fig 054) above it is obvious that apple would appear maximum times because Apple: Banana = 3:1 , if you wish to give equal preference set the object 3 and the object 4 field to 'No Object'.

Usage

1)This event can be used for creating bonus object .

2)For creating missiles

3)For games like mines(Fig 056) shown besides where the bomb must appear or a number.

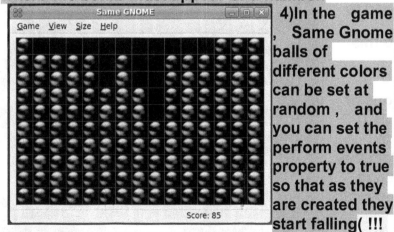

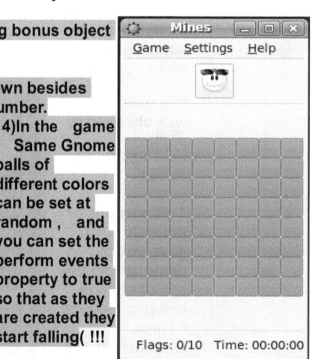

4)In the game , Same Gnome balls of different colors can be set at random , and you can set the perform events property to true so that as they are created they start falling(!!! means very very very important)

d)Change instance :- With this action you can change the current instance into instances of other objects.

Note :- This action would convert an instance into other for uses view the screenshots provided below.

Explanation :- The idea behind the game :- You have to collect all the coins to reach the next level but if you collide with any monster a life would be reduced , to weaken the monster you have to eat the bonus coins , when you eat the bonus coin the monsters turn from to . !!! this is where the change instance action comes into the picture , the instance of was changed to using this action

This was one of the example I gave you to demonstrate the use of change instance action. (These screenshots are taken from a game provided as a sample with Game Maker version 6 , these sprites can be downloaded from the game maker website)

Note:- If the perform events is set to yes events such as create of

the instance would be executed.

e)Destroy instance:- As the name suggests this action would destroy an instance(Fig 057)

f)Destroy at position :- You can use this action for destroying all the objects in a given area at the same time.(Fig 058)

(Fig 057)   (Fig 058)

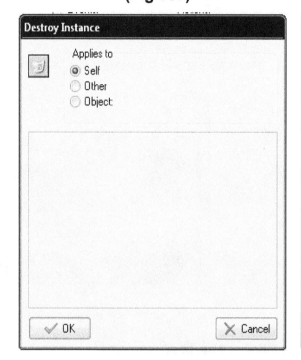

Destroying at position can be used when anything explodes and a particular area has to be cleared
Note:- This action would not spare anyone , it would destroy everything in that particular area.

The second part contains 3 actions

a)Change sprite

b)Transform sprite

c)Color sprite

a)Change Sprite:- Change sprite would change the sprite of that particular instance into other sprite but all the events and actions would remain unchanged.Game Maker even Let us you specify which subimage of a particular sprite should be used and the speed of the animation. If you want only a particular subimage then set the speed to zero. If your speed of animation is larger than one the subimages may be skipped. If you set a negative speed the subimages are shown in reverse order ,   this can be used if you haven't made subimages in the reverse order ,   doing so would also reduce the filesize of your game .

Changing sprite is an important feature , this action can be used to change the sprite of a bomb into the sprite of an explosion , don't be surprised even explosion requires a sprite , observe the strip below

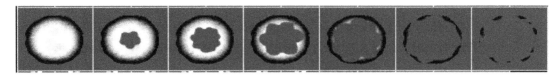

(Fig 059)

(Fig 059) clearly proves that even explosion contains a sprite.

(Fig 060)   (Fig 061)

Observe (Fig 060) and (Fig 061), the first one contains the original sprite and the second one contains changed sprite. For changing that sprite this action was used.The change sprite window appears like one given below.

b)Transform Sprite :- You can use this action to change the size and proportion of the sprite , use the angle to rotate the sprite , you can even specify whether it should be mirrored horizontally or flipped or you may apply both at one and the same time.(Fig 064)

c)Color Sprite :- Use this action to change the color of your sprite , you can choose   the new color from any of the available colors , the new color would merge(blend) with the original color of the sprite , you may even specify the alpha value for transparency 0 is completely transparent whereas 1 is completely opaque , if you want to add transparency effect you must choose a value between them.(example :- 0.245 ,   0.786 ,   0.50)You would be able to see the background partially while using transparency effect. (Fig 063).

Note:- If you use a negative value your sprite would become transparent.

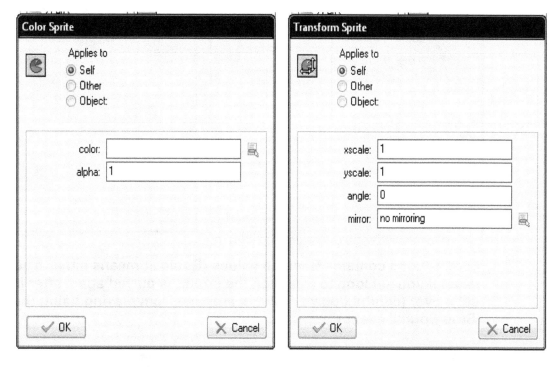

(Fig 06   (Fig 064)

The 3rd part deals with sounds ,   it contains 3 types of actions

a)Play sound

b)Stop sound

c)Check sound

Play sound:- As the name suggests play sound plays sound in your games(Game maker supports only .midi and .wav files ,   it can play multiple .wav files simultaneously but it cannot play more than one .midi file at one and the same time ,   this is one drawback of Game Maker)(Fig 065)

Note :- .wav files are the most uncompressed music files and they require more disk space than other formats.

Stop Sound :- This action stops playing the specified sound , It does not matter whether single instance of the sound is being played or multiple instances are being played , If multiple instances are being played at the one and same time all are stopped. (Fig 066)

(Fig 065)   (Fig 066)

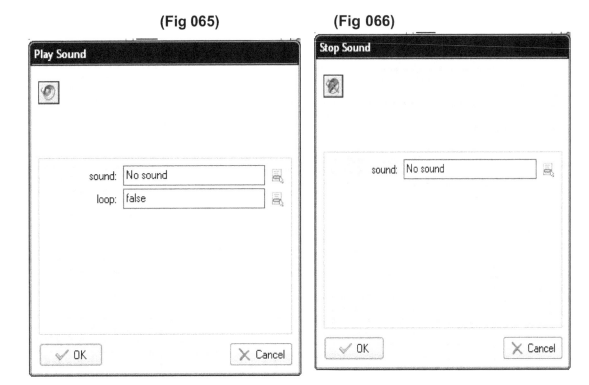

Loop :- Loop contains Boolean values (Boolean means either true or false) If you set loop to true then the sound is played again after it get's over (continuously , till it is stopped from playing using the 'Stop Sound' event.)

Usage

a)Loop(set to true) is generally used for adding background music in your game.

Check Sound :- If the specified sound is being played (you can listen it through your speakers) then the next action is performed otherwise it is not performed , you can even check NOT so that the next action is not executed , but there is no use if you check whether a particular sound is playing and select NOT , instead of selecting NOT it is recommended to avoid using this action . This action is not flawless it contains certain flaws which are as follows.

a)   If you select this action to start playing a sound , the sound doesn't reach the speakers at that particular moment hence it may still return false for sometime

b) If you select this action to stop a sound the sound is not stopped at that particular moment and you may hear the sound and this action will return true.

(Fig 067)   **(Fig 068)**

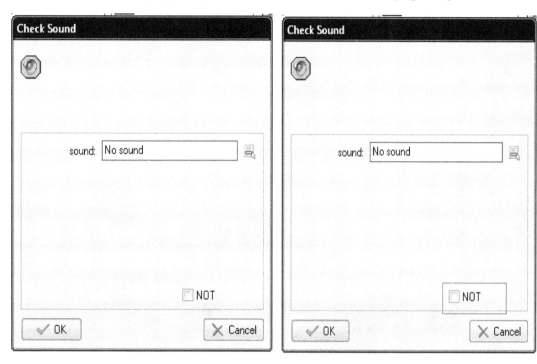

(Check Sound Window)   **(Not checkbox is marked)**

The next part help's you deal with all types of action associated with rooms

The actions contained in the Rooms part are as follows

a) Previous room

b) Next room

c) Restart room

d) Different room

e) Check Previous

f) Check Next

a) Previous room :- This action let's you go to the previous room (level) ,   you can select any one transition effect or no transition effect version 8 of Game Maker has 21 different types of transitions , try using all the transitions and select the one you like ,   you may even opt for no transition(not recommended) ,   using transition effect would create an impression on the person playing your game.(Fig 069)

Note :- If you are in the first room and if you use this event your game would stop working abruptly with an error. (Fig 070)

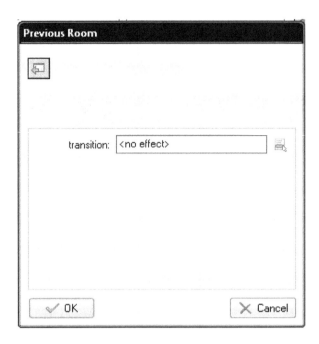

(Fig 069)

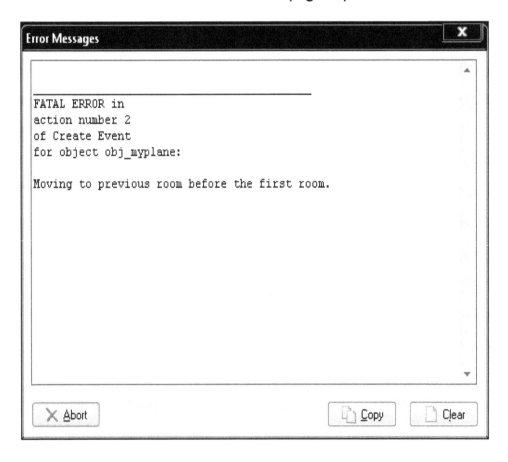

Fig 070 given above shows how an error is displayed in Games created by Game Maker , Game Maker can also be programmed to handle errors occurring in your Games , it is a very useful tool because no one would like if a Game stops abruptly.

Errors are explained in detail further in this book.

Reason :- Errors have to be dealt in a proper way and for dealing with errors one has to know at least the basics of programming

b) Next Room :- The next room action is same as that of Previous Room only difference being instead of going to the previous room you would go to the next room.

Note:- If you are in the last room and this action is executed your game would encounter an error.

c) Restart room :- The same room is started again.

Note :- Even if you change your room the scores and the number of levels would remain unchanged.

b)The screenshots for the windows of 'Next Room' and 'Restart Room' are not provided as they are similar to 'Previous Room'.

d)Different room :- You can use this action to go to a room you desire. (The chances of Failure of this action is less compared to others as you specify the room then and there ,   this action fails if you specify an existing room and then delete that particular room).

(Fig 071)

e) Check previous :- This action checks if there is a room before the current one and if there is ,   the next actions are executed.

f) Check next :- This action checks if there is a room after the current one and if there is ,   the next actions are executed.

Note:- There are no parameters for 'Check previous' and 'Check next' actions , they can be used to avoid errors.

The third Tab named 'Main 2' consists of 4 parts

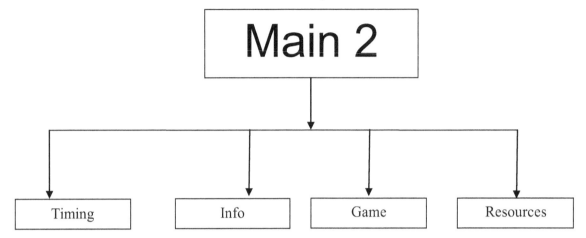

Timing contains 8 actions

a)Set Alarm

b)Sleep

c)Set timeline

d)Timeline position

e)Timeline speed

f)Start timeline

g)Pause timeline

h)Stop timeline

Let us have a brief idea about each of them

a)Set alarm :- Using this action you can set one of the twelve available alarms , you have to specify the number of events and the alarm no , you can even specify the number of steps to be relative , when the number of steps are over the associated actions with that particular alarm event take place.(Fig 073)

b)Sleep :- Using this event you freeze the game for a paricular time period you can even specify whether the screen should be drawn(The redraw parameter doesn't make much difference)(Fig 074)

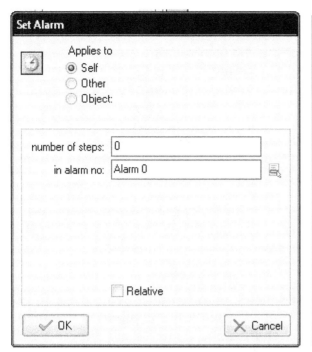

(Fig 073)   (Fig 074)

To understand the actions dealing with timelines it is necessary to understand timelines first , they are explained in (Chapter No 10).

The second part (Info) contains 7 actions a)Display a message , b)Show Info , c)Splash Text , d)Splash Image , e)Splash Webpage , f)splash video , g)Splash settings

Note :- 1) # is a new line character , Suppose you type 'I am programming # a game' it would appear as 'I am programming

a game'
If you want the # character to be displayed type '\#'
Type this sentence 'I am programming \# a game' , the message would appear as 'I am programming # a game' but if there is a space between '\' and '#' the line would not be displayed as desired , this is known as syntax for using expression where syntax means the rules to be followed and the expression means a particular symbol in that particular language , Syntaxes of different languages are different and the expressions in a particular language may or may not be different in different versions.

2)Game Maker doesn't provide in built codecs for playing video files so it is recommended to use video types which are frequently used , if your users machine is not having the specific codec your game would encounter an error , If you use codecs which are not in common use it is advised to supply a codec pack like the 'K-Lite Mega Codec pack' , K-Lite mega codec pack can be downloaded from the website "Free-Codecs.com", you may even convert videos from one codec to another.(Converting videos is explained in Chapter 7)(Converting video is a topic by itself and cannot be dealt with here, however it is mentioned here as it has linkage with the topic on hand.

3)The show text action let's you display text from a file but it's functionality is limited because you cannot use , .doc , .docx , .odt or any other format except the .txt format , this means that you cannot add pictures, word-arts, format the text ! , the text must accommodate in the window because the remaining text document is not shown.

4) Splash Image action doesn't show animated images, to show animated images it is required that you convert all the images into a single video file and use the splash video action.

5)Splash webpage can be used to show an internet webpage , for example you own a company named 'XXX Game Programmers' and your website's address is 'www.xxxgameprogrammers.com' you can use this action to splash webpage.

6) If you use text files and video files it is better to provide them in the executable (.exe file) itself instead of providing it separately because someone may delete the file by chance and game would encounter an error, moreover a file which is included with the executable cannot be extracted from it, but this function comes at a cost which means that files cannot be included in the games made by Lite edition of Game Maker.(More the number o included files more the time required to load the game).If you don't include the file in Included files , the file and the game must be in the same directory / folder.

a)Display a message :- This action would display a specified message , but you cannot use any font nor you can specify size , color for the text.

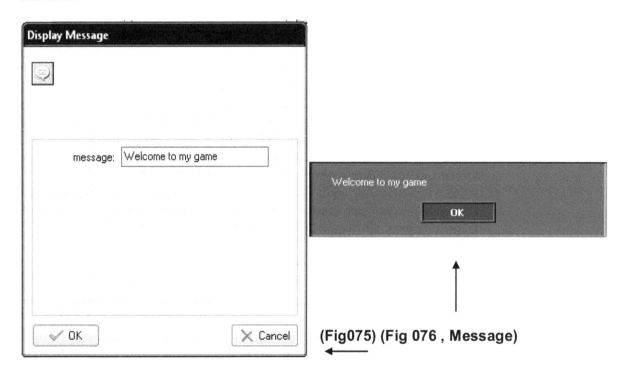

(Fig075) (Fig 076 , Message)

Fig 075 displays the window and Fig 076 displays the message, Fig 076 would definitely give you a rough idea about how your message would appear on the screen.

b) Show info :- This action would show the documentation (digital help) of your game.

Note :- The player can access the digital information by pressing the key F1

(Fig 077)

Fig 077 is the screenshot of one of the documentation made by me for one of my game.

c)Splash text :- This action would display text on the screen. (this action is not a substitute for display message because 'Splash text' would not display the text in the form of a message box) .

Note :- 1)You have to specify the name of the text or the rtf file without any mistake ,   if you enter wrong name game maker would prompt an error.

2) If you enter the correct name of the file but someone renames it later you would encounter an error.

3)If that particular file is edited(or damaged/corrupted) by any virus/other program/the user himself , your game would prompt an error.

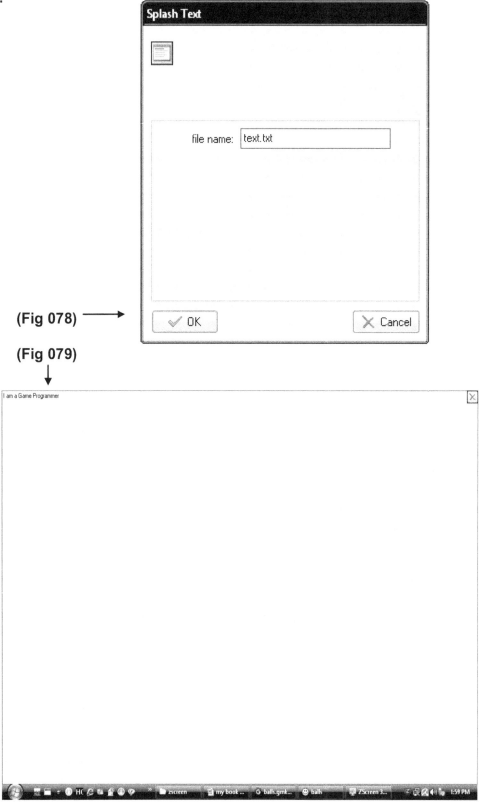

(Fig 078) ⟶

(Fig 079)

↓

Fig 078 shows the window associated with the show text action , Fig 079 demonstrates the appearance of text on the screen.(This action should be used if you want to display huge amount of information in a window).

d) Splash image :- This action would display an image (graphic) on the screen , us filetypes which are used frequently (.bmp , .gif , .png , .jpg)(Fig 080)

e)Splash webpage :- This action displays a webpage on the users screen.(You can display your companies webpage containing additional info about other games made by you or display some news through your website)

Note :- You cannot use the above mentioned action to display a html file

b)You can even program your game in such a way that your webpage would be displayed in a browser (example :- Internet Explorer).(Fig 081)

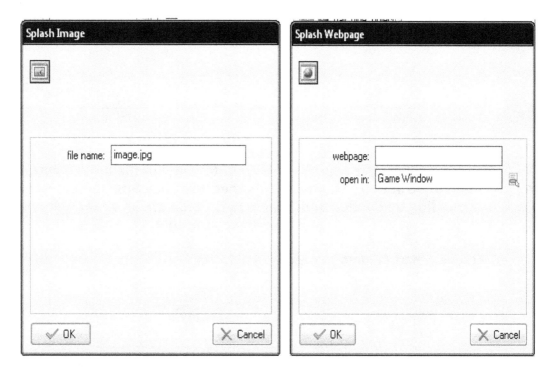

(Fig 080 and 081)

f) Splash video :- This action would splash a video on the screen , it is recommended to provided a codec pack if you are using X-vid, Div-X or mpeg/mpg videos you may provide a video containing your companies name and/or info about your game.If you are unable to provide a codec pack it is recommended to convert the videos before distributing them.(Chapter 7 explains How to convert videos , Chapter 5 will help you learn animation so rejoice!!!)

g)Splash settings :- You can change any settings(caption , window , buttons and even mouse) for splash actions(splash text / image / webpage / video)

Note :- Splash settings can only be applied to the actions preceeding this action.

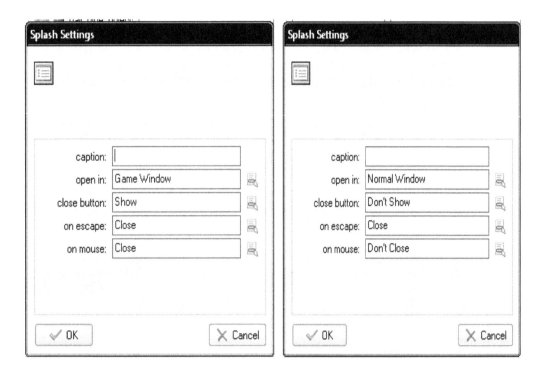

(Fig 082 and 083)
Tip :- Whenever your game encounters any of the splash actions mentioned above , it checks whether there is a Splash setting action succeding that action and if there is it would check all the parameters and fuction accordingly.

The next part (Game) contains 4 actions.

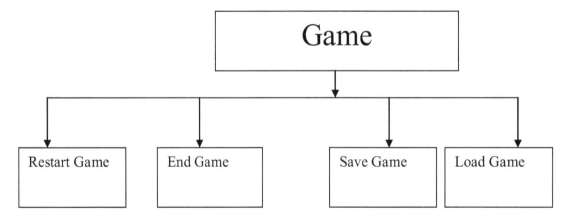

There is no need to explain the first and second action because their name suggests what they can do , they third and the fourth are explained on the next page.

Save Game :- This action saves the game in a file with the specified name(Fig 086)

Load game :- This action loads a file with the specified name(Fig 087)

Note :- If you save your game more than once with the same name , your game would overwrite the previous file without confirmation !

2)It is essential to use (assign) an unique extension.   (Extension means the character after the '.'character ,   eg :- .wav ,   .mp3 ,   .mov ,   .sav   )

Tip :- Some files contain more than one extension for example Calc.ResourceFile.Dll

3)If any game tries to load the game file of any other game ,   Game Maker would prompt the window shown below.

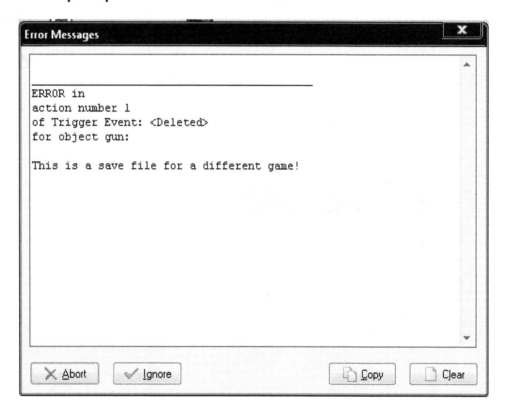

(Fig 085)

How does Game Maker know that a file is saved by a particular game ? read   the point given below carefully

4) There is a catch over here , you would understand it better when you would learn 'Game Indentifier' , On each saved file the Game Indentifier of the game which wrote it is written down , if your Game Identifier doesn't match with the game identifier of the saved file

(Fig 086)

(Fig 087 given below)

Game Maker would prompt the error shown above , it is possible that another game consisting of the same sprites, events, actions, object may prompt an error because of the difference in the Game Indentifier.

The third part 'Resources' contain 3 actions

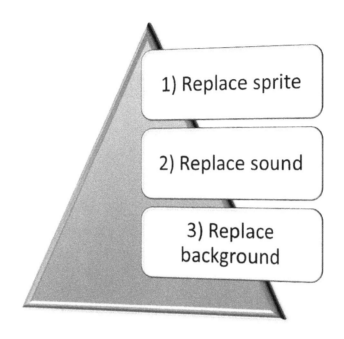

(Fig 088)

1)Replace Sprite :- With this action you can replace a sprite with another sprite , Game Maker accepts many of the available image formats available , it also let's you set the subimage for the sprite , it is again reminded that it is recommended to include the sprite file through the included files option.(Fig 089)

2)Replace Sound :- With this action you can replace a sound , (use .wav files) (Fig 090)

(Fig 089)   (Fig 090)

3)Replace Background :- As the name suggests , this would change the background , this feature can be used for converting day to night.(This action supports more formats compared to Replace sprites)

Next comes the control tab which is divided into 4 parts

a)Questions , b)Other , c)Code , d)Variables

Questions contain 9 actions , majority of them return a boolean value (true/false which is synonymous to yes/no , computer cannot differentiate between yes and no , it can understand(let's assume) true or false to some extent , wherever there is yes/no mentioned in this book it means true/false)

Some actions even deals with mouse and grids , there is one more interesting action which groups one or more than one actions nothing else but still it is very useful , read further to learn it's utility.

2) All the actions contain a parameter NOT , if NOT is activated (checked) the succeding actions would be executed if the condition is false and if the condition is true the succeding actions would not be executed.

a)Check empty :- 1) This action returns 'true' if the object (actually instance) doesn't collide with any other object at the position , you can even specify the position to be relative or non-relative , Game Maker even let's you specify whether you want to consider collision only with solid objects or with all the objects.(Fig 092)

b)Check collision :- This action is completely opposite of the one mentioned above.(Fig 093)

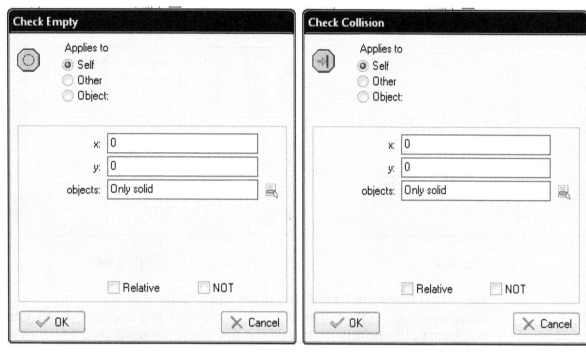

(Fig 092)   (Fig 093)

c)Check Object :- This action checks whether the instance collides with another instance(of the object   you specify) at a position (you specify) which may be relative or may not be.

d)Test instance count :- This action contains 3 parameters 1)Object , 2)Number ,   3)Operation ,   you specify an object and a number ,   this action would compare the number and the number of instances of that object which exist in that particular room when this action is executed ,   you have to even specify an operation ,   there are three available operations a)Equal to ,   b)More than ,   c)Less than .

Note :- This action returns a boolean value depending upon the operation you specify.

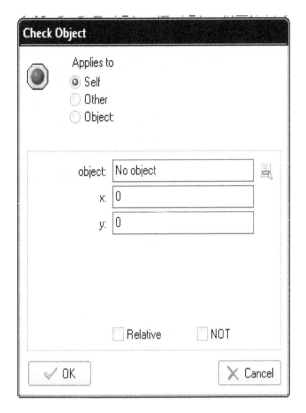

(Fig 094)   (Fig 095)

Tip :- Test Instance Count has many applications in Game Programming , with this action you can check the number of monsters in a game , the bonus points which are yet to be collected and much more

The Game (whose screenshot is Fig 096) uses this 'Test Instance Count' for checking the number of dots , if they are zero (all of them are collected) then the level progresses

e)Test Chance :- This action is simple probablity , lesser the number you enter more is your chance , even decimal values are accepted 2.5 means 2 chances out of 5 , 3.5 means 2 chances out of seven etc .

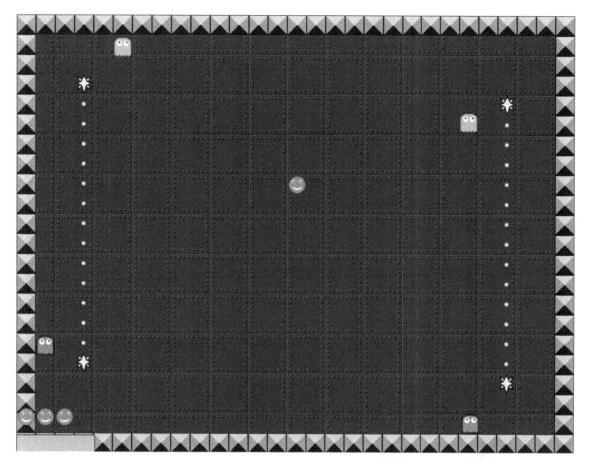

(Fig 096)

f)Check question :- This action would let you ask a question to the player ,   if he replies Yes ,   'True' is returned and false is returned for 'No' ,   common example of a question is 'Are you sure you want to quit   ?'

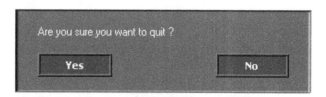

(Fig 097)

g)Test expression :- If the expression returns a value >= 0.5 the next action is performed('True' is returned).(Fig 102)

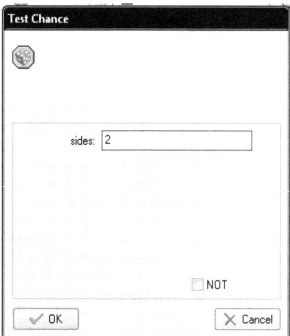

(Fig 098)   (Fig 099)

(Fig 100)   (Fig 101)

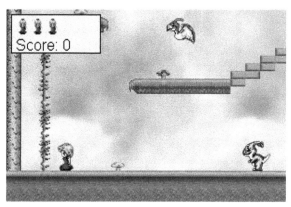

Usage :- The game shown above used this action to check whether the collision was taking place from upward direction(girl jumps on monster) or any other direction , if the collision would take place in the upward direction , the monster would be killed otherwise a life would be reduced.

Note :- It was not possible to accommodate the screenshot of the 'Test Expression' window on this page so it is provided on the next page.

h)Check Mouse :- This action returns true if the specified button on the mouse is pressed , Game Maker supports mouse containg even the middle button(old ones , difficult to be found nowadays) .(It is not recommended to use the check mouse for middle button because

many of the computers are not shipped with mouse possesing middle button (they contain a scroll instead).) (Fig 102)

(Fig 102)

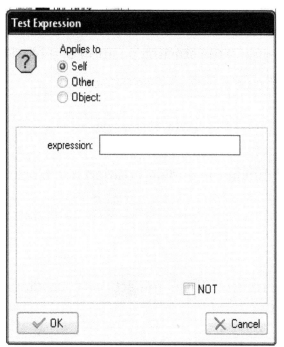 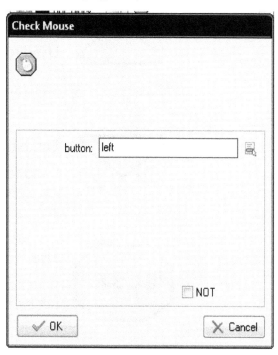

(Fig 103)

i)Check Grid :- This action returns false if the instance is not on the grid , you even have to enter the snap values , this is useful when you don't want the instance to change directions.

The next part 'others' contain 6 actions

Start block

Used for defining the starting position of a block

End block

Used for defining the ending position of a block

Else

If an action returns 'False' the actions succeding the else action are executed.

Repeat

This action repeats the actions succeding this actions a number of times (you specify)

Exit Event

This action is used to move the control outside that particular event

Call Event

This action calls the corresponding event in the parent object

Parent Objects

We inherit the characteristics of our parents , the same way Object intherit their events from their parents , their parents are objects too. If you define 'a' as the parent of 'b' , 'b' as the parent of 'c' , 'c' would inherit all the events from 'a' and it would also inherit all the events of 'b' which are not present in 'a' object 'a' (main parent)

object 'b' (inherits events from 'a')

object 'c' (inherits events from 'a' & 'b')

How to define parent object ?

Parent ojects can be only defined in the advanced mode.(advanced mode is explained later in this chapter)

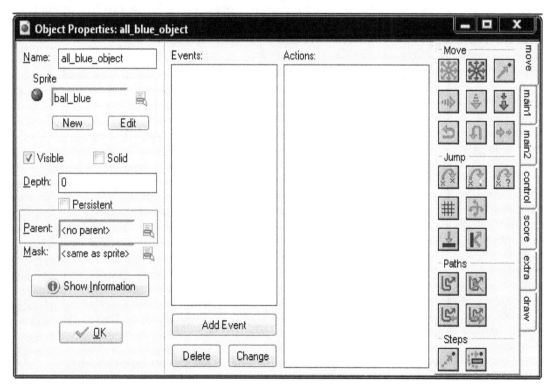

[(Fig 107) Observe the red marking]

Depth :- Preference for creating the object in the room is given depending on their irrespective depth's , instances with more depth are drawn first , suppose you want to draw the planet object above the meteorite ,

Planet

Meteorite

The depth of planet must be < depth of meteroite , your image would appear as (Fig 110)

(Fig 110)

How to define depth ?

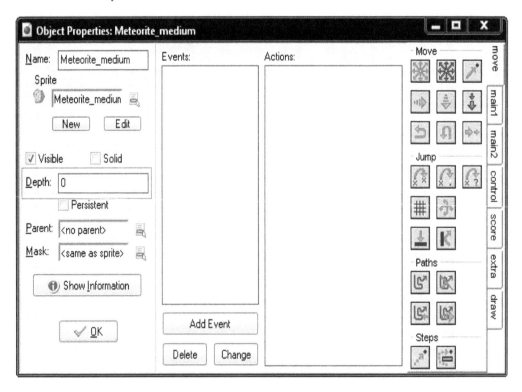

[(Fig 111) Observe the red marking]

Mask :- If you want to define differnent sprites for collisions and appearance(picture on the screen) you use masks , the sprites used for mask may be the sprite used for that object or any other sprite.

How to define Mask ?

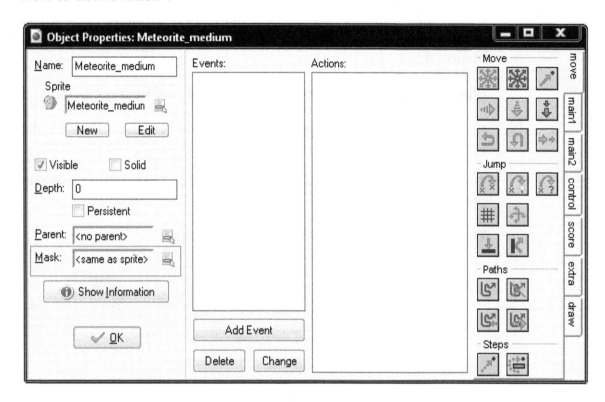

[(Fig 112) Observe the red marking]

Persistent :- If an object is persistent , it would appear in all the room , you just have to place it in the first room.

Usage

1)You can use this feature for objects which deal with background music.

Show information :- If you press this button game maker would show all the information of that object in a window , using that window you can save the information(write to a file) or you may even print it.

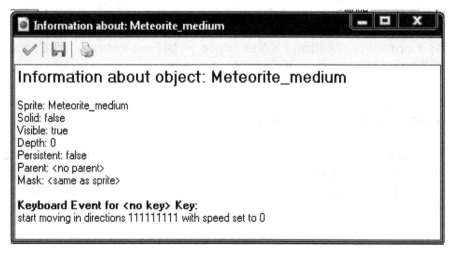

Visible :- If you uncheck the visible box your object would become completely invisible (it would be in the room) but you (or user of your game) would not be able to see it because it's transparency (alpha value) would be 0 , and you would be able to see the background behind it.

Solid :- If you check this box your object would become solid.

Note :- The checkboxes for visible and solid are just above the depth text box.

The third part named 'code' and fourth named 'Variables' deal with programming so they are explained in the later chapters.

The 5th tab Score is divided into three parts.

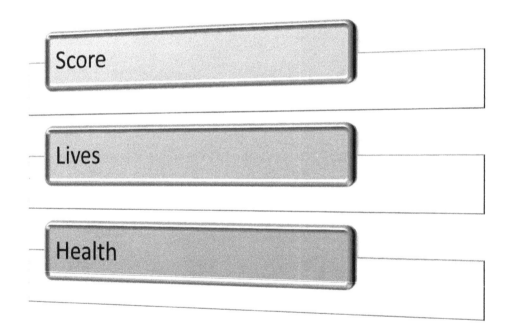

Let's learn the score part

1) It contains 5 actions a)Set score , b)Test score , c) Draw score , d)Show highscore , e)Clear highscore

a)Set score :- This action can be used to increase or decrease the score , the score can be relative or non-relative.(Fig 115)

b)Test score :- This action can be used to trigger other actions depending on the score(Fig 116) you just have to specify a value and the operation you want to perform a)Equal to , b)More than , c) Less than

Testscore is very important , this action has many application , you may even program your game to increase the difficulty if the score goes beyond a certain limit or value for example 1000

Usage

If the score is => a specified value the game must switch to a new level or more monsters should be included etc

(Fig 115)   (Fig 116)

c)Draw score :- This action draws the score on the screen.(It is compulsory to include this action in the draw event of an object.).You must even know the x and y co-ordinates of a particular point on the room for you have to mention the x and the y co-ordinate , you must even provide a suitable(catchy) caption.

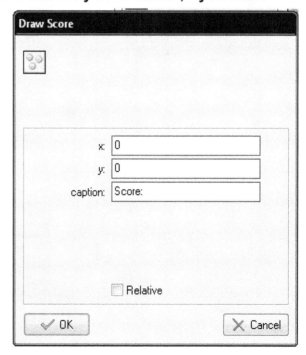

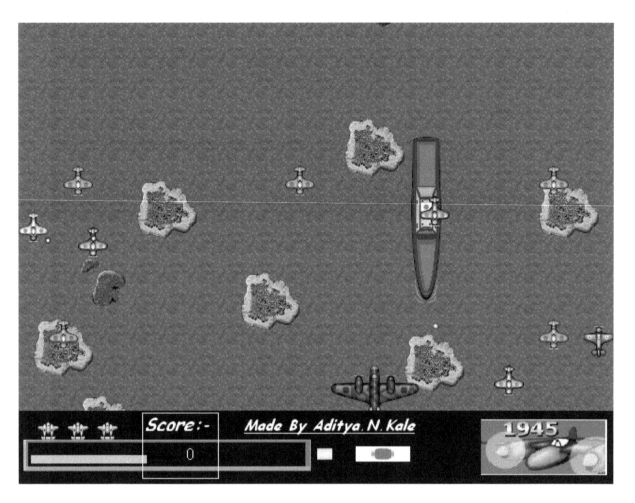

[(Fig 118) Observe the yellow marking]

d)Show Highscore :- This action must be used when the game ends .

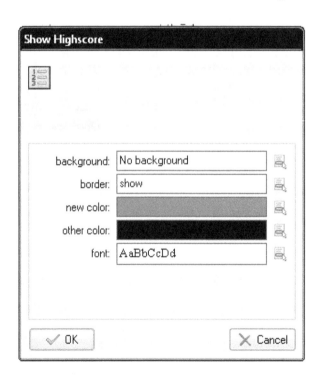

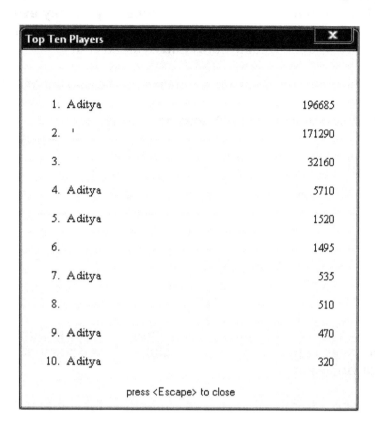

Top Ten Players	
1. Aditya	196685
2. '	171290
3.	32160
4. Aditya	5710
5. Aditya	1520
6.	1495
7. Aditya	535
8.	510
9. Aditya	470
10. Aditya	320

press <Escape> to close

[(Fig 120) A sample high score chart (table), Next table shows the high score with a background]

Top Ten Players	
	Scores
1.	1760
2.	603
3.	437
4.	400
5.	395
6.	395
7.	350
8.	333
9. dddddddd	328
10. d	305

press <Escape> to close

The new color indicates the color of the new entry , other color indicates the color of other (old) entries , you may even specify whether the window should have a border or not , Game Maker even allows you to set a background and select a font.

e)Clear highscore :- This action clears all the entries of the high score.

The next part lives contain 4 actions.

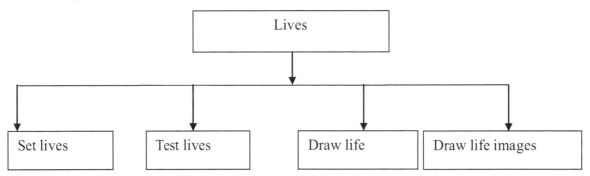

a)Set lives :- You can specify the number of lives using this action , you may even specify them to be relative to the present number of lives or non-relative.

Experience :- In one of my game I specified the value to be -1 but I forgot to check relatively hence the 'No more lives' action used to be triggered.

b)Test Lives :- Test lives is similar to Test score , instead of the score the lives are tested.

c)Draw lives :- The parameters used in this action is same as that of 'Draw score'.

Note :- This action will draw only figures (1 , 2 , 3 , 4 , ...)

(Fig 123)   (Fig 124)

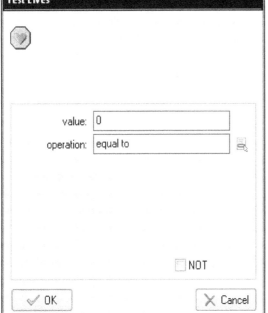

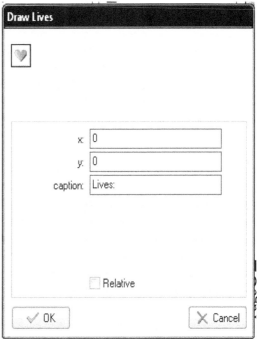

d)Draw life images :- This action draws the lives on the screen(figures are not drawn , sprites are drawn).

The balls shown above are from one of my game , I specified the sprites to that ball sprites , 1 ball = 1 life.

The next part 'Health' contains 4 actions a)Set Health , b)Test Health , c)Draw Health , d)Score caption.

a)Set health :- Use this action to change the health in your game.

Note :- If you specify a value > 100 , the health which would be applicable is 100 because Game Maker is programmed in such a way that it would not accept Health above 100 , the lower limit is 0 , values such as 100/2 , 200/5 or 45.6789 are also accepted.

2)The + point of game maker is that it won't generate error if the health value exceeds maximum limit (100).

b)Test health :- Test health is similar to test score , instead of score health is tested.

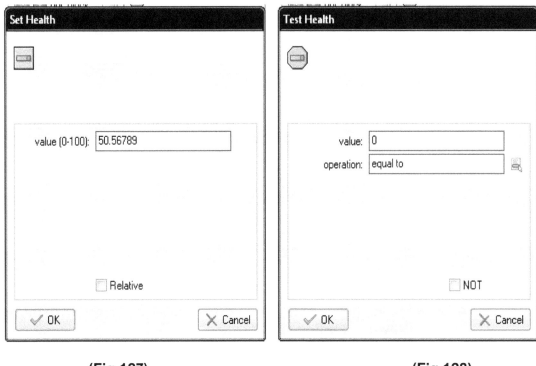

(Fig 127)   (Fig 128)

You may use test health for displaying a warning when the health decreases beyond a certain value

c)Draw health :- This action would draw a bar on the screen (similar to a progress bar) indicating health.

Note :- Samples are provided on the next page , Game Maker even let's you choose the color for your Health bar , try each one and select the one which suits your needs the best , some of the available colors are 1)Blue , 2)Yellow , 3)Lime , 4)Fuchsia , 5)Black , 6)Gray , 7)Silver , 8) White , 9)Maroon , you may even specify a combination of colors for example green to red , white to black .

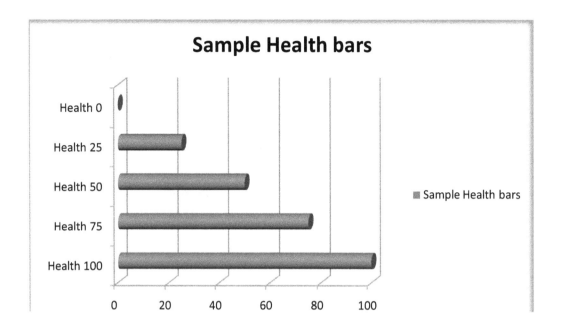

Sample Health bars

Health 0

Health 25

Health 50

Health 75

Health 100

■ Sample Health bars

0   20   40   60   80   100

The graph shown above is for mere demonstration , the health bars which would appear on the screen would not be cyrindrical but rectangular in shape.

d)Score Caption :- This action is applicable to the window settings , you can specify whether the score should be shown as the window title it even deals with lives , health.

Score Caption

SLH

show score: | show
score caption: | score:
show lives: | don't show
lives caption: | lives:
show health: | don't show
health caption: | health:

✓ OK   ✗ Cancel

(Fig 130)

Move on to the next tab extra , it contains 3 parts .

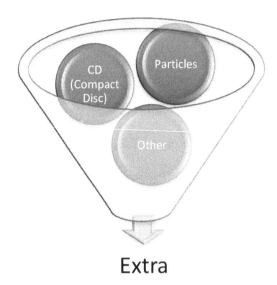

(Fig 131)

The particles part is explained in the 13th Chapter .

Let us gain some information about the Cd part

a)Play CD :- with this action you can play the tracks on the CD you just have to mention the start track and the final track.

Note :- There would be a possibility that the user of your game may have two CD-drives.

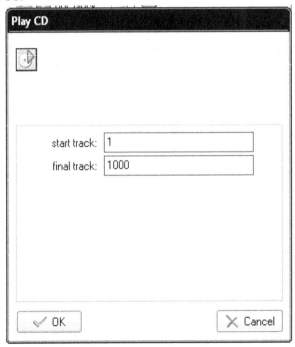

b)Stop CD :- Stops the current CD playing.

c)Pause CD :- This action pauses a track which was playing before this action was executed.

d)Resume CD :- As the name suggests this action resumes (continues) a paused disc.

e)Check CD :- If there is a cd in the default drive the actions succeding this action are executed

Note :- This action cannot be used for DRM protection.

f)Check CD playing :- If a track is playing on the CD the succeding actions are executed.

Note :- These actions come at a cost which means that they are available only in the PRO edition of Game Maker.

The next part **Other** contains just one action

a)Set Cursor :- This action replaces the windows cursor with a sprite (of your choice) , the sprite may be animated or inanimate , the effect of this action nullifies out of the Game Window which means that the sprite would be shown only within the borders of your game. (Fig 133 shown below)

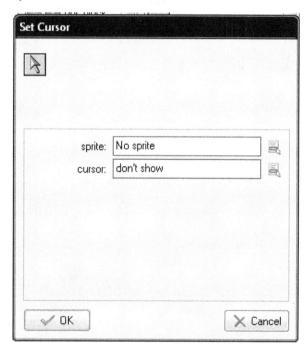

Let us proceed to the last tab **draw** , as the name suggests this tab contains actions which deal with drawing (text , sprites , scaling etc). It is compulsory to define all the draw action in the draw event This tab is

divided into 3 parts

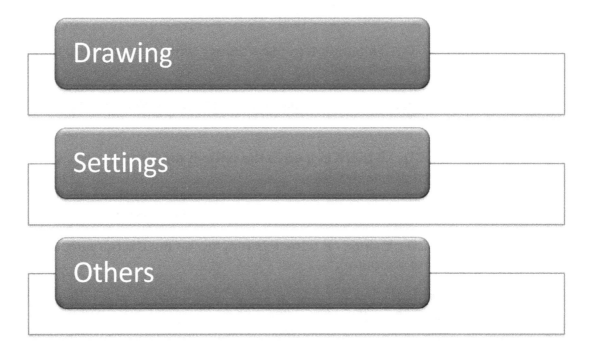

Drawing contains 11 actions
1)Draw sprite :- This action draws a sprite at a particular position on the screen.

2)Draw background :- This action draws background at a particular position on the screen.

3)Draw text :- This action draws text at a particular position on the screen (you cannot select font !)

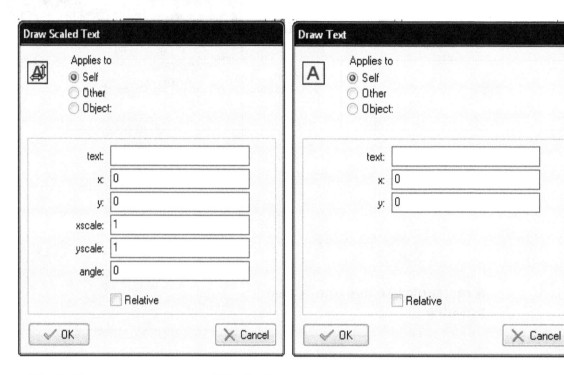

(Fig 136)   (Fig 137)

4)Draw scaled text :- This action is same as the previous one only difference being you can scale(change the width ,   height) the text , some parameters are same as that of transform sprite.

5)Draw rectangle :- This action draws a rectangle on the screen ,   you just have to specify the co-ordinates of two opposite points. To understand the difference between filled and outlined rectangle view the illustrations provided below.(Fig 144)

(Outlined rectangle)

(Filled rectangle)

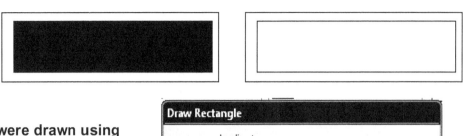

These
rectangles were drawn using
two actions

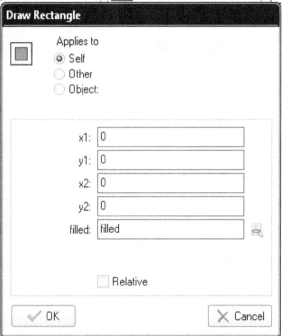

A rectangle like this one is also
possible

(Fig 144)

Like rectangles you would be able to draw everything once you learn
GML ,   you would be able to draw figures like the one given below

6)Horizontal gradient :- This action draws rectangle with a gradient
colour (the shade of the color changes from left to right).

A horizontally gradient rectangle

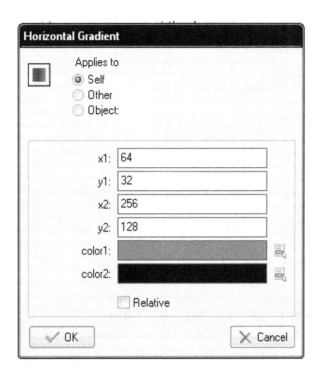

Note :- The color which is mentioned first appears at the left whereas the color mentioned second (color2) appears at the right , in the middle there is a mixture of both the colors , it is obvious that if the same color is mentioned twice the rectangle would be evenly painted by that particular color .This is useful if you want the rectangle to be painted with only one color , if you choose two colors very similar to each other it would be difficult to observe the color merging.

7)Vertical gradient :- This action draws rectangle with a gradient colour (the shade of the color changes from top to bottom).

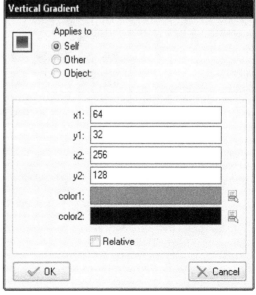

A vertically gradient rectangle

Everything remains the same instead of left to right the shade changes from right to left.

Note :- The further contains invaluable extra information (tip) don't commit the mistake of neglecting it (it is a separate article all together but information is provided just to enhance your knowledge and increase your skills)

Detailed Info about colours

What is the use of this information ?

This information would enhance your knowledge related to RGB index and heus , sat , lums . RGB means the proportion of Red-Green-Blue in a paricular color .

If RGB = {0, 0, 0} the shade(color) you obtain is black whereas if RGB = {255, 255, 255} is white . RGB = {25, 25, 25} and RGB = {25, 25, 24} are different , even if you feel they are same they aren't , you may feel they are same because it is one of the limitation of the Human Eye , Human Eye cannot identify such minute differences .You would be able to differentiate between RGB = {255, 255, 0} and RGB = {255, 255, 255} because here there is a lot of differene in the colors obtained(The Hue , Sat , Lum values must remain the same). (Even computer monitors use RGB for displaying images , Computer monitor is divided into many dots , each dot shows a color and when we look at the screen we are simultaneously looking at 1000's of dots and these dots appear to us as an image) . But what's the reason for learning this ? , You would require this knowledge while selecting colors for your rectangle.Press the 🖻 button on the Horizontal Gradient window, The following window(Fig 149) would appear on the screen.

(Fig 149)

(Fig 150)

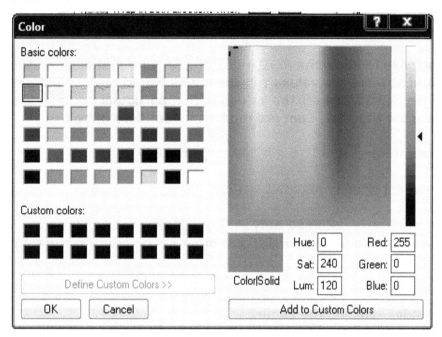

To choose more colors press , 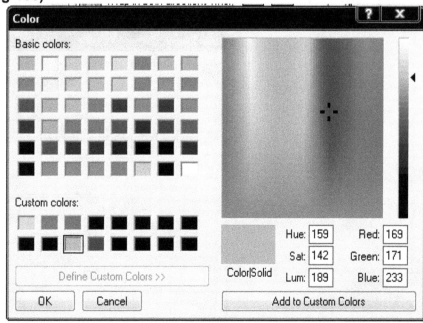 **Define Custom Colors >>** after
pressing the button Fig 150 would appear o the screen . (48 Basic
colors are provided to you , you can add 16 more colors , these 16
colors would be added to the custom colors.)

To define custom colors just select
a color and press the **Add to Custom Colors**

Button. Your colors would be
added.(Fig 153)

Note :- Each color has a RGB index (value) and Hue ,   Sat ,   Lum . According to dictionary hue means (I have provided meanings from 2 dictionaries) a color or a tint ,   a variety or shade of a color ,   The quality of a color as determined by its dominant wavelength.

Tip :- Each color has a wavelength .   Examples a)Red = 0.0008 mm , b)Violet = 0.0004.

2) If you wish to know the RGB index of any color just click on the color and observe the values ,   new values would replace old ones and these new values are the values of that particular color ,   the RGB and the Hue, Sat, Lum are the true indentifiers of colors.

3)Maximum Hue = 239 ,   Sat = 240 ,   Lum = 240

4)You cannot specify negative values.

5)Thus window is not used only in Game Maker ,   such type of windows are also used by Paint and other image editor programmes.

6)RGB index remains the same ,
            it is irrespective whether on a computer ,   mobile , dvd player ,
programming languages.

7)You can move the bar up/down.

8)Draw ellipse(circle or an oval shape). :- This action is used for draw an elliptical shape ,   you just have to specify the co-ordinates of the opposite sides.
(Fig 155)

9)Gradient ellipse :- This action draws an ellipse with gradient colors.

(Fig 156) ⟶

(The colors of these windows may appear different on your computer , these colors depend upon the theme on your computer)

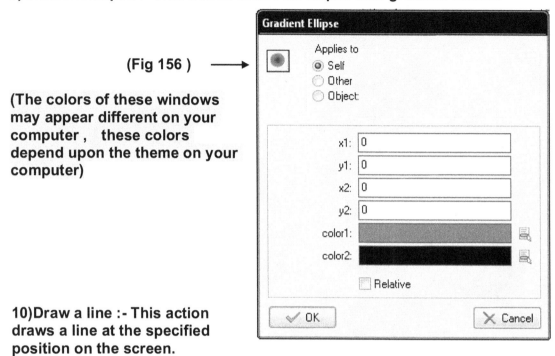

10)Draw a line :- This action draws a line at the specified position on the screen.

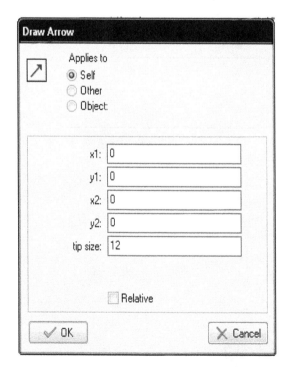

11)Draw an arrow :- You have to specify the co-ordinates of the end points and the tip size.

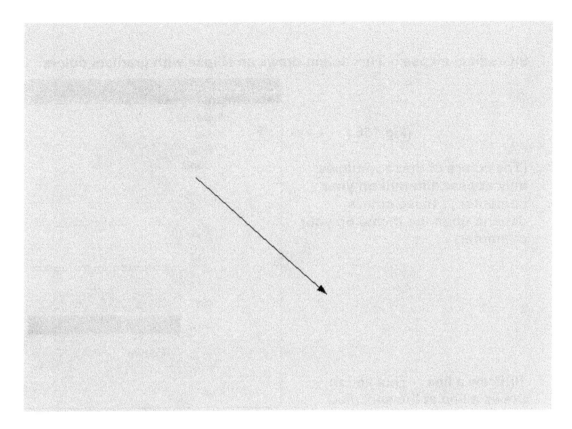

(Fig 158 ,   this is an example of an arrow)

The drawing part ends over here ,   Let us move to the settings part.

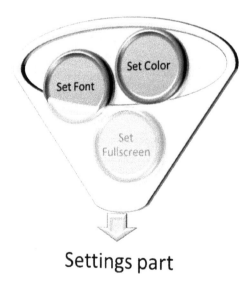

Settings part

a)Set Color :- Let us you specify color for lines ,   rectangles , ellipses and text

b)Set font :- With this action you can change the font and even specify the alignment of the text.

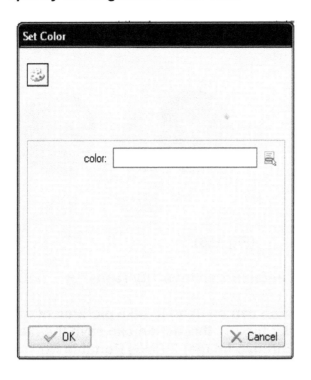

c)Set fullscreen :- This action is used to change the screen-mode , the action parameter contains 3 options 1)Switch ,   2)Window , 3)Fullscreen.

(Fig 162)

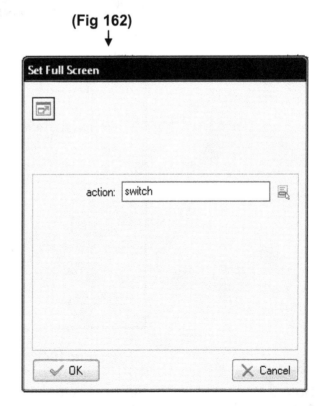

If you specify switch (before the switchig the window is windowed.) then the window would become fullscreen.If you specify switch (

before the switchig the window is in fullscreen mode.) then the game would run in a window.

The settings part ends over here ,   Let us move onto the next part Other.

(Fig 163)

Fig 163 shows that Other contains 2 actions 1)Screenshot ,   2)Other

1)Take snapshot :- This action can be used to take pictures of a game(game window) at a particular time ,   this action can save the file in 2 formats 1)BMP(Windows Bit-map Image) 2)PNG(Portable Network Graphics).

Tip :- Use PNG instead of bitmap because a bitmap image requires less hard disk space than a BMP image

(Fig 164)

Note :- You must not forget to specify an extension(extension must follow the filename for example snapshot.bmp or snapshot.png , extension is that part after the character '.') if you specify any other extension or you don't specify any extension then game maker would not change the filename but the actual format of file would remain

BMP (This means that Game Maker would save the file with the name you have specified but the file-structure would be that of BMP.)

Tip :- If a file already exists with that particular name , Game Maker would overwrite without a prompt !!!.

2)This action should not be defined in the step event !!!

2)Create Effect :- This action does majority of your work (Do you know that this action can save nearly 500 lines of code if the same game is written in any other programming language !!!). This action can create 12 different types of effect , you just have to select the effect , specify the position and select a color , if you select above objects for the where parameter the effect would be drawn above all the sprites (instances infact) and if you select below objects this action would draw the effect below the instances but this works only for objects whose depth is in the range of -100000 to 100000.

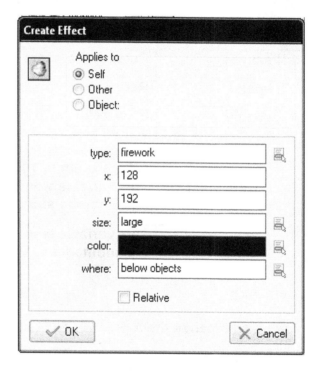

(Fig 165)

Here the explanation of the actions ends but you have to wait to learn the actions that deal with code , variables and particles , thay are explained later in this book

I have introduced a part of programming here as it is important while dealing with (some) actions , Suppose you want to create an effect at the position where an object named apple lies what would be your x and y ? in such a case the variables mentioned below are used.

Note :- Game Maker is case sensitive , which means that Depth , depth and DEPTH are not the same for Game Maker.

Variable name	Function
1) Depth	This variable is used to change the depth
2) hspeed	Horizontal speed of the instance of an object
3) vspeed	Vertical speed of the instance of an object
4) x	Returns the value of x co-ordinateof the instance
5) y	Returns the value of y co-ordinate of the instance
6) direction	The direction in which the instance is moving (in degrees)
7) mouse_x	The x co-ordinate of the mouse pointer
8) mouse_y	The y co-ordinate of the mouse
9) lives	Returns the number of lives
10) health	Returns the health
11) score	Returns the score
12) speed	Returns the current speed in of the instance
13) visible	If 1 is returned it means that the instance is visible and if instance is invisible it means that the instance is invisible (It wouldn't return a value except 0, 1)
14) image_index	This variable would return a value which is the nmber of the subimage being shown
15)image_speed	This variable is used to change the pace at which the subinages are shown

Summary

Let us summarize the topics we dealt with in this chapter

In this chapter we learned about the difference between an absolute and a relative value. Besides we briefly discussed about majority of the actions we even discussed about paths and dealt with actions associated with paths.

Towards the later half of this chapter we discussed about depth , creating effects using the action Create Effect and case-sensitivity

Chapter 3 Create your First Game !

Now you are equipped with all the knowledge you require for actually creating a Game so let us start (this chapter would be too small compared to the earlier one , we would create the game Space which we left half way in the second chapter)

Creating games is like making a food item , we have added all the ingredients for making a game(sounds , sprites , backgrounds) so let's start our cooking process. (actual creation , adding events , actions).

We have already discussed that 14 objects are for decorating , following is a list of objects and their purpose , for the objects marked as N there is no need for events and actions(Two objects with same name cannot exist)

Object	Purpose
1)Alien_green	N
2)Alien_purple	N
3)Meteorite_large	N
4)Meteorite_large2	N
5)Meteorite_medium	N
6) Meteorite_medium2	N
7)Meteroite_small	N
8)Meteorite_small2	N
9)Planet1	N
10)Planet2	N
11)Planet3	N
12)Planet3_cloudy	N
13)Planet4_cloudy	N
14)Rocket	Y
15)Saturn	N
16)Triangle	Y
17)UFO_simple	Y
18)Lazer_blue	Y
19) Lazer_green	Y

20) Lazer_red	Y
21) Lazer_yellow	Y
22)Manager	Y

Open the rocket object

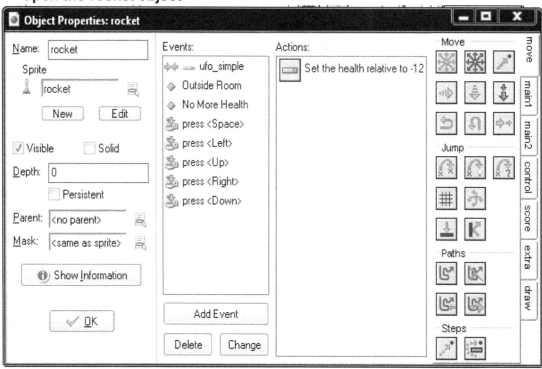

(Fig 168 ,   some of the tables are also considered as Figures , These events would not appear automatically we have to add each of them)

To add an event press [Add Event] **,   then Press** [Collision] **specify the other object as UFO ,   the collision event would be added into the events list ,   from the score tab drag the action Set health specify the value parameter as -12 and remember to check the relative checkbox. Though there is mentioned value(0-100) a negative value is accepted.**

2)To add the second event press [Add Event] **then press** [Other] **next select 'Outside Room'. ,   from the**

move tab drag the action 'Wrap Screen' specify the direction parameter as 'in both the direction'

(Fig 170)

3)From the Other event add one more action 'No More Health' , From the main1 tab drag the action 'Destroy instance' and 'Play sound' specify the sound parameter as explosion and specify the loop property to false , From the sore tab add Show the Highscore (don't change the parameters) then at last from the main2 tab drag 'Restart Game'

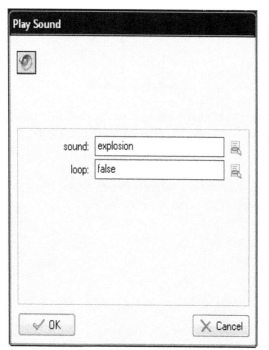

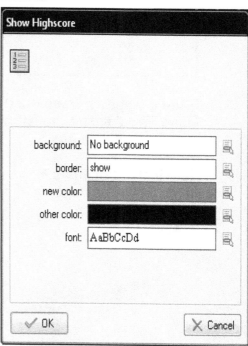

4)Add the event Key Press <space> , from the main1 tab drag the action 'Create Moving' specify the following parameters a)Object: Lazer_red , b) x : 4 , c) y : 4 , d) Speed : 3 , e) direction :90 and check relative , Drag one more action 'create moving' everything must be same as the previous one change the Object to Lazer_yellow , x : -4 , and y : -4.

(Fig 172 and 173)

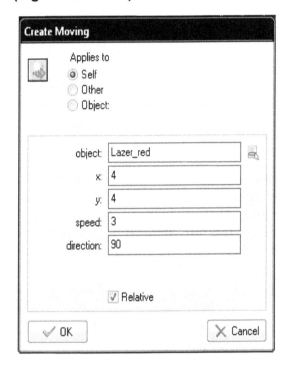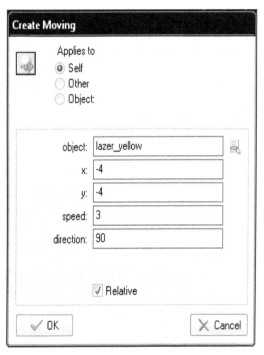

5)Add event Key Press <Left> from the move tab drag the action 'Move Fixed' select the left arrow , specify the speed as 3 don't check the relative box.

Tip :- Instead of Move Fixed you can drag 'Move Free' specify the direction as 180 degrees , speed as 3 and non-relative.

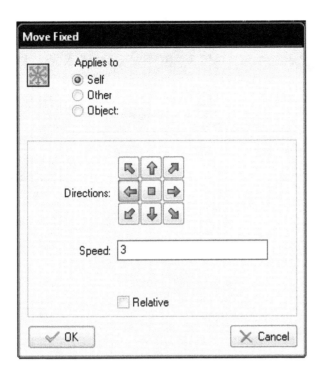

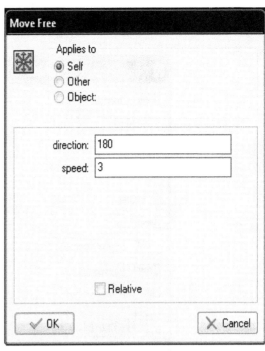

6)Add event Key Press <up> drag the 'Move fixed' action press the upward arrow , speed :3 non-relative

Tip :- Instead of Move Fixed you can drag 'Move Free' specify the direction as 90 degrees , speed as 3 and non-relative.

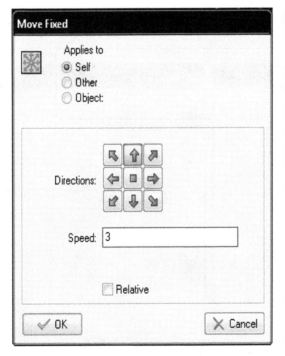

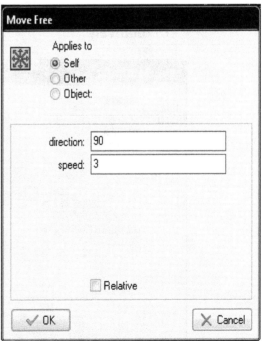

(Fig 176 and 177)

Similarly add the events 'Key Press'<down> , and 'Key Press'<right> and drag the action Move Fixed or Free and specify the corresponding direction.

Open the object triangle

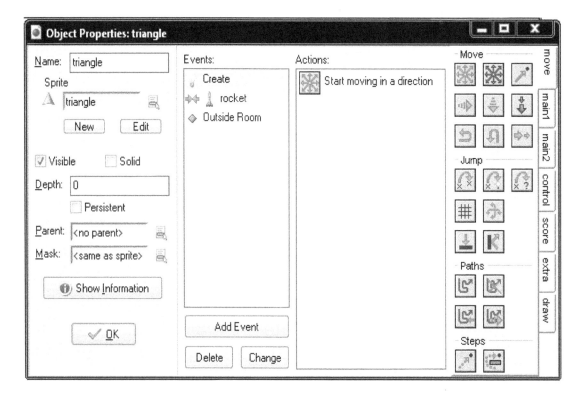

1) Add event Create , drag the action 'move fixed' specify the upward direction and speed 5 non-relative.

2) Add event collision with 'rocket' , drag the action 'set health' value = -15 relatively

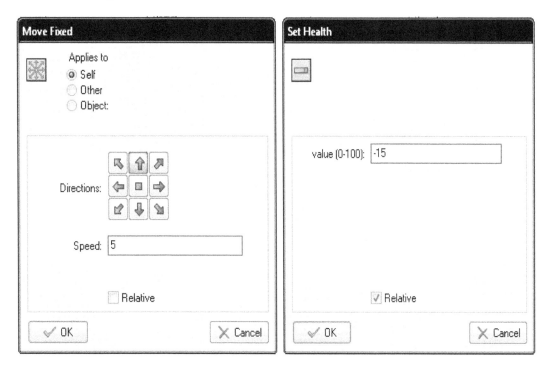

(Fig 179 and 180)

3)Add event 'Outside Room' and drag the action 'Jump to random position' **Note :- Let the snap values be 0 in both the cases x and y**

Open the object   UFO_simple

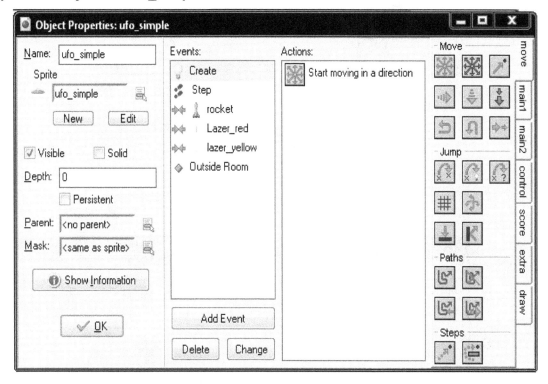

Add event 'Create' drag the action Start moving in a direction(Move Fixed) and select all the directions excluding the middle one and let speed = 3 non-relative

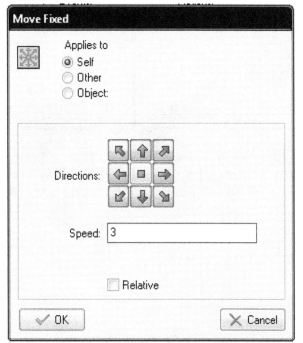

(Fig 182)

Add event 'Step' drag the action test chance let the sides be 12 ,
start a block drag an action 'Create instance of object'
Object:Lazer_blue ,   x : 14 ,   y : 8 relatively ,   drag one more action
'Create instance' Object:Lazer_green ,   x : -14 ,   y : -8 relatively .

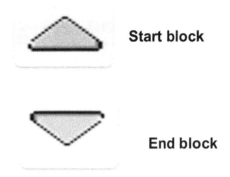 **Start block**

End block

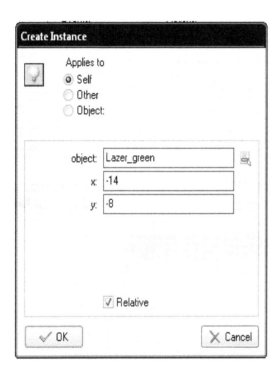

Add event 'collision with rocket'
and drag destroy instance (self) ,   the drag 'Play sound' explosion
without looping ,   drag set health let the value be '-10' relatively

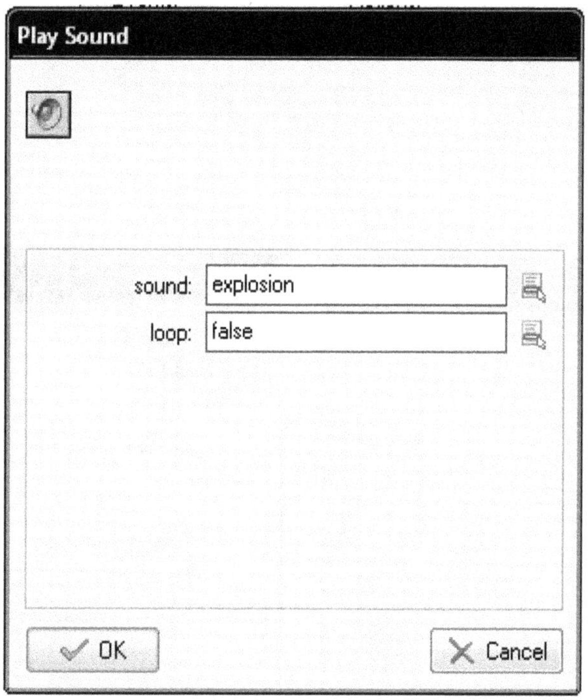

Play Sound

sound: explosion

loop: false

✓ OK   ✗ Cancel

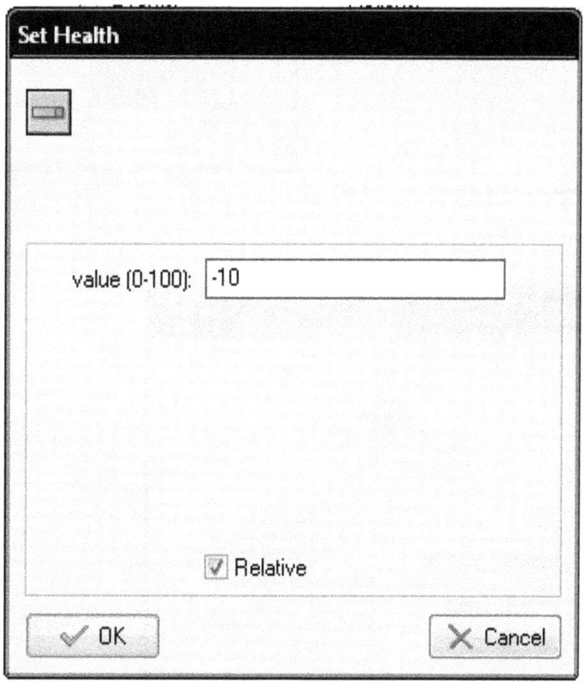

Set Health

value (0-100): -10

☑ Relative

✓ OK   ✗ Cancel

(Fig 187 and 188)

Drag create instance object : UFO_simple , x : your choice , y : your choice . (this action is important because , if a player collides his space ship with all the UFO's the number of UFO's would be zero !!!).

Add one more event 'Collision with Lazer Red' , drag actions 'destroy instance' (self). , drag action 'Play sound'(explosion) without looping , Drag Create instance of Object UFO (anywhere you desire , this is important for the reason highlighted on the previous page , then drag set score value = 5 relatively.

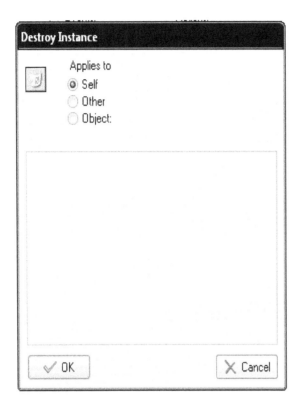

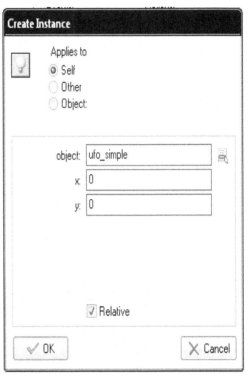

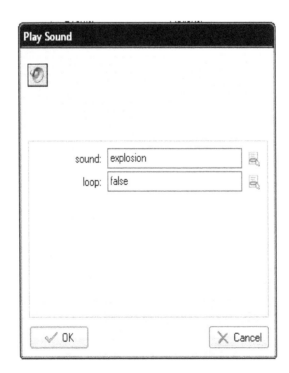

(Fig 192)

Add event 'collision with Lazer_yellow' all the actions should be same as the previous event(select all of them using your mouse and 'ctrl' then right click on any one select copy and then paste them)

Tip :- The actions are executed in the order placed by you

Tip :- Suppose you drag 'Test chance' and you don't place the succeding actions in a block then the action after the 'test chance' is affected but other's are not ,   if you want 'Test Chance' to apply for suppose 3 actions the 3 actions must be placed in a block after the 'Test Chance' .

Add event 'Outside Room' ,   drag the action 'Wrap Screen' and specify 'both the directions' .

Next open the 'Lazer_blue' object.

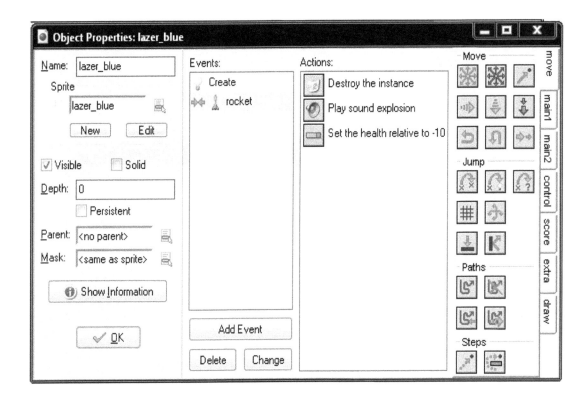

(Fig 193)

Add event 'create' drag the action ,   drag the action move fixed ,
select the downward arrow with speed 3 non-relative.

2)Add event 'Collision' with rocket ,   drag action destroy instance (
self) ,   drag action playsound with loop set to false ,   drag action set
health and let the value be -10 relatively.

3)Define the same events and actions for 'Lazer_green'.

Move Fixed

Applies to
⦿ Self
○ Other
○ Object:

Directions:

Speed: 3

☐ Relative

✓ OK   ✕ Cancel

(Fig 194)

Now it's time to create the last object 'manager' this object would not possess any sprite .

Open the object manager (Fig 195)

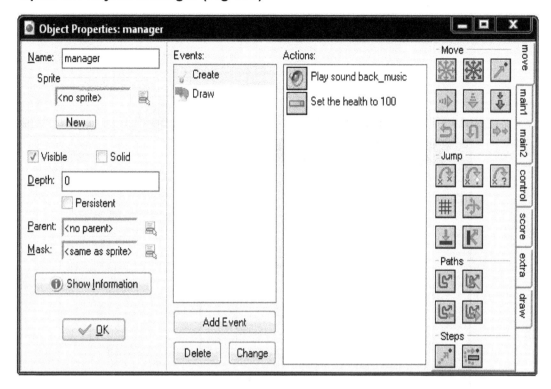

Add event create , drag the action playsound (back_music) with looping set to true because we want the background music to be running continuosly.

Drag 1 more action 'Set Health',   let the value be 100 non_relatively

Note :- Health property cannot be applied to other objects.

Tip :- When you define actions some actions can be defined in such a way that they apply to others ,   but it is always advisable to apply the action for self.(For example if you drag move_fixed action and mention other object for applies to , the other object would move in that direction).

Add event 'Draw'(This is the first time we are using draw !) drag the action draw health and specify the values as shown in the (Fig 196 and Fig 197))

(Fig 196) ⟶

These values may differ depending upon the room settings and the place where you want that bar to be displayed ,   you may specify backcolor if you want .

Note:- The backcolor and the bar color must be different otherwise

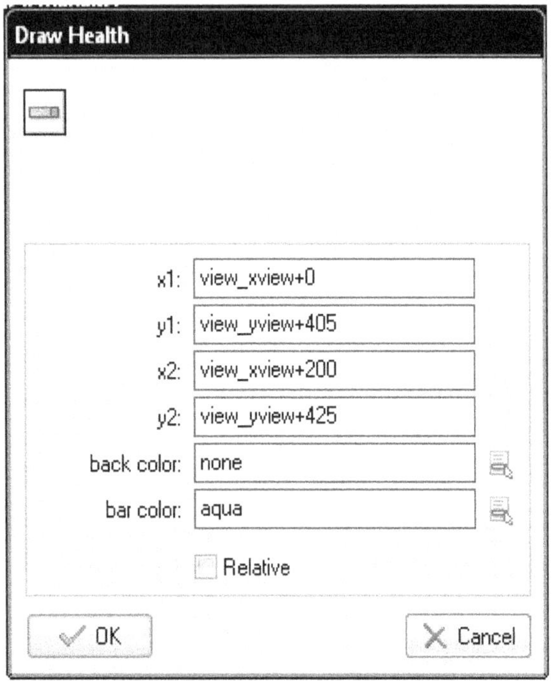

Draw Health

x1:	view_xview+0
y1:	view_yview+405
x2:	view_xview+200
y2:	view_yview+425
back color:	none
bar color:	aqua

☐ Relative

✓ OK   ✕ Cancel

there is no use of the health bar.

2)Game Maker allows you to choose from among 16 colors or combination example :- Green to Red.

Designing Room

This is a basic game so we would create only 1 room.

Follow the procedure to create room
a)From the resource menu press Create Room.

b)A window like Fig 198 would appear.

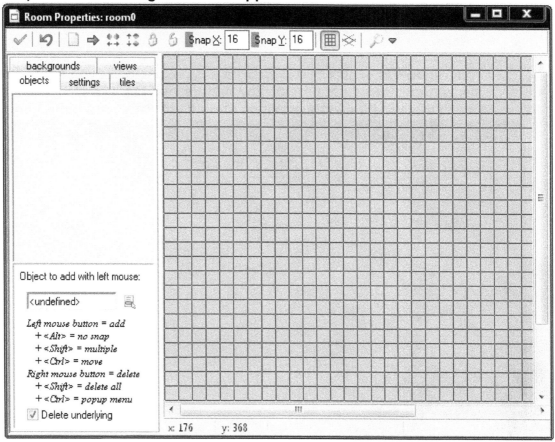

(Fig 198)

Press the settings tab ,   Let the Name be Space ,   Caption be space , width and Height be 640 and 480 respectively ,   Let the speed be 30

Press the backgrounds tab Check the following boxes 1)Draw background color 2)Visible when room starts ,   3)Tile Horizontal , 4)Tile Vertical 5)Stretch.

Press the objects tab ,   select an object press on the area containing the room (left button) and decorate your room

Note :- There should be only one instance of Rocket and Manager(Manager doesn't contain sprite so a question mark would be shown).

Tip :- To remove an instance right click on it.

The game is not over ! ,   we are moving to a bit boring part (Documentation). Majority of the programmers hate documentation but they don't have an option and even you don't have.

From the resource menu press 'Change Game Information' .

(Fig 199)

This window is similar to a Word Pad , you can load even a RTF file , this window would not provide you feature rich tool like MS-word or Open Office but the tools provided should suffice your needs. You

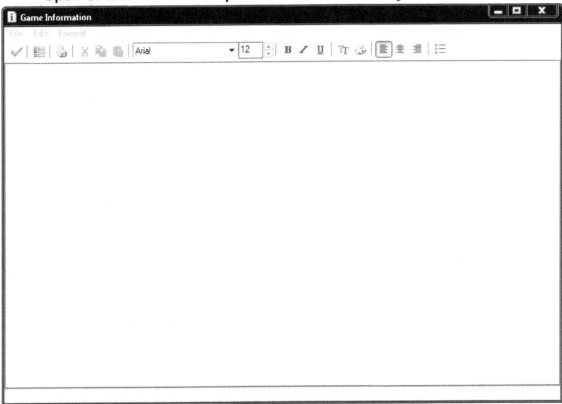

must divide the documentation into categories like Objective :- , Rules :- , Controls:- , Cheats , Hacks (If any) you don't have to specify system requirements in this case because if the user can read it means that your game is running on his machine.

Note :- The user would be able to view help by pressing F1 key. F you don't want F1 to display help open the Global Game Settings window (Resources   Change Global Game Settings) Open Other tab and uncheck the Let < F1 > show game Information box .

Save the changes (Game Info) by File ⟶   Close Saving Changes.

Now it's time to change/modify the Settings

Follow the procedure (Resources ⟶   Change Global Game Settings)

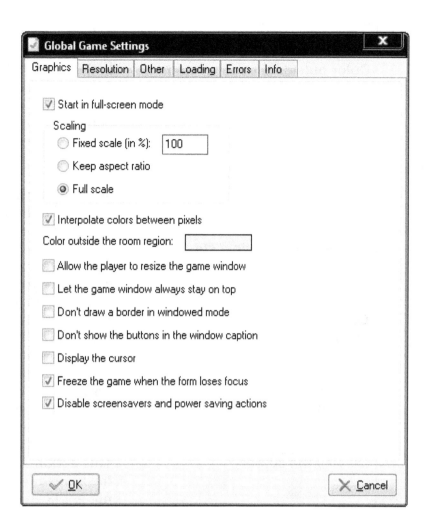

(Fig 200)

The table below will provide you all the detailed information regarding Game settings.

Name	*Usage*
Start in fullscreen mode	**Starts the game in fullscreen mode.**
Scaling	**Scaling is used to adjust the room size , you can use scaling for specifying what to do if the size of room is > size of the screen etc . If your value is > 100 the room is strecthed to the value(you specify) . If your value < 100 then some part of the room remains blank . The 2nd part is Keep aspect ratio (in this action the ratio of the width/height is maintained) The 3rd option sees to it that the window is completely filled.**
Interpolate colors between pixels	**Interpolation of colors has it's white and grey side , white side :- creates a better picture , grey**

	sides :- cause havoc if not used wisely!
Color outside the room region	In this field you specify the color which you would like to be the color of the region left blank(in scaling I have mentioned that some parts remain blank , this color would be filled in that part .)
Allow the player to resize the window	This action would let the player of your game change the size of the window(there is no need for the player to specify the dimensions)
Let the game window stay on top	In fig 110 we see how the earth lies above the meteorite , the same way your game window would lie on other window.
Don't draw a border in the windowed mode	This action would draw the game window without a border (This action is meaningless for games running in fullscreen mode)
Don't show the buttons in the window caption	This action would draw a window would the 3 standard buttons (minimize , maximize , close) present on the title bar
Display the cursor	This action would let you display the mouse pointer (this action is not applicable to cursors customised using the Set Cursor action.
Freeze the game when form loses control	Here 'form' literally means window , freeze means like paused , focus lost means you start using another application.(This action is really important because many a times antivirus triggers something and the window of antivirus is given preference , if this action is not checked and such a thing happens the player may even lose which is very much annoying .)
Display screensavers and power saving options	If you check this option the screensavers and power saving options would be displayed even during the game so I recommend don't go for this one.

Using the 'Other' tab specify the process priority , default keys and the version information

Use the 'Loading' tab for changing the icon

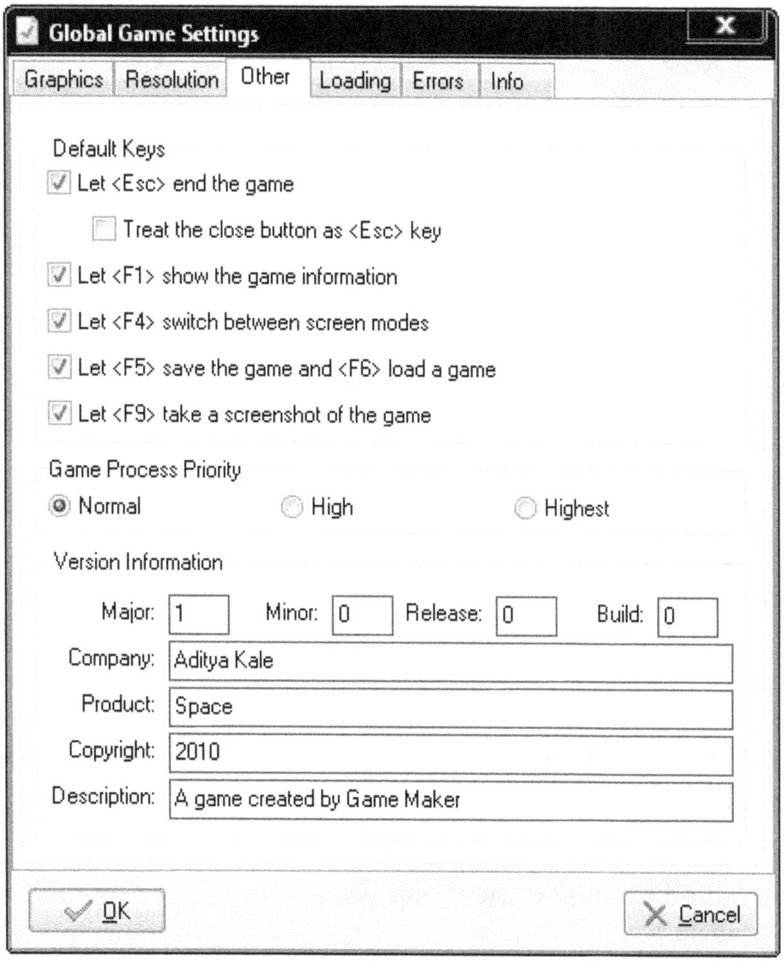

Global Game Settings

| Graphics | Resolution | Other | Loading | Errors | Info |

Default Keys

☑ Let <Esc> end the game

☐ Treat the close button as <Esc> key

☑ Let <F1> show the game information

☑ Let <F4> switch between screen modes

☑ Let <F5> save the game and <F6> load a game

☑ Let <F9> take a screenshot of the game

Game Process Priority

◉ Normal   ○ High   ○ Highest

Version Information

Major: 1   Minor: 0   Release: 0   Build: 0

Company: Aditya Kale

Product: Space

Copyright: 2010

Description: A game created by Game Maker

✓ OK   ✗ Cancel

(Fig 201)

To save open the file menu then press save , save the file to a suitable location , to play press F5.Your game is complete , go share it with your friends and earn appreciation for the knowledge you have gained.(If you are using the BETA version don't commit the mistake of distributing the game , distribute the game only if LITE or PRO edition is installed on your system.)

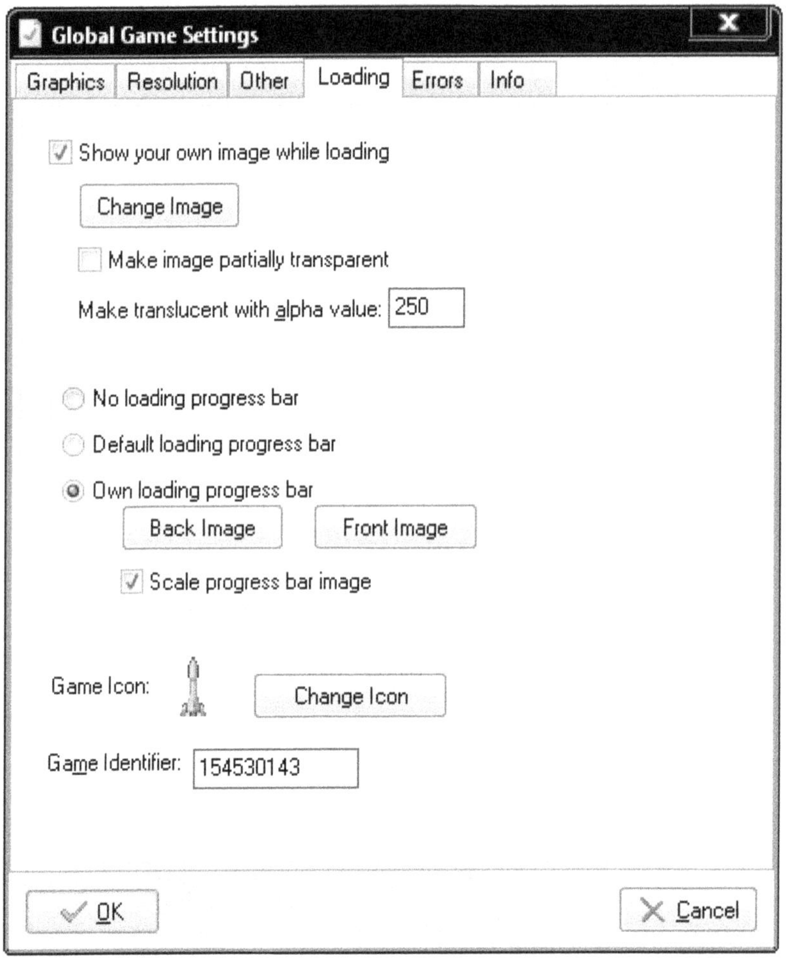

(Fig 202).

Now we have completed our game so let us understand how the actions , events and the objects co-operated with each other (How everything happened ? , Why it happened that particular way ? , How to increase the difficulty level ? , How to save a game or how to load a saved game ? if these are your doubts read further to clarify these doubts)

understand each object in the manner in which they were created(tabular method of explaining used.)

1)First we created the 'Rocket' object.

Events	Actions	Description
1)Collision(UFO _simple)	Set health to -12 (relatively)	When the Rocket collides(sprites/masks overlap) with the UFO reduce the health by 12 pixels per step.
2)Outside room	Wrap screen in both the directions	When the rocket goes out of the screen it returns from the otherside of the screen.
3)No more health	1)Destroy the instance	When the health becomes 0 or negative(health can be negative eg:-

	2)Play sound explosion(without looping) 3)Show the highscore table 4)Restart the game	the health is 8 and the rocket collides with the UFO the resultant health becomes 8 – 12 = -4) the rocket is destroyed , explosion sound is played , highscore is shown and the game is restarted.
4)Key press<space>	1)Create moving instance of lazer_red 2) Create moving instance of lazer_yellow	When the person playing the game presses the space bar two lazer's are fired in the 90 degree direction
5)Press <left>	Move in a direction (left with speed = 3)	When the person presses the left key the rocket moves in the left direction
6)Press<up>	Move in a direction (up with speed = 3)	When the person presses the up key the rocket moves in the upward direction
7)Press<down>	Move in a direction (down with speed = 3)	When the person presses the down key the rocket moves in the downward direction
8)Press<right>	Move in a direction (right with speed = 3)	When the person presses the right key the rocket moves in the right direction

One would ask the reason for using the Key_press event instead of Keyboard , the Answer is if you use Keyboard event the instance would move in that diretion even if the key is released , in that case you must make separate arrangement for braking.

You cannot specify health for more than one object (at this level , it is possible to some extent , you will learn this when you learn programming and gml) , here the health is only for the rocket object.

2nd object triangle

Events	Actions	Description
1)Create	Start moving in the upward direction with speed = 5	As soon as the instance is created it starts moving in the upward direction with speed of 5 pixels per step
2)Outside room	Jump to a radom position	If the instance goes out of the room the triangle jumps to a random position

Here we din't drag the action 'wrap Screen' because we want the movement of the triangle to be random.

3rd object UFO

Events	Actions	Description

| 1)Create | Start moving in a direction with speed 3 | As soon as the UFO is made it randomly selects any of the direction shown besides and starts moving in that direction with speed = 3 pixels per step.

(we have not selected the middle square) |
|---|---|---|
| 2)Step | With chance 1/12 create instance of object 'Lazer blue and green' | This action just creates the Lazer's this action is not 'create moving' so the lazer's would not move as soon as they are created.(If the lazer doesn't move as soon as it is created then how does the lazer move ? , you would find Answer to this questions afterwards. |
| 3)Collision(Lazer_red) | 1)Destroy the instance

2)Play sound explosion

3)Create instance of Object(UFO)

4)Set the score relatively to 5 | As soon as the instances of Lazer_red and UFO collide the UFO is destroyed , explosion.wav is played , another UFO pops up (otherwise the number of UFO's would become 0 and there would be nothing to do in the game) and the last action increases the score by 5 |
| 4)Collision with (Lazer_yellow) | 1)Destroy the instance

2)Play sound explosion

3)Create instance of Object(UFO)

4)Set the score relatively to 5 | As soon as the instances of Lazer_yellow and UFO collide the UFO is destroyed , explosion.wav is played , another UFO pops up (otherwise the number of UFO's would become 0 and there would be nothing to do in the game) and the last action increases the score by 5 |
| 5)Outside room | Wrap direction | If the instance goes out of the room it reappears from the other side. |

4th object Lazer_blue

Events	Actions	Description
1)Create	Start moving in the downward direction with speed = 3	(Lazer_blue and green are fired by the UFO so they should move in the downward direction , even if the Rocket is above the UFO the lazer would move in the downward direction) as soon as the Lazer is created ot starts moving in the downward direction

2)Collision (Rocket)	1)Destroy the instance(self) 2)Play sound explosion 3)Set the health relatively to - 10	In the case of UFO we have programmed in such a way that the UFO would be destroyed , but this is not the case here the Lazer would be destroyed instead you must always check the 'Applies to' property and the object in which this action is placed , a bit of negligence can waste a lot of time .

6th object manager

Events	Actions	Description
1)Create	1)Play_sound(backmusic , looping = false) 2)Set the health to 100	Plays the sound 'background music' without looping and specifies the health as 100
2)Draw	Draw the Health bar	Draws the Health bar (ike a progress bar) , the size of the bar and the health are directly proportional to each another.

Sometimes there are numerous ways to write the same game , It is even possible to write the actions for all in one object but it is not recommended as it would become a complete mess and you would waste time searching for the actions relating to a particular object , It is even posible to write the whole game without any actions but it would require a lot of scripts(program code in GML).

We have examined two queries(How everything happened ? , Why it happened that particular way ?) the next query was how to increase the difficulty level ? , it is possible to increase the difficulty of any of the game made by Game Maker , but it is difficult to make a game which let's the user adjust the difficulty level(tedious , time consuming but possible).

First let's understand what happens behind the screen when difficulty is increased . In our game the difficulty would increase if 1) The speed of the rocket is reduced , 2) The UFO's fire more bullet (here bullet mean Lazer's) , 3)The bullet fired by the UFO move towards the rocket , 4) The lazers fired by the UFO have more speed , 5) The number of UFO's and/or Triangle rockets is increased , 6) The aliens too attack the rocket , 7) Instead of 10 the Lazer's reduce the health by 12 or 15 after collision. 8)The size of rocket is increased(as the size increases the number of collisions with lazers increases too!!!. It becomes difficult to dodge the rocket) These are few of the possibilities (there may be even more)

1) To reduce the speed of the rocket reduce the speed in all the Move Fixed actions (of the rocket object)

2) If you want the UFO's to fire more Lazers Open the UFO
Go to the step event   Open the action test chance
reduce the number specified for the sides parameter (don't forget 'as
the number of sides decreases probablity increase ,   as the
probablity increases more lazers are fired')

3)To accomplish the 3rd point perform the following task Open the
Object Lazer_blue   ⟶   Go to the create event
Replace the Move Fixed action with Move Towards (x = rocket.x ,   y =
rocket.y ,   speed = 3) apply the same for Lazer_green

4) (It assumes that you have performed the 3rd one) open the move
towards action(let the x and y be the same just increase the speed.)

5)When we made the room we saw how to add objects to the room ,
add few more.

6)Add the collision event with aliens(in rocket) and drag an action
Change Health and specify a negative value.

7)Open the Lazer (blue and then green) ⟶   Open the event
'Collision with rocket'   Open the action set health change
the value to -12 or -15

8)Open the Object Rocket ⟶   Add event create   ⟶
Drag action transform sprite (main1 ⟶   sprite) let the xscale
and the yscale > 1

        Apply these changes and feel the difference but remember the
user/player would not like if you increase the difficulty too much or
the game is too easy. There are many ways of increasing the difficulty
, to understand in detail you must know what is AI (Artificial
Intelligence) A common example of a game which uses AI is a chess
game (the computer knows how to make a move / attack / defend and
sometimes even defeat.)(AI is needed for increasing the difficulty in
such games ,   AI cannot be applied to the game we made (space)

Note :- AI requires a lot of programming.

So we have made our first game but we can add much more to it so
let's modify.

1) We would add the save/load feature ,   2) We would make the
window adjustable(user can switch between fullscreen and windowed
) ,   3) Add effects ,   4)We would let the player change the color of the
rocket ,   5) We would change the number of Lives ,   6) Lives would
be drawn ,   7) We would change Resolution ,   8) We would add
bonus lives after a collision takes place,   9)We would add a loader ,
10) We would change the background of the Highscore table

Note :- These changes will not affect the difficulty level ,   these
changes would improve the appearance of our game .

2) After the appearance is improved the games would require more processing power (they would require more physical memory comparatively . Physical memory means RAM ,   for example if your game consumed 200 mb after improving the looks it would consume approx 225 – 250 mb)

1)Open the global game settings ———➤   Other tab ———➤ put a check on the box ' Let <F5> save a game and <F6> load a game Press Ok

Note :- F5 would save and F6 would load

Note :- You can't save multiple games and select one of them for loading , this feature is not supported by Game Maker

2)Open the object manager ———➤   Add event Keyboard(Letters ———➤ F) drag action set fullscreen (draw tab settings part) Specify the action parameter to switch

Note :- F was selected randomly ,   you can specify any other key (totally your choice) ,   on pressing the 'F' key it would switch between the window and fullscreen mode.

3)Open UFO_simple———➤   collison_Lazer red ———➤ Drag action 'Create Effect' (draw tab others part) specify the parameters as shown in the figure below. Apply the same to Collision_Lazer yellow (the Create effect action must be placed before all the other actions as they are executed in the order in which they are placed)

Tip :- Explosions must also be above the objects , to get a feel of explosion

Note :- Explosions drawn above the objects seem more realistic

4)(We would program in such a way that pressing 'w' changes the rocket color to yellow , you can specify any other key or color)

The screenshots of some actions are not provided as some of the actions contain no window

Open the rocket object   add event keyboard(letters ——→ W) drag the action color sprite (main1 tab sprite part) specify the yellow color let the alpha value be 1 (Selecting white color won't work)

5)If we don't feed any information about the lives , the number of lives is taken to be as   1 , (We would program in such a way that there are 3 lives)

Open the manager object ——→   Open the create event ——→
Drag the action set lives (new lives : 3)

Game Maker cannot make out what must happen if the lives get over , we have to add 2 more events

a)No more lives

b)No more health (this is already added we have to modify the actions corresponding this event)

Note:- These events must be added in the rocket object only

In the event 'No more health' drag action Set Lives , let the lives be -1 (relatively) and drag action Set Health , let the new health be 100 (absolutely)

Explanation :- When the health is no more on of the lives is reduced and the new health is set to be 100

6)As the health is drawn you would even like if lives are displayed.(Observe Fig 204 given below)

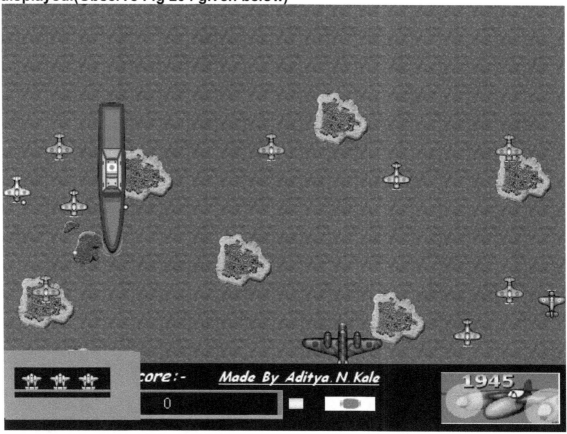

(Observe the area marked in red fig 204)

1)Open the object manager 2)Open the event Draw 3) Drag the action draw life images (score tab lives part) (x:16 ,   y:368 image:rocket , non-relative)

Note:- The lives should appear slightly above the bar if they don't you have either checked the relative box ,   not placed the manager object in the room or you have not selected the image as rocket and last but not the least your room settings are different than mine.

7)To change the resolution (Resources ⟶ Change Global Game Settings) then Open the 'Resolution' tab , select the box 'Set the resolution of the screen'

Just compare (Fig 205 and 206 for the difference)

Note :- More the resolution better the effect and more processing required. (Use 32-bit as it gives a better effect compared to 16-bit , 32 requires more processing compared to 16-bit)

 (Fig 205 and 206 of Global Game Settings are given on the next page)

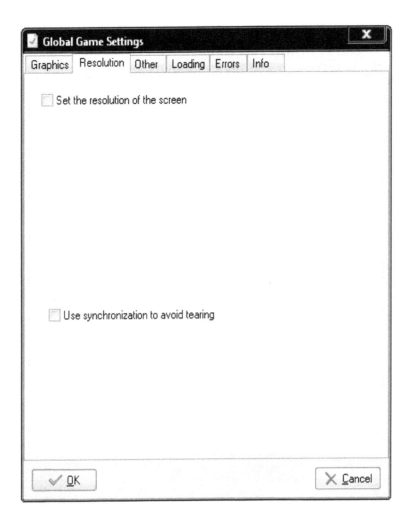

2)Resolution is always in the form X x Y (x > y) the maximum resolution supported by Game Maker(ver 8 in this case) is 1600 x 1200.   (don't change the frequency we would deal with freuency in the later part of this book)

Select 1600 x 1200 and press Ok

8)The idea is to increase the lives when a player collects a heart ,   but for that it is necessary to add a sprite (any sprite of your choice but name the sprite as bonus),   we would program in such a way that if the player doesn't collect the life(in 250 steps) it would expire (disappear)(we even want a new bonus to be created after 250 steps)

Note :- The bonus would appear randomly on the screen it wouldn't appear at a fixed place

Follow this procedure(we would use Alarm1 and Alarm2 ,   create an object bonus with the sprite as bonus).

1)Open the object 'manager' ,   2)Open the event 'create' ,   3)Drag action set alarm (main2 tab ,   timing part) Parameters are (number of steps : 500 ,   in alarm no 'Alarm 0')

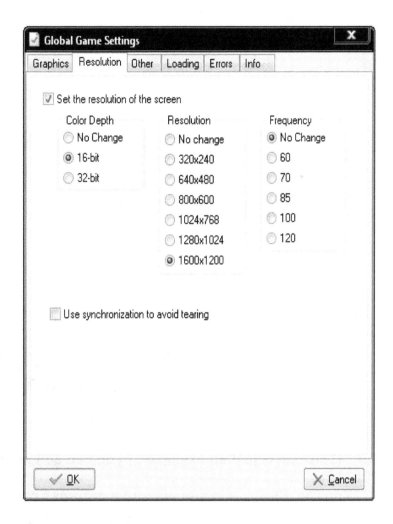

2)Add event 'Alarm 0' ,   2)Drag action 'Create Instance'(main1 tab , objects part) Parameters(object : bonus ,   x : 0 , y : 0) 3) Drag action set alarm (main2 tab ,   timing part) Parameters are (number of steps : 500 ,   in alarm no 'Alarm 0')

3)Open the object 'bonus' ,   Add event 'create' drag action set alarm (main2 tab ,   timing part) Parameters are (number of steps : 125 ,   in alarm no 'Alarm 1') drag action 'Jump to a random position (move tab ,   jump part) parameters (snap hor : 0 ,   snap vert : 0)

4)Add event 'Alarm1' ,   drag action 'destroy instance' applies to : self (main1 tab ,   objects part)

5)Add event 'Collision ,   with rocket' ,   drag action 'destroy instance' applies to : self (main1 tab ,   objects part) 2) Drag action 'set lives' (new lives : 1 ,   relatively) Add one more sound 'Applause' (provided on the disc) and name it the same,   3) Drag action 'Play sound' (main1 tab ,   sounds part) (Parameters   sound : Apllause ,   Loop : false)

9) Loader means the 'Progress Bar or the image shown at the beginning of the game'

Default Loader of Game Maker

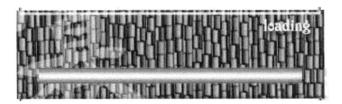

Changed Loader

(This one is just an example ,   you can add anything)

You can display a loader without a progress bar (Fig 209)

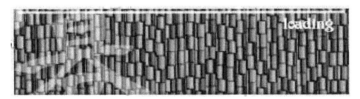

(Fig 209)

To add a loader open the Global Game Settings Check the box ' show your own image while loading'   Press the button change image and then browse to the location where you have saved the picture you want to save as the Loader

Note :- the browse window would appear like (Fig 210)

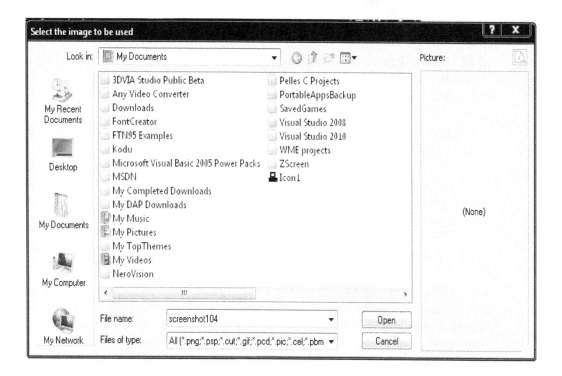

(Fig 210)

Tip :- You can make the Loader transparent (fully or partially) (Fig 211 shows a partially transparent Loader)

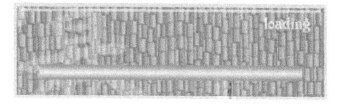

(Fig 211)

To make the Loader transparent , check the box 'Make image partially transparent' , Lesser the alpha value greater is the transparency and vice versa

Note :- Alpha value must be (0 to 255 , 0 means fully transparent and 255 means fully opaque)

2) If you are specifying the Alpha value as 0 there is no sense as the progress bar would not be shown (I recommend a value between 25 to 250)

Note :- 4 loaders are provided on the disc and over and above that many themes have also been provided.

10)To understand this point observe Fig 120.

To add background to your Highscore table you have to add a background , It is not recommended to specify the same background for the Room as well as the High score table , In the themes folder I have provided a lot of Backgrounds

Add the background which you want to use for your highscore and open the action 'Show the Highscore table' where it is already dragged and change the very first parameter.

We have to add the Event 'No more lives' and modify the event 'No more Health'

Note :- To delete an action , right click on the action and select delete or select the action by left click and press the delete button on your keyboard .

2)Game maker wouldn't prompt for confirmation

Open the oject 'Rocket' , Open the event 'No more health' , delete the actions show the Highscore table, Destroy the instance and Restart Game drag the action Set lives (new lives : -1 , relatively) then add event 'No more lives' , drag the actions 'show the Highscore table, Set health (value : 100) and Restart Game'

Note :- You can even add a sound which would be played when the game ends , Just add a sound and drag the action 'Play Sound' (This action should be placed before the actions 'show the Highscore table and Restart Game'

Summary

Let's recollect the main points discussed in this chapter

In this chapter we have actually created a game , we learnt the true application of the actions 'Start Block' and 'End Block' , we discussed about drawing lives and health , we even discussed about progress bars and the transparency effect

Chapter 4 Font , Icons and Tiles

i) Font

What is a Font ? , well that's a very simple question to Answer , according to dictionary a font is 'A specific size and style of writing' but the actual definition for font used in a computer would be 'A specific style of writing' , because the font size can be adjusted in a word processor .

This book will not explain you how to make a font!!! , this book just deals with settings associated with font's in Game Maker. If you remember we have learnt the action 'Set Font' in the 2nd lesson(draw tab / settings part) , This action uses fonts which we create using Game Maker.

Note :- There is a catch over here , Game Maker doesn't let you make a font(.fnt) it would let you select a style , the size and the character range , you can say that Game Maker let's you modify and use a font upto a certain extent.

To create a font select 'resources' menu and press 'create font' the following window would appear(Fig 212)

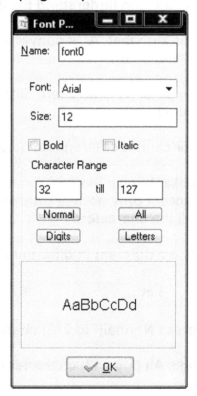

(Fig 212)

In the first box you have to specify a font name , in the second one you have to select a font (Game Maker would show all the installed font's , don't use a font installed by some other program as the other program may have the copyright of that font)

To understand character range first you need to know Binary Numbers and ASCII , there are three types of number systems binary, octal and decimal , generally we follow decimal number systems

For example

$2 + 10 = 12$, $45 - 5 = 40$, $32 + 9 = 41$ etc these numbers are to the base 10 , because the decimal number system contains 10 numbers 0 , 1 , 2 , 3 , 4 .... 9 . $2 + 10 = 12$ can also be written as $2_{10} + 10_{10} = 12_{10}$, the numbers in the octal system are to the base 8 , computers can calculate $2_{10} + 10_{10} = 12_{10}$ but computer would calculate in the form $10_2 + 1010_2 = 1100_2$ (10_2 stands for 2_{10} , 1010_2 stands for 10_{10} and 1100_2 stands for 12_{10}.)

Note :- 1 means on and 0 means off , binary is a combination of on and off.

It is very easy for a computer to convert a decimal value into binary but computer cannot convert an alphabet (a , b , N etc) into binary , therefore alphabets are converted into a number known as the ASCII (American Standard Code for Information Interchange) , this code is universal and used by all the computers globally (Computers even cover mobiles , tablet us , PDA's etc Infact anything which can understand the digital language is a computer)

Note :- If the alphabet 'A' is converted into ASCII it's value would be 65 , 'B' is 66 and so on

2)For a computer 'A' and 'a' are different , same is the case with other alphabets

3)Computer cannot differentiate between Alphabets and Symbols.

4)Game Maker knows the ASCII values , you can program game maker to accept on;y normal Characters , Letters(Alphabets) , Digits or all the characters

5)Symbols are different in different font's for example :-

$, **$** , $, $ etc.

6) If you press Normal(Fig 212) character range is 32 till 127

If you press All (Fig 212) character range is 0 till 255

If you press Digits(Fig 212) character range is 48 till 57

If you press Letters(Fig 212) character range is 65 till 122

The following chart provides ASCII code. (65 to 122 Letters)

ASCII Code	Character
65	A
66	B
67	C
68	D
69	E
70	F
71	G
72	H
73	I
74	J
75	K
76	L
77	M
78	N
79	O
80	P
81	Q
82	R
83	S
84	T
85	U
86	V
87	W
88	X
89	Y
90	Z
91	[Note [, { , (are different.
92	\
93	]
94	^
95	_

96	`
97	a
98	b
99	c
100	d
101	e
102	f
103	g
104	h
105	i
106	j
107	k
108	l
109	m
110	n
111	o
112	p
113	q
114	r
115	s
116	t
117	u
118	v
119	w
120	x
121	y
122	z

91 , 92 , 93 , 94 , 95 , 96 are not alphabetic (refer to the table) , you may not want to include them in your font but you may want to include 65, ..., 89 , 90 , 97 but Game Maker provides you no facility to skip some characters which you don't want , you have to include them.

The following chart provides ASCII code. (48 to 57 Digits)

ASCII code	Character

48	0
49	1
50	2
51	3
52	4
53	5
54	6
55	7
56	8
57	9

ASCII code	Character
0	Note :- Character is not shown as 0 stands for blank .
1	☺
2	☻
3	♥
4	♦
5	♣
6	♠
7	•
8	▫
9	○
10	◙
11	♂
12	♀
13	♪
14	♫
15	☼
16	►
17	◄
18	↕

19	‼
20	¶
21	§
22	▬
23	↕
24	↑
25	↓
26	→
27	←
28	∟
29	↔
30	▲
31	▼
32	Tip :- When you press the space bar this character is generated in the editor. Note :- There is a difference between ACII character 0 and 32 . Difference :- Character 0 is not at all generated but character 32 is generated.
33	!
34	"
35	#
36	$
37	%
38	and
39	'
40	(
41	)
42	*
43	+
44	,
45	-

46	.
47	/
Refer the earlier table for characters in the range 48 – 57	**Refer the earlier table for characters in the range 48 – 57**
58	:
59	;
60	<
61	=
62	>
63	?
64	@
Refer the earlier table for characters in the range 65 – 122	**Refer the earlier table for characters in the range 65 – 122**
123	{
124	|
125	}
126	~
127	⌂
128	Ç
129	Ü
130	É
131	â
132	ä
133	à
134	å
135	ç
136	ê
137	ë
138	è
139	ï
140	î
141	ì
142	Ä
143	Å
144	É

145	æ
146	Æ
147	ô
148	ö
149	ò
150	û
151	ù
152	ÿ
153	Ö
154	Ü
155	¢
156	£
157	¥
158	Pts
159	*f*
160	á
161	í
162	ó
163	ú
164	ñ
165	Ñ
166	a
167	o
168	¿
169	⌐
170	¬
171	½
172	¼
173	¡
174	«
175	»
176	░
177	▒
178	▓

179	│
180	┤
181	╡
182	╢
183	╖
184	╕
185	╣
186	║
187	╗
188	╝
189	╜
190	╛
191	┐
192	└
193	┴
194	┬
195	├
196	─
197	┼
198	╞
199	╟
200	╚
201	╔
202	╩
203	╦
204	╠
205	═
206	╬
207	╧
208	╨
209	╤
210	╥
211	╙
212	╘

213	╞
214	╥
215	╬
216	╪
217	╝
218	╔
219	█
220	▪
221	▌
222	▐
223	▪
224	α
225	ß
226	Γ
227	π
228	Σ
229	σ
230	µ
231	τ
232	Φ
233	Θ
234	Ω
235	δ
236	∞
237	φ
238	ε
239	∩
240	≡
241	±
242	≥
243	≤
244	⌠
245	⌡
246	÷

247	≈
248	°
249	·
250	·
251	√
252	ⁿ
253	²
254	■
255	Unable to display the symbol.

Note :- (Only for Windows Users) If you want to view any of the symbols press alt and punch the ASCII number in an editor like MS Word.

Note :- For punching the ASCII code use the keys(buttons of the Keyboard) situated on the extreme right of your keyboard , don't use the keys situated above the Alphabets of your keyboard.

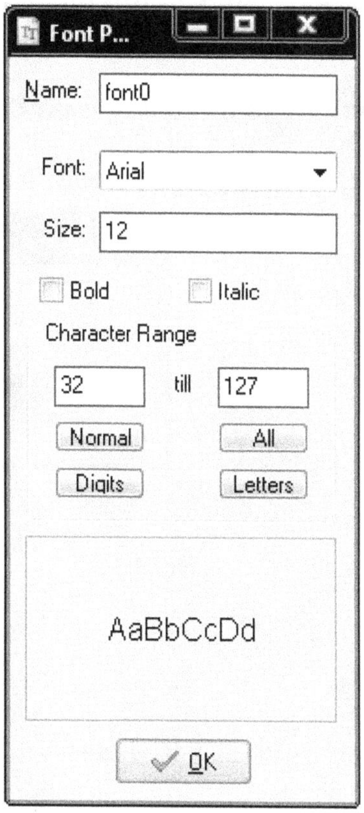

(Fig 213)

Note :- Your game would work even if the user of your game hasn't installed that particular font , Game Maker would include the font (not the font file , It would make a copy of the font in binary) with your game (in the .exe file) , Game Maker wouldn't even bother to

check whether that particular font is installed or not , it would just do it's work by displaying the font , this is one of the major plus point of Game Maker.

2)You can have more than 1 font file with the same name in your game ! , Game Maker would give preference to the one arranged first , This is not at all recommended .

3)The set font action should be dragged only in the draw event and in that particular event there must be at least one Draw Text or Draw Scaled Text action.

The Font part ends here .

ii)Icons

This book will explain you the way to make , edit and save icon with icon suite .

Note :- Icon Suite can be downloaded from "brothersoft.com" or "tucows.com"(Please note that you download version 2.1.12"

Credits :- Icon Suite is not made by me , Icon Suite is made by Mike Bouffler

License :- While installing Icon Suite the License is displayed.

Installing :- Follow the screenshots.

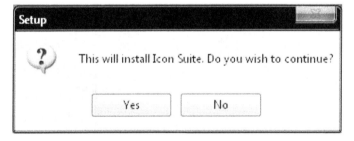

(Fig 214)

Press Yes

Tip :- Icon Suite is a freeware

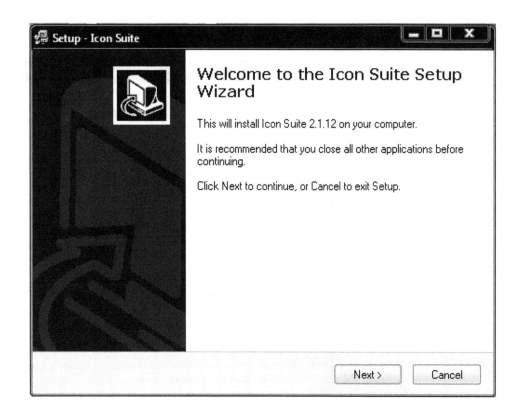

(Fig 215 Press 'NEXT')

(Fig 216 Press 'NEXT')

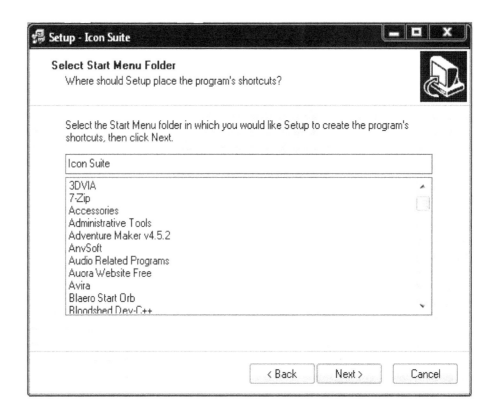

(Fig 217 Press 'Next')

Setup - Icon Suite

Select Start Menu Folder
Where should Setup place the program's shortcuts?

Select the Start Menu folder in which you would like Setup to create the program's shortcuts, then click Next.

Icon Suite

3DVIA
7-Zip
Accessories
Administrative Tools
Adventure Maker v4.5.2
AnvSoft
Audio Related Programs
Auora Website Free
Avira
Blaero Start Orb
Bloodshed Dev-C++

< Back   Next >   Cancel

(Fig 218 Press 'Next')

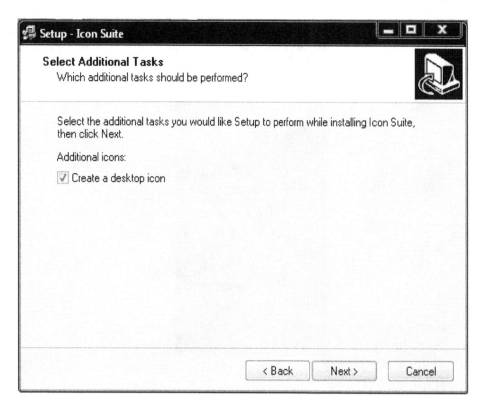

(Fig 219 Press 'Next')

Note :- Uncheck the box if you don't want to make a desktop icon.

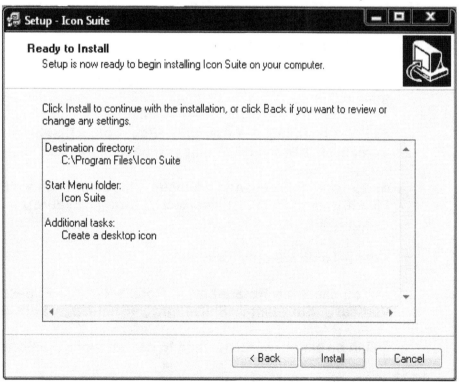

(Press 'Back' if you want to change any settings or else press 'Install' to proceed)

(Fig 221 , Final Window , Press 'Finish')

Reasons for selecting Icon Suite

a)Meets our requirement

b)Free for commercial , non-commercial purposes , any use we can think of.

c) No Advertising, Timeouts, Pop Ups, Disabled functions, Nag Screens or a Pro version that you have to pay for.

d) 15 tools (Freehand , Erase , Floodfill , FloodErase , Circle , FilledCircle , Rect , FilledRect , Line , Eyedrop , Select , Flood , HotSpot , Invert)

Note :- Tools are only for drawing.

e) You can even Rotate-Left , Rotate-Right , Flip-Horizontal , Flip-Vertical , Shift-Left , Shift-Right , Shift-Up , Shift-Down .

f) Can be simultaneously used to design more than one icon.

g) Provides Undo option.

h) Supports sizes 16 x 16 , 24 x 24 , 32 x 32 , 48 x 48

i)Supports color depths true color , 256 color , 16 color , 2 color

j)Provides preview even before the icon is saved.

(Fig 222 Icon Edit window)

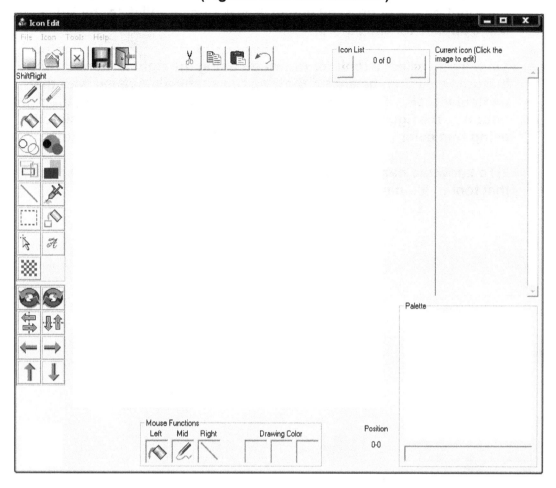

To the extreme right are the tools for drawing and others (flip , rotate etc) , Toolbar provides nine tools (New , Open , Close , Save , Exit , Cut , Copy , Paste , Undo) and there is an icon list , you can navigate to the other windows by pressing the buttons

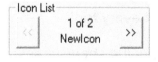

(Fig 223)

To the extreme right downward corner is the palette , In the above window the palette is not showing any colors , colors would be shown when you press new in the file menu or open an existing icon , Pallete provides 256 colors (different shades actually) but you cannot define custom colors , the color which you select is shown(displayed) in the box located below the palette.

The mouse functions support 3 buttons 'Left , Mid and Right'

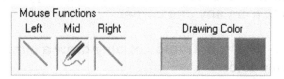

The image above shows a line for the right button which means that if the Right button is pressed line is drawn same applies to the left .The same applies for the colors.

Tip :- If you select a tool(for drawing) using the right button ,   right button would then be set for drawing the shape associated with that particular tool ,   If you select a color(from the palette) using the right button ,   the figures drawn using the right button would be painted using that color ,   same applies to the Left and the Middle button.

2)To know the name of a particular tool just hover your mouse over that tool ,   it's name would be displayed above the toolbox.

(Fig 225 'Toolbox')

Now let's learn about every tool

a)Free Hand :- No specific shape is associated with this particular tool ,   you can draw anything freely.

b)Erase :- As the name suggests this tool works like an eraser.

c)FloodFill :- This tool is used for coloring a large area provided a region is bounded by other color or else it would color the entire drawing are with that particular color.

d)FloodErase :- This tool is the exact opposite of FloodFill ,   it would erase the region covered with a particular color.

e)Circle :- This tool is used to draw circles ,   If you want to draw arcs start your circle from any one corner.

f)Filled Circle :- This tool would not only draw a circle but also fill it with a particular color.

g)Rect :- This tool is used to draw rectangles.

h)Filled Rectangle :- This tool would not only draw a rectangle but also fill it with a particular color.

i)Line :- You can draw lines using this tool but one must take care sometimes the lines appear crooked.

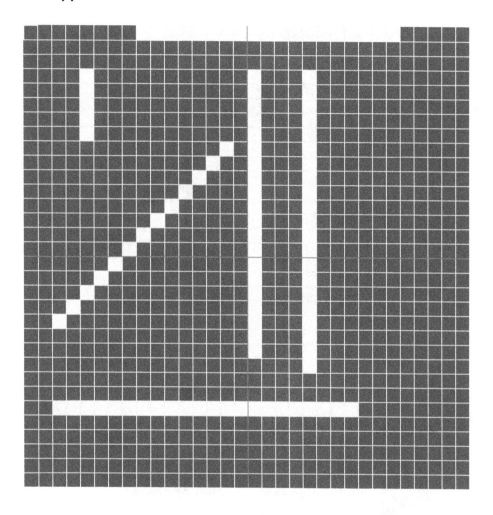

(Lines like a diagonals are also considered as straight lines , while drawing lines you must have a lot of control on your mouse)

Tip :- If you commit a mistake immediately press undo but remember there is no redo !!!

The button located to the extreme right is the undo button.

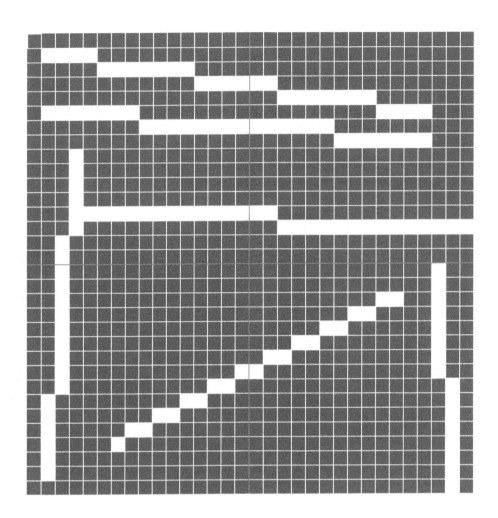

(Fig 228)

(These are examples of Crooked Lines)

j)Eye drop :- This tool is used to pick up a color already present on the drawing area.

k)Select :- This tool is used for selecting an area on the icon which can then be cut , copied or pasted.

l)Flood :- This tool is a bit different , this tool cannot be used for drawing a particular shape as no shape is associated with it , you have to select between square fill , and diagonal fill

   i)Square :- this is the Flood function used for normal flooding.

   ii)Diagonal :- this is the Flood function used for flooding diagonally.

m)Hotspot :- This function let's you select a block which could be clicked using your mouse

n)Text :- Allows you to write something (makes your writing work easier) , when you click on text a window appears (Fig 229)

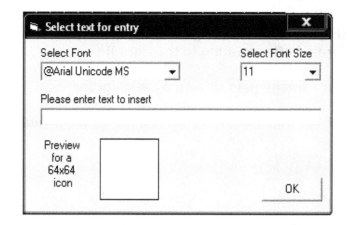

(Fig 229)

You can select a font , font size and then you have to type the text , Icon Suite can even show you the preview of your text.

o)Invert :- This tool would invert the color of a selected square.

Tip :- Some part of an icon is transparent (actually every icon is a square , you cannot make out the other part as it is transparent) , if you invert a particular region that region wouldn't be transparent.

Other tools (there are 8 other tools)

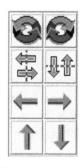

(Fig 230)

a)Rotate Left :- This action rotates the image to the left.

[Fig 231 (Original image)]   [Fig 232 (Image formed after rotating to the left)]

Tip :- Image gets rotated by 270 degrees.

b)Rotate Right :- This action rotates the image to the right.

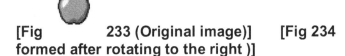

[Fig 233 (Original image)]   [Fig 234   (Image formed after rotating to the right)]

Tip :- Image gets rotated by 90 degrees

c)Flip Horizontally :- Flips the image horizontally

[Fig 235 (Original image)]   [Fig 236 (Image formed after horizontal flip)]

Tip :- Mirror image is shown after an image is horizontally flipped

d)Flip Vertical :- Flips the image vertically

[Fig 237 (Original image)]   [Fig 238 (Image formed after vertical flip)]

The remaining four tools are used to shift the image to the left ,   right , up and down

   You can save an icon through the file menu (or presss Ctrl and S together) . Icons acan be made in the following sizes 16 x 16 ,   24 x 24 ,   32 x 32 ,   48 x 48 . (48 x 48 is better than 32 x 32 ,   similarly 32 x 32 is better than 24 x 24 ,   icons of the size 16 x 16 are the ugliest looking icons.

 Tip :- To change the size / color depth go to the icon menu and select Copy to new size / depth .

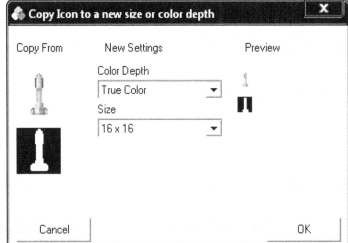

iii)Tiles

Tiles are something like incomplete images useful for designing games, tiles are like foreground images which are displayed on the background in a room.(Fig 240 is a tile)

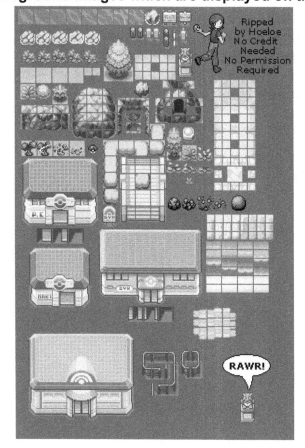

(Fig 240 'A tile made by Hoeloe)

Fig 240 clearly shows that the image is incomplete or we can even define tiles as a set of incomplete images arranged as a single images.

Uses of tiles

Tiles are of great importance as they reduce a lot of time and efforts , tiles are created in the same way as the background is created , in Game Maker there is nothing like 'Create Tile'. Moreover same tile-sets can be used for different versions of a game, hence there is a kind of similarity in the versions of a particular game.

Note :- Tiles are drawn on the background(actually this is not applicable but for the sake of explaining : 'Depth of backgrounds > Depth of tiles')

Advanced game programming.

We can use the tiles for defining obstacles, barriers etc, but one may ask 'How does game maker know that there is an obstacle as tiles are drawn on the background ?(or 'tiles / part of tiles are not objects ?') the Answer to this question is 'You have to create an object (with a sprite or at least a mask)defining the events and actions of an obstacle and uncheck the visible box , and place your objects where you have drawn the tile' , the person who plays the game feels that there is no object but the object is there , the player is not able to recognize because we have unchecked the visible property.

Note :- It is obvious that the sprite or mask of the sprite must be similar to the tile.

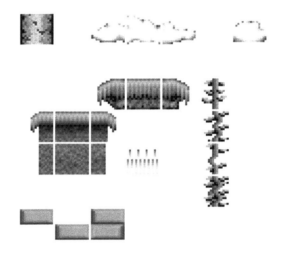

(Fig 241 'This tile was used in the game whose screenshots are given below)

(Fig 242 and 243 , 'From a tutorial by Mark Overmars')

The girl displayed in Fig 242 can stand on the cloud as shown in Fig 243 even though the cloud is a tile , this happened because there is an object(having a sprite or a mask) at the same place where there is the cloud and the object is designed in such a way that the girl can stand on them(the object's visible property is unchecked)

Note :- Even if you have unchecked the visible property of an object you can view that object while designing the room but you cannot see the object when the game is in progress.

While designing the room appears like Fig 244

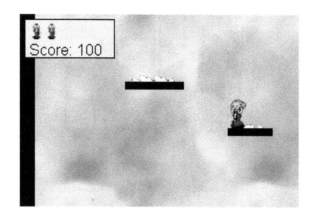

(Fig 244)

The blackish part is actually an object which was turned invisible by un-checking the visible property.

To load a tile you have to load it as a background , once you load a background (you can make the tile transparent , smoothen the edges , remove the background of that particular image , these options are available on the 'Open a Background Image' window , observe fig 245)

Look in:	tilesets				Image Information
	marioType_Tileset_Castle	marioType_Tileset_Skys-dark			☑ Show Preview
My Recent Documents	marioType_Tileset_Coco	marioType_Tileset_Subterranean			
	marioType_Tileset_Coco-dark				
	marioType_Tileset_Desert				
	marioType_Tileset_Desert-dark				
	marioType_Tileset_Fortress				
Desktop	marioType_Tileset_Icy				
	marioType_Tileset_Icy-dark				
	marioType_Tileset_PIPES1a				
	marioType_Tileset_PIPES1a-dark				Size: 192 x 320
My Documents	marioType_Tileset_PIPES1b				
	marioType_Tileset_PIPES1b-dark				
	marioType_Tileset_Plains				☐ Make Opaque
	marioType_Tileset_Plains-dark				☐ Remove Background
My Computer	marioType_Tileset_Skys				☐ Smooth Edges
	File name:	marioType_Tileset_Coco		Open	
My Network	Files of type:	All Supported File Types		Cancel	

(Fig 245)

(Fig 246 and 247 , Fig 246 is original , Fig247 is formed if the background is removed)

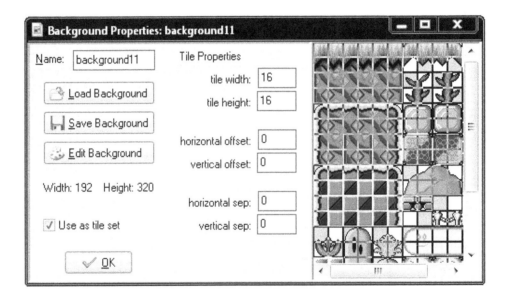

To use a background as a tile check the box 'Use as tile set' , observe Fig 248 given above

Specify the width, height and other values according to your needs.

To use a tile create a room , press the tiles tab , select a region of the tile and draw the tile in the room , sometimes you want to use a particular part of a tile in that case press the <Ctrl> or <Alt> (I would prefer the later one as Alt doesn't restrict me upto the grid) and drag your cursor over the area you want to use in your room.

You can change the depth of your tiles (Default value is 1000000) , You can add a new tile layer , change an existing layer and even delete a particular layer)

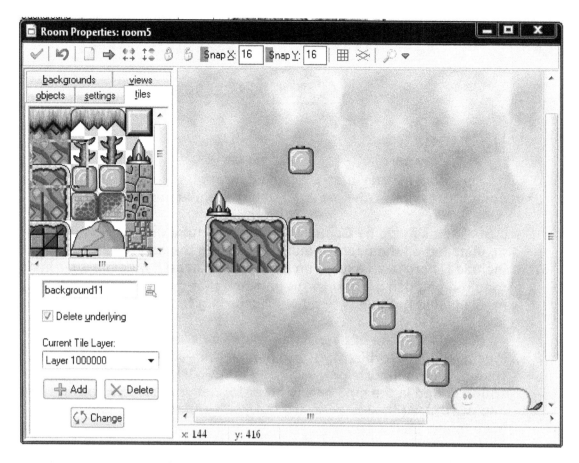

If you check the box 'Delete underlying' the underlying (one tile lying beneath the other) tiles are deleted , Ability of specifying tiles at different depths is one of the biggest positive feature of Game Maker.

Summary

Let's summarize the important points which we discussed in this chapter

At the beginning we learnt about fonts , binary numbers and ASCII , later we discussed about icons , we even discussed the process of installation of Icon Suite and the process of creating icons using Icon Suite and finally we discussed about the application of tiles

Chapter 5 Sounds and Animation

i)Sounds

Sounds are files which are played through the speakers of your computer (or any other device) using a media player.

Tip:- Games made by Game Maker don't require any media player to be installed on the users system for playing the sounds you include.(There is an exception over here , even if media player is not required you can program your game so that it may play sound using media player but this is of no use according to me.)

Sounds files are of different formats like Wave(. Wav) , Music(.Midi) , Vorbis(.Ogg) and many others like mp3 , wma etc but Game Maker supports only .wav and midi , if you want to include sound coded in the mp3 or any other format you have to convert them into .wav files.(mp3 is accepted but you cannot add effects and you have to use media player)

Tip :- Wave files are uncompressed files and the same file requires more disk space compared to other formats (Example :- a mp3 file of the duration 3 min may require 3 MB disk space but the same file in wav format may require approx 4.45 – 5.00 MB)

To record sound you require a microphone , it is possible to record a part of any other sound file. Microsoft includes a sound recorder with ever version of windows to open the sound recorder carry on the following procedure (Press 'Start Button' select 'All Programs' then select 'Accessories' next 'Entertainment' and finally 'Sound Recorder')

Note :- If you already know how to record sound using any other program and you are comfortable with that program you may use that program provided that the program can record sound in .wav format.

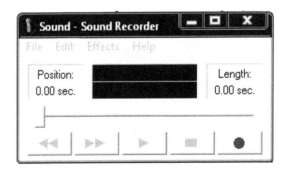

(Fig 250, Sound Recorder)

 **Press this button to start the recorder (You have to press this button after every minute)**

This button must be pressed after the recording is over

Tip :- From the effects menu you can add a few effects like (Increase Volume by 25 % , Decrease volume , Increase/Decrease speed , Add Echo and Reverse)

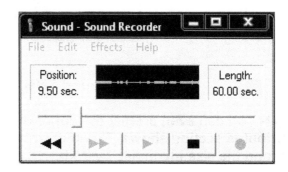

The fluctuation of the above graph shows that the sound is being recorded. If fluctuation is not observed sound is not being recorded in that case a plain(without information) file would be recorded , though sound is not recorded such files require disk space!

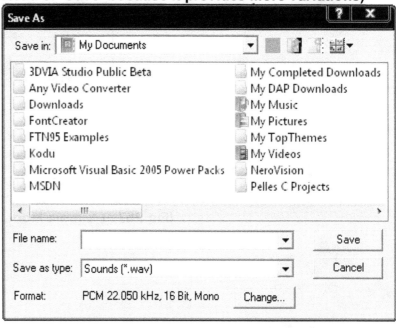

(Fig 254 , Recorder in progress)

'Save' and 'Save As' options are available in the file menu (It is better to use 'Save As' instead of 'Save' because it provides more variations)

(Fig 255, Save As Window)

Press the change button for changing format,　Observe the fig 256 'Sound Selection' window provided on the next page.

Note :- Experiment with each one of them and select the combination you wish ,　Better the effect more the disk space required.

Note :- Three formats are already provided 'CD quality' ,　'Radio quality' and 'Telephone quality'.

2)You can even create your own.

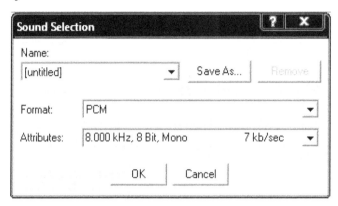

(Fig 256 Sound Selection Window)

Tip :- You can even predict the approximate size of the image ,　the Attributes section shows '7kb/sec' which means that for every one second file size increases by 7 kb.

To add sounds follow the procedure

a)From the Resources menu select Create Sound

(Fig 257 , (Simple Mode))

(Fig 258 , (Advanced Mode))

To add sound files press 'Load Sound' , You can even edit sounds but Game Maker doesn't include an internal sound editor (version 8.0 , hope an editor is added) , you have to specify an external sound editor. To specify an external sound editor open Preferences from the File menu and select the Editors tab

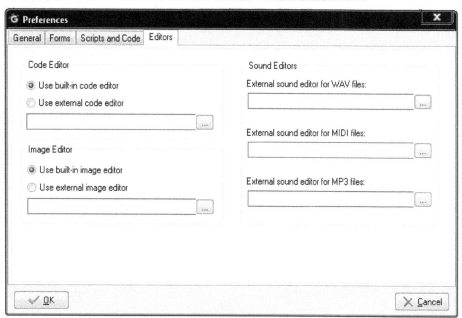

Press the button placed besides the textbox or enter (type) the filename without any mistake , you can even use external editors for editing backgrounds and images (I am providing an external image editing program GIMP (GNU Image Manipulation Programme) Gimp is available on www.gimp.org.

ii)Animation

The animation referred to in this book is just basic, covering animation in detail is beyond the scope of this book. Some games for example 'Age of Empires II' display an animation before beginning the game, the animation gives info about the credentials of the game , we are learning animation so that even would be able to make a simple video displaying credentials . Some games even play a short animated film before the game (Example :- The Game 'The House Of The Dead' shows a story type film) , using films like these improve the impression of your game and makes them marketable.

We would use Windows Movie Maker(Reason :- Movie Maker comes preinstalled with a windows installation , to start Movie Maker press the start button → All Programs → Movie Maker

(Fig 260)

Note :- The Start Button may appear different depending upon the version of Windows installed on your system.

Additional benefits

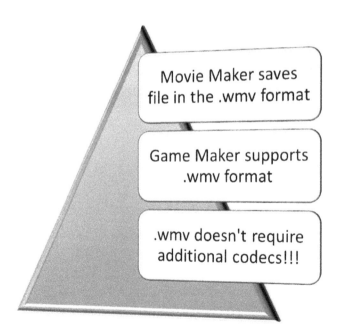

Movie Maker saves file in the .wmv format

Game Maker supports .wmv format

.wmv doesn't require additional codecs!!!

Start Movie Maker

(Fig 262 Movie Maker)

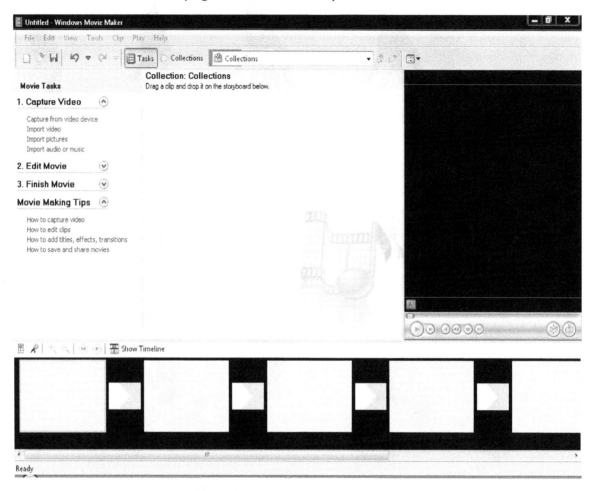

Before Proceeding it's essential to remember a few points

1) Every film is a series of still pictures.

2) FPS is a commonly used term in Animation, FPS means Frames Per Second , More the FPS better the picture but limit your FPS from 25 to 30 , More the FPS more is the file size , A good animator has to adjust between file size and FPS.

3) It is important to add sounds.

4) It is advisable to add 2 or more screenshots of the game in the video.

5) Don't add any sounds from the game.

6) A story type introduction is a fantastic idea.

7) Add credentials about your company or watermarks if possible(this discourages others from using a part of your video)

You may be wondering 'How can Animation be a series of still pictures?' observe the screenshots given below.

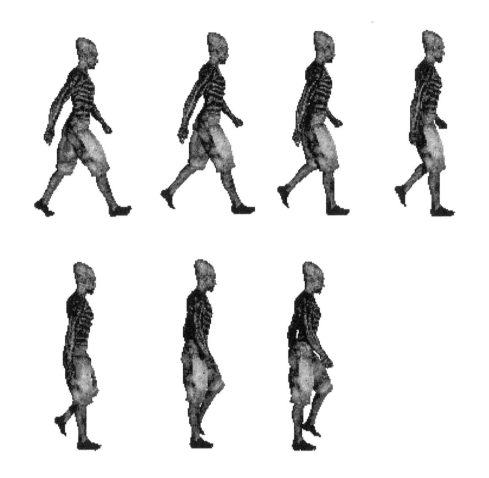

(Fig 262)

Even when a particular image is removed the illusion of that image remains for 1/16th of a second and if a series of such pictures are produced before the eyes within 1/16th of a second we feel that the person is moving , when such a series of pictures is accompanied by sound/voice the series of pictures is known as an animation.

Thus we can define animation as 'A set or a series of still images accompanied by sound'.

Now you are ready to learn the real art of animation.

Note :- Even our motion pictures are a series of still images , if it's possible observe the film of a cine camera.

You must draw all the images you want to use in your film.

Note :- It is even possible to merge an existing video with your film.

Open Movie Maker.

Press Ctrl + I, select the graphic files or the videos you wish to import.

Note :- You must include at least 5 images.

Drag the images to the storyboard situated at the bottom.

Each rectangular box is a frame , go on adding the images in the required order.(Figure 264 is only an example)

(Fig 264)

To the extreme right is a media player, this player let's you play the file even before it is made!!!.

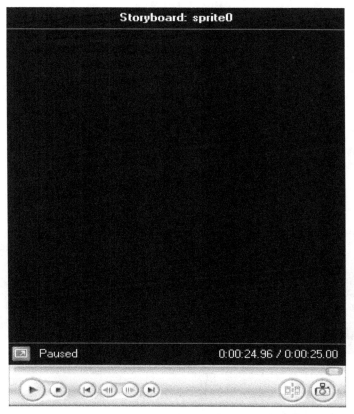

The graphic shown besides shows the media player , you can even take screenshots of a video when the playing is in progress by pressing the button located on the extreme right.

To know the names of the buttons hover your cursor over the buttons.

Tip :- Such type of help is known as Tool Tip Text in the language Visual Basic.

a)Play :- Play button is used for playing(starting) a video.

Note :- To pause a video press the Play button again.

b)Stop :- As the name suggests this button stops the animation.

c)Back :- Goes to the previous image.

d)Previous Frame :- Shows the previous frame.

e)Next Frame :- this is just the opposite of the previous button.

f)Forward :- goes to the next image.

Tip :- For Fast Forward or Rewind use the bar located above the media buttons.

Let's move on to the Time Line.

Story Board	Timeline
a)Less Accurate	More Accurate
b)Doesn't display time	Displays time
c)Doesn't display information about audio tracks	Displays information about audio tracks
d)Non-adjustable	Adjustable
e)Provides less information	Provides much more information compared to Storyboard

A timeline is shown below

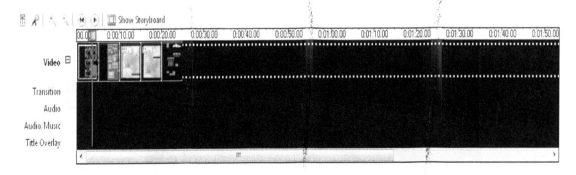

(Fig 267)

Stretch the images on the timeline according to the duration required.

Adding Sounds

As mentioned earlier one must own a microphone for adding sounds , attach your microphone to your computer and press the button narrate timeline.(Shown Below)

Start Narration

Press the button

Adjust the input level according to your needs.

(Fig 270)

Note :- you don't require a microphone if you wish to record from an existing audio file.

Tip :- To record from an existing file play that file and Press the start button

(Tip :- This applies only for the Sound Recorder taught earlier)

Press the button 'Stop Narration' when you wish to end.

Note :- Some microphones are very sensitive they even record the sound of breathing and external noises. See to it that you record sound where there are less noises.

When you stop the narration Movie Maker will request you to save the sound.

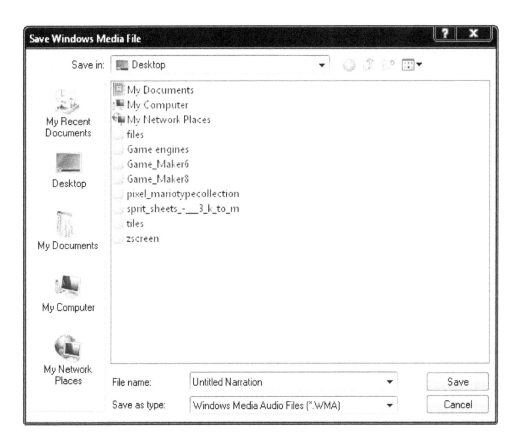

Save the file at a suitable location.

After adding sounds it's time to test the film , test the film using the media player.

To save the final file press Ctrl + P(Follow the screenshots)

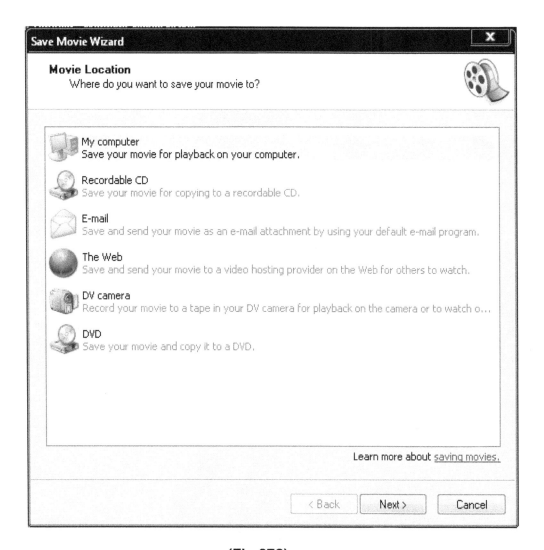

(Fig 272)

Press `Next >`

Choose Filename and Location.

Press the Link Label 'Show more choices....'

Fig 274 would appear.

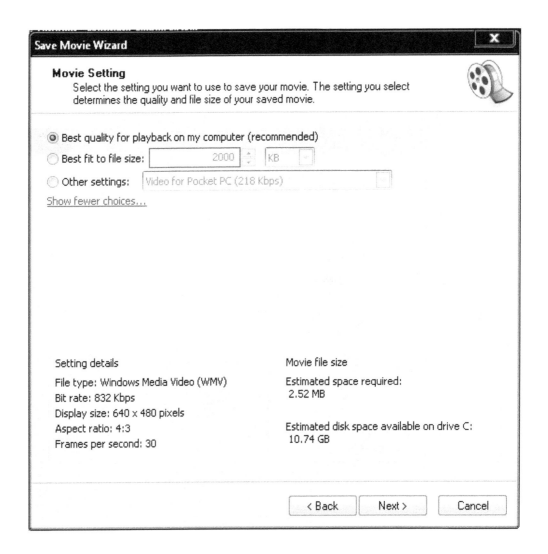

(Fig 274)

Adjust the settings according to your needs. Press 'Next >'

CONGRATULATIONS !!Your movie is complete ! you have learnt the Basics of animation , Use the action 'Splash Video' for using such videos in your game.

Chapter 6 Editing Sprites and Backgrounds

Open the sprite editor.(In this tutorial we have used the 3D ship sprite)

Note :- If you are editing sprites you must edit even the subimages or else the total animation may appear disjoint.(This is not the case when there is a single sprite)

The sprite editor let's you edit all the sprites (It is a tedious process to edit many subimages) (Given below is Fig 275) the preview column shows the preview of the sprites in the arrangement of their order. (it is not advisable to delete any of the images at all)

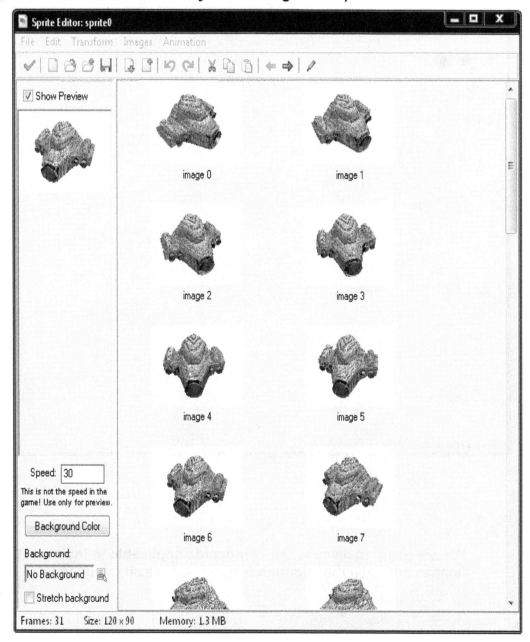

Fig 275 Sprite Editor

Press any of the images to edit,   the editor looks like Fig 276

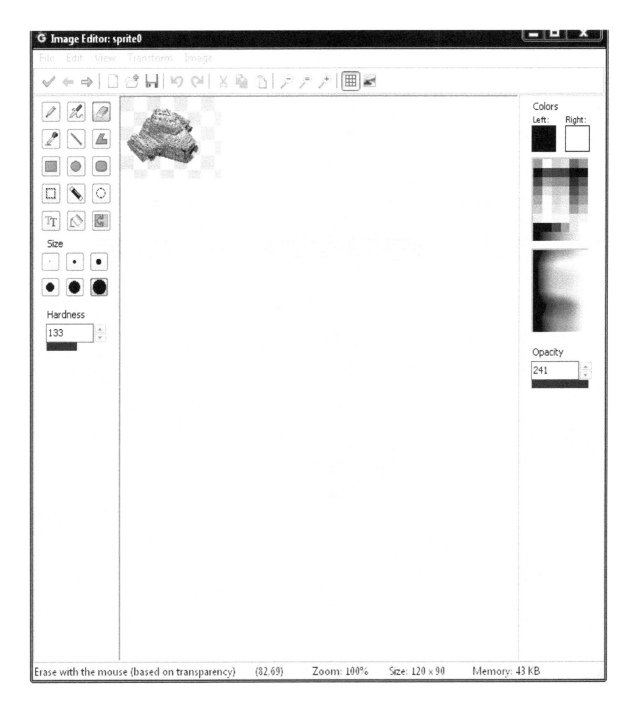

(Fig 276)

We are going to discuss the commands applicable to individual
images and then the commands applicable to all the images.

Menu Bar

Menu bar contains 5 menus

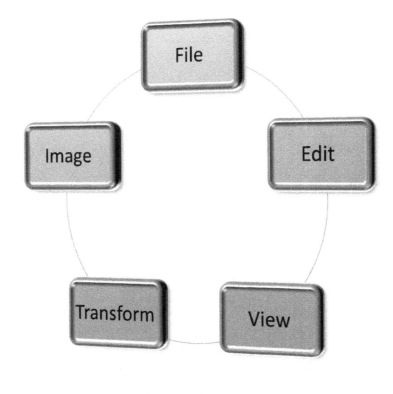

(Fig 277)

a)File :- File menu let's you open a new image , save the graphic in PNG (Portable Network Graphic) format open a next image and exit.

b)Edit :- Edit let's you perform clipboard operations like Cut , Copy , Paste , Select.

c)View :- View enables you to zoom in/out and other allied functions

d)Transform :- Transform let's you skew , flip , rotate etc

e)Image :- Image provides many options and it is almost impossible to describe them all in short.

The tools available in the editor are linked with an alphabet , to know the alphabet linked with each tool hover your mouse over the tool(Example :- Draw an image is associated with the alphabet 'D')

There are 15 tools all of them are explained on the next page

Tool	Function
1)Draw on image	This tool is like a pencil
2)Spray paint on the image	Sprays a paint on the image
3)Erase part of the image	Works as an eraser
4)Pick a color	This tool works like the Eye drop tool of Icon Suite which is explained earlier
5)Draw a line	Draws on the line on the screen
6)Draw a polygon	Used to draw irregular shapes.
7)Draw a rectangle	Draws a rectangle
8)Draw an ellipse	Used to draw a circle or an oval shape
9)Draw a rounded rectangle	Used to draw a rectangle which is curved and doesn't contain vertices
10)Selecting a region	Used to select a region for performing clipboard activities like cut , copy , paste
11)Selecting using a magic wand	A type of the above mentioned tool
12)Selecting by spraying	Used to select a particular region
13)Font	Used to draw text
14)Fill an area	Completely fills an area with a particular color
15)Change all pixels with a particular color	Changes all the pixels of a particular shade with the other color

To choose a color just select from the area shown below(located to the right)

(Fig 278)

You may even choose a color from the palette which provides 54 shades

(Fig 279)

Now lets us study the view menu

Menu	Shortcut	Function
1)Zoom Out	Ctrl + -	Enlarges the image
2)No Zoom	Ctrl + 0	Adjusts the image to it's original size
3)Zoom In	Ctrl + =	Reduces the size of the image
4)Grid Options	Ctrl + R	Let's you modify the grid settings
5)Show Preview	Ctrl + P	Shows the preview before saving the image
6)Set Transparency Background	Ctrl + T	Let's you adjust the background color and block size(blocks are only squares)

Let's proceed to the Transform Menu

1)Shift (Ctrl + Alt +S)

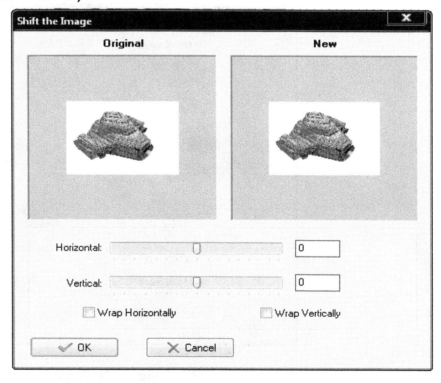

Adjust the scroll bars to shift the image , the range starts from -255 to 255

2) Mirror/Flip(Ctrl + Alt +M)

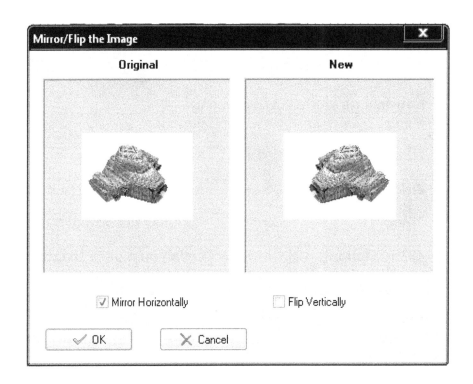

(Fig 281 , Mirrored Horizontally)

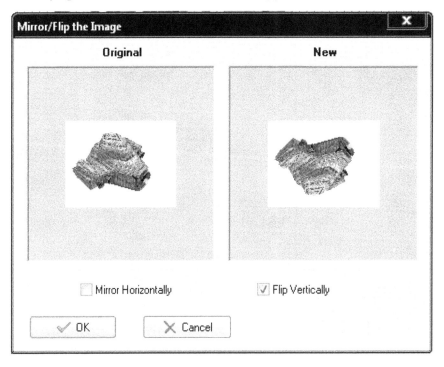

(Fig 282, Flipped Vertically)

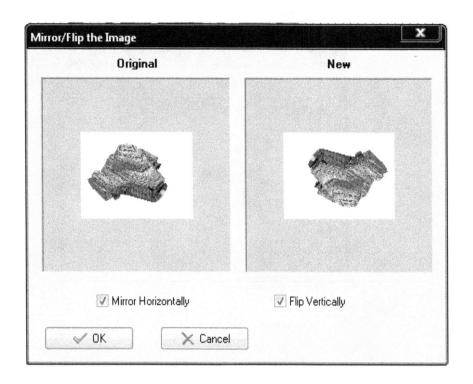

(Fig 283, when both are applied)

3)Rotate (Ctrl + Alt +R)

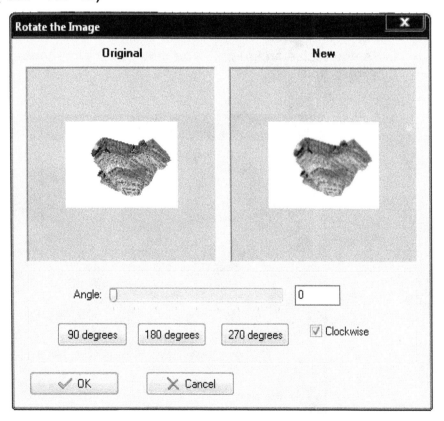

(Fig 284)

Let's you rotate an image clockwise as well as anti-clockwise

4)Scale (Ctrl + Alt + A)

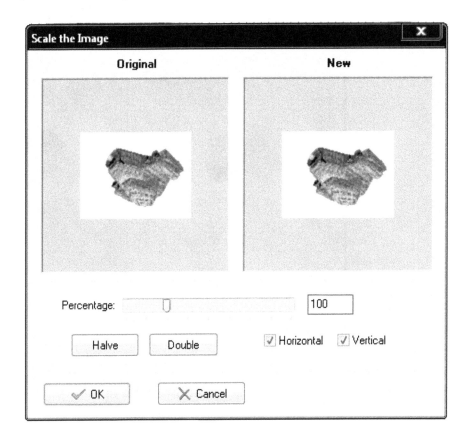

(Fig 285)

Let's you resize an image,   you may use the percentage bar to resize by proportion.

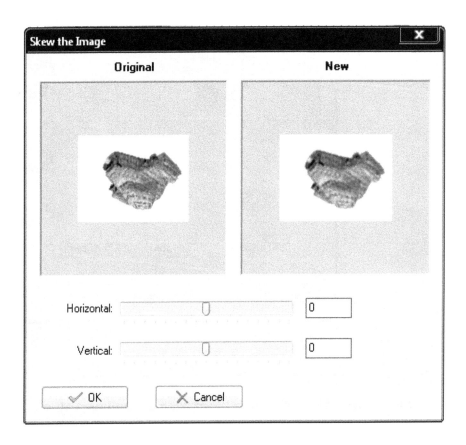

5)Skew(Ctrl +Alt + K)

Skew means to turn that image or make it slant or place at an angle.

The Image Menu (This is a huge topic)

1)Black and White (shift + Ctrl + W)

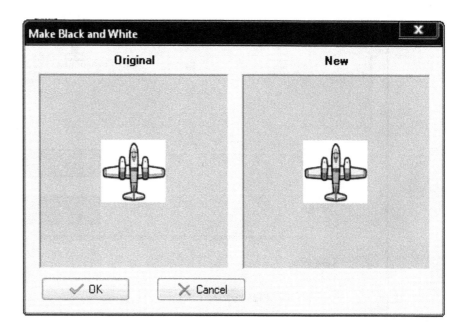

(Fig 287 , Converts an image into a monochrome image)

2)Colorize(Shift + Ctrl + C)

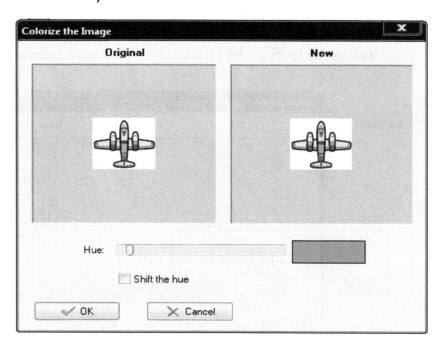

(Fig 288 , Move the bar and observe the color change)

3)Colorize Partial(Shift + Ctrl + O)

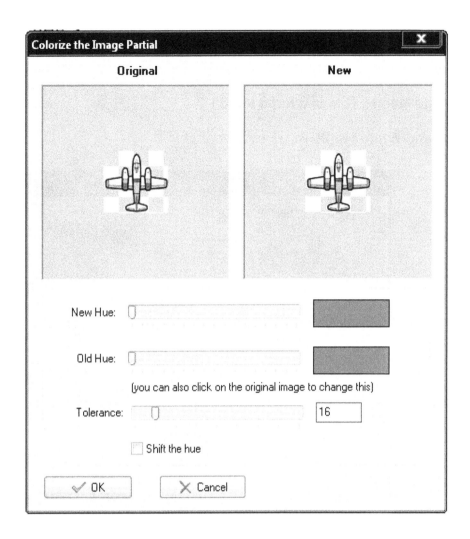

This one is better than the previous , this one provides more and better settings than the previous one , you may even specify the tolerance level , the tolerance level ranges between 0 to 128.

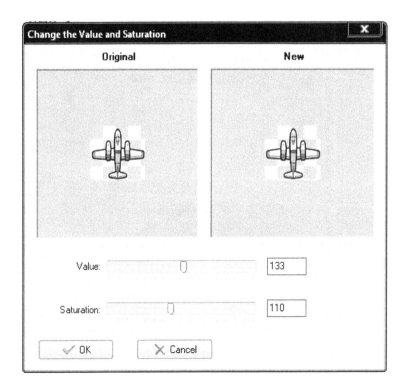

You may click on the original to change the hue , but you must click on the region required

If you want to Shift the Hue check the checkbox 'Shift the Hue'

The colors are shown besides the scroll bars(used to adjust the hue level)

4)Intensity(Shift + Ctrl + I) Intensity provides two parameters(Value and Saturation) both ranging from 0 to 255.

Adjust them according to your need and select the one which suits your requirements.

The Fig given besides is Fig 290

5)Invert (Shift + Ctrl + V)

Inverts the color (example :- white is changed to black and vice – versa , every color has an opposite color)

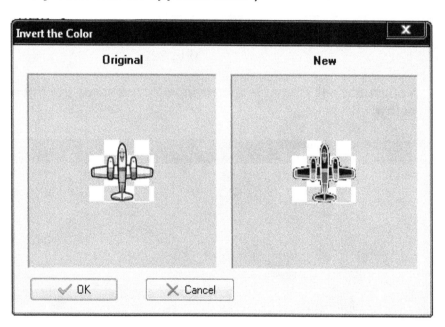

(Fig 291)

6)Make Opaque(Shift + Ctrl + M)

Removes every transparent color and makes completely opaque.

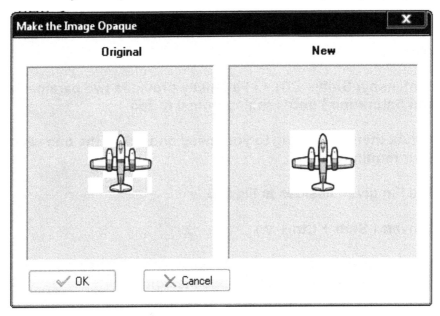

(Fig 292)

You would ask ' What is the change ?'   observe the figure given below.

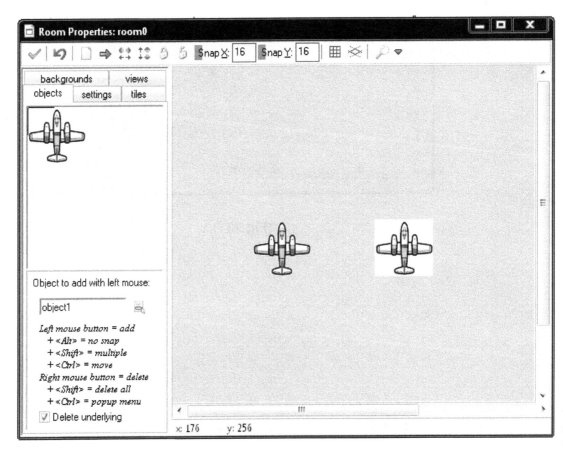

(Fig 293)

Can you make out the difference now ? , the white part of the second image is also considered to be the part of the sprite , this has no advantages but has the following disadvantages

a)The second sprite would increase the chances of collision

b)The white part would mismatch with the background , the over all look would be unpleasant and would annoy the person playing your game.

7)Erase a color(Shift + Ctrl + E)

Removes a particular color entirely from the image , If you set the tolerance level to maximum the image would fade away completely.

Note :- Observe Fig 294 given on the next page.

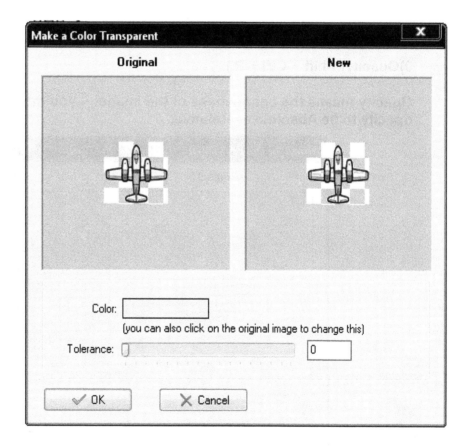

(Fig 294)

8)Smooth Edges(Shift + Ctrl + S) :- Smoothens the edges , Fig 278 is not able to show the difference as the plane is already smooth.

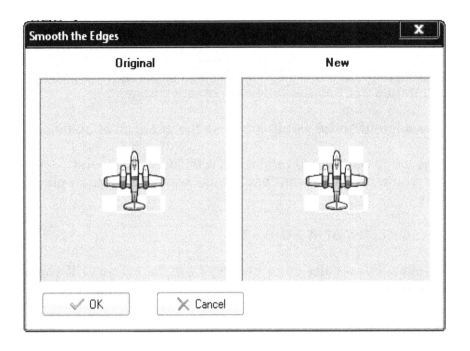

(Fig 295)

9)Opacity(Shift + Ctrl + P)

Opacity means the opaqueness of the image , you may specify the opacity to be Absolute or Relative.

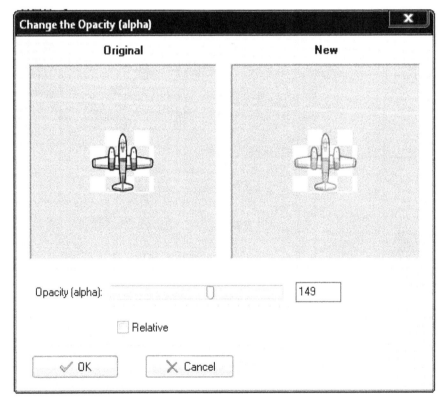

(Fig 296)

10)Set Alpha from File(Shift + Ctrl + A) :- This would select Alpha value from a file (Image)

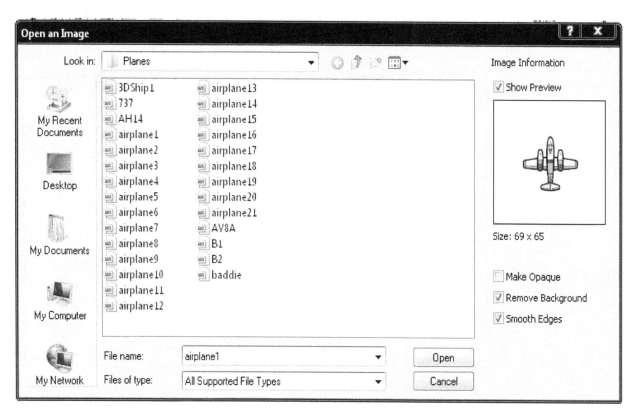

11)Fade(Shift + Ctrl + F) :- Fades to a particular color to the amount specified (0 to 255)

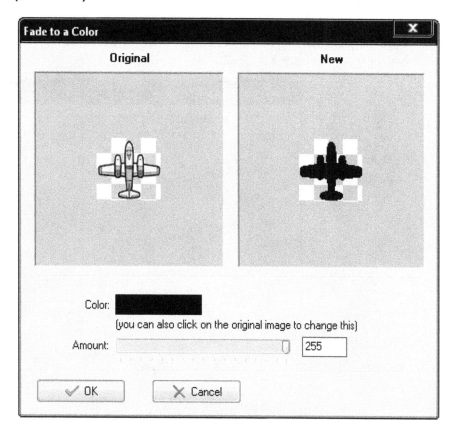

(Fig 297)

12)Blur (Shift + Ctrl + B):- Creates a blur effect , you have to choose the intensity (Small , Medium , Large) and whether to Blur colors , transparency or both , It's useless if you uncheck both of them. Observe (Fig 298 given below)

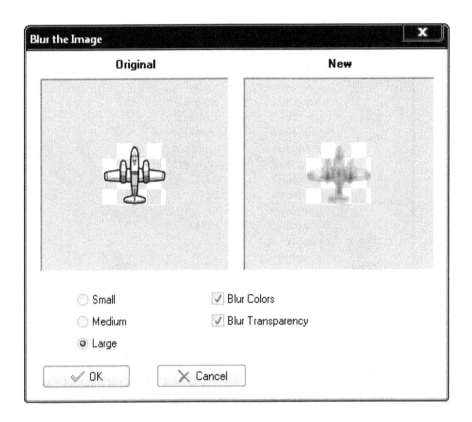

13)Sharpen(Shift + Ctrl + H) :- Sharpens the color , transparency or both (your choice)

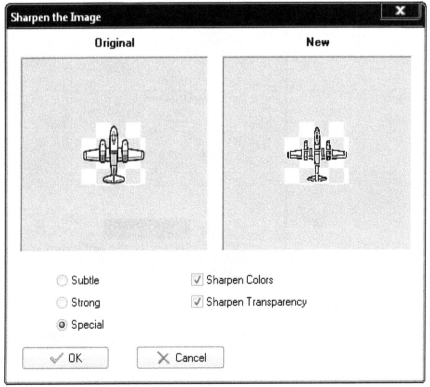

Note:- We chose 'Special' because we want to see the difference .

14)Outline(Shift + Ctrl + U) :- Provides settings to deal with outlines

Place inside image   **Remove the image**   **Smooth Image**

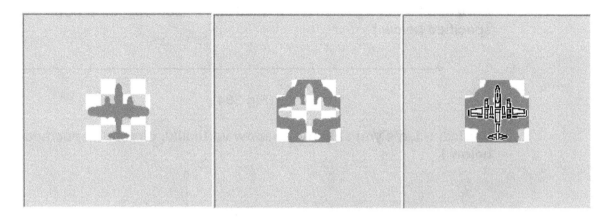

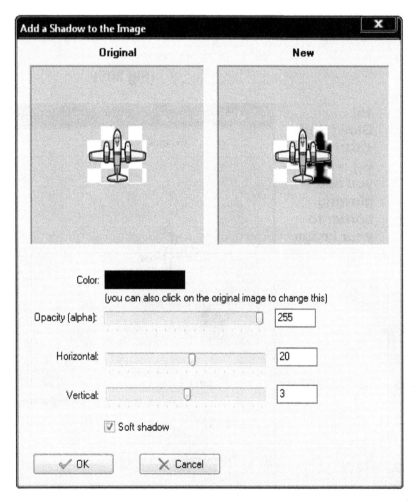

15)Shadow(Shift + Ctrl + D) :- Provides all the necessary functions to deal with shadows observe (Fig 287) provided on the next page.

Color :- Press on the box and select the color of the shadow

Opacity :- Opacity is directly proportional to the darkness of the shadow

Horizontal :- Let's you shift the shadow horizontally(direction specified below)

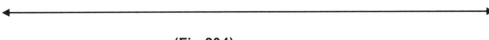

(Fig 304)

Vertical :- Let's you shift the shadow vertically(direction specified below)

(Fig 305)

15) Glow(Shift + Ctrl + G) :- let's you add a glowing border to your image.

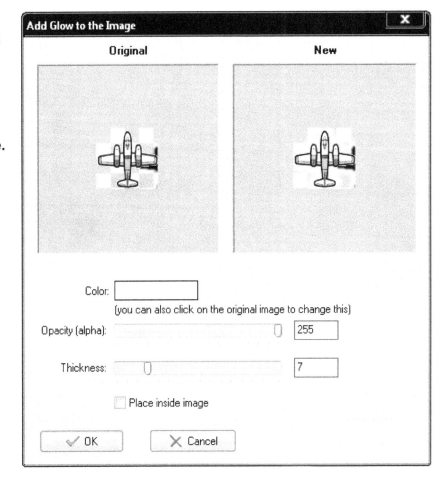

16)Buttonize(Shift + Ctrl + U) :- Buttonizes the image parameters described below.

Color :- Let's you select a color for applying the effect.

Opacity :- It's the degree to which the color would be applied.

Thickness :- Adjust the thickness and select a suitable one for you.

Note :- The thickness and the opacity must be balanced otherwise the result would be Fig 307

(Fig 307)

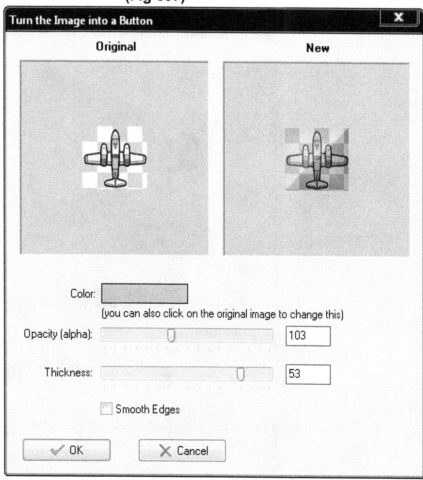

(Fig 308 ,   Buttonize Window)

17)Gradient Fill (Shift + Ctrl + R) :- Let's you choose from among multiple options for applying the desired effect.

You can select any one among the twelve kinds (types of effects)

(Fig 293,   The color combination of the effects depend open the 2 colors selected)

You may select Replace ,   change transparency or both ,   You must adjust the opacity according to your needs and select the two colors according to your needs.

The range of Opacity is 0 to 255

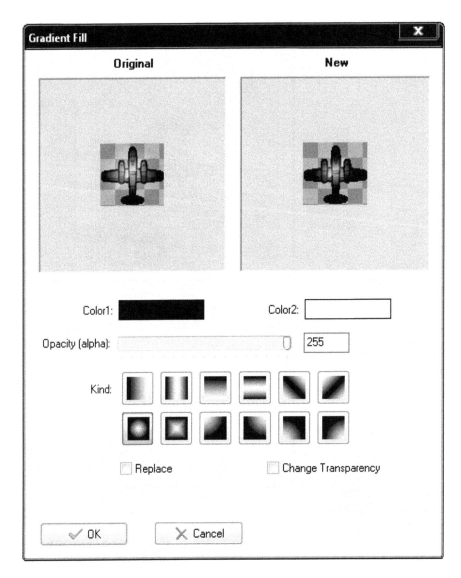

Here we dealt we the effects which are applicable to just one sprite now we would deal with the effects which are applicable to all the subimages as well.

Note :- The effects once selected are applied to all the subimages of a particular picture.

2)We have already studied all the effects which would therefore not be repeated over here

3)It is recommended to go through the animation part before proceeding as the further part requires basic knowledge of animation

4)This book will explain you many aspects related to Game Maker

5)Here you don't have to select a particular image for editing

Menu Bar

Menu bar contains five items shown below

1)File Menu

a)New :- Let's you select a new sprite ,   you have to specify the width and the height.

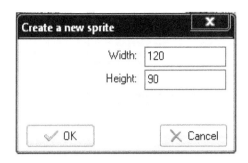

(Fig 312)

b)Create from file :- Let's you open a new sprite file for editing through the browse window.

c)Add from file :- Let's you add an image or images for editing

Precaution :- The size of the new image may not be equal to the size of the previous   image even the placement may differ , interfering or tampering these settings may not load the sprite properly so it's important. If you use new size the sizes of all the sprites would change ,   this would not matter much if the sprite has a transparent background.

Tip :- The browse window provides the size of the image below the preview.

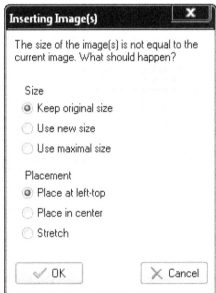

(Fig 313)

d)Save as PNG :- This option let's you save the file in the PNG (Portable Network Graphics) format.

e)Create from strip :- Let's you add/import an image from a strip.

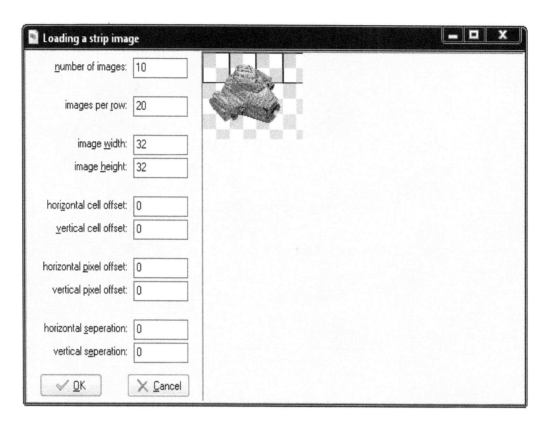

(Fig 314)

f)Add from strip :- Same as the previous one.

g)Close saving changes :- Closes the window and saves the changes.

Precaution :- It wouldn't prompt for confirmation so check whether all the changes are favorable.

Tip :- If you commit a mistake press Ctrl + Z

2)Edit Menu

a)Undo :- Deletes the changes caused to previous action.

b)Redo :- Restores the changes done by using undo

Cut , Copy , Paste are the clipboard settings , when you cut or copy a particular text or graphic that text or graphic is copied to a place called the clipboard , when you select paste the matter present on the clipboard is copied to the place you want if the matter is compatible with the software you are using.

f)Erase :- Used to erase the picture.

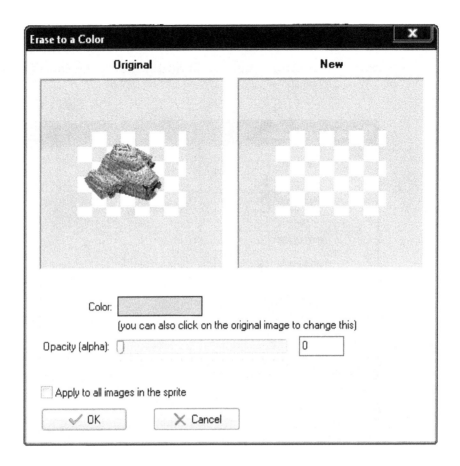

(Fig 315)

g)Delete :- Deletes a particular image from the set of pictures.

h)Move Left :- I will explain this function with an example 'Suppose you apply thus function for subimage number 4 , it's number would change to 3 and the picture whose image number was 3 would become 4.

i)Move Right :- This is just the opposite of the previous one.

j)Add Empty :- Adds an empty image at the end.

k)Insert Empty :- Same as the previous one

l)Edit :- Opens the window used for editing individual images

m)Set transparency background :- Opens the following window

Blocksize :- Set's the size of the block , blocks are square shaped hence their length and breadth are the same.

Single color :- Transparent background is generally shown in two colors(Fig 301) this would change it to one.

(Fig 317)

3)Transform Menu :- The first 5 functions are explained earlier the remaining are explained now.

a)New size :- Let's you change the size of all the images.

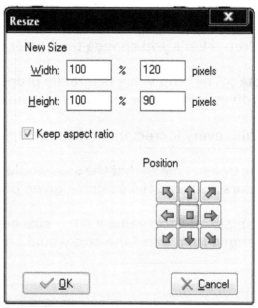

Keep aspect ratio :-
Maintains the ratio of the width and the height of the image , there are nine different positions available for placing the images you have to choose one of them.

b)Stretch :- Stretch is similar to resize only difference being 'One can set the position in stretch and one cannot set the quality in resize.'

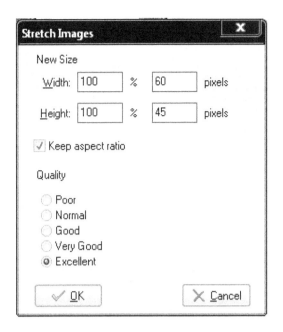

(Fig 319)

c)Crop :- Let's you change the border size

Note :- The crop value is directly proportional to the size of the image , If you specify a very high value Game Maker may stop responding.

2)With every increment in the crop value the size increases by 2 x 2

This doesn't mean that the size would increase by 4 (2 x 2) to understand read the example given below

Example :- (Crop value = 0) ,   size = 98 x 98 ,   when the crop value is changed from 0 to 1 the size would become 100 x 100 (98 + 2 x 98 + 2)

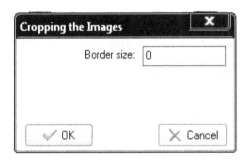

(Fig 320)

Images

a)Cycle Left :- To understand it better read the example given below carefully

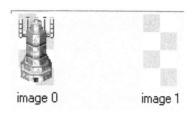

image 0   image 1

(Fig 321)

The sprite shown above has two subimages image0 and image1 , when you select this action the image1 would become image0 and vice-versa ,   but there is a catch over here read the further part to understand.

b)Cycle Right :- If you would apply this effect to the earlier one you would get the same result ,   then what is the difference ?

Answer :- When you cycle left the first image becomes the last , 2nd one becomes the 3rd and so on ,   but when you cycle right the last image becomes the first ,   the 1st image becomes the 2nd , 2nd becomes the 3rd and so on.

Animation

a)Set Length :- Let's you adjust the number of frames.

Note :- If the number of subimages is 9 and you specify the new length to be 5 then the last four ($9 – 4 = 5$) images are deleted.

2)If the number of subimages is 5 and you specify the new length to be 7 then the first two images are copied and pasted after the 5th images

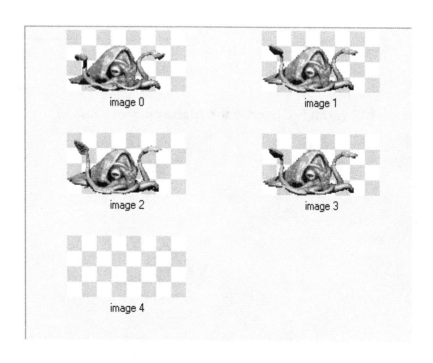

image 0   image 1

image 2   image 3

image 4

(Fig 322 above and fig 323 below)

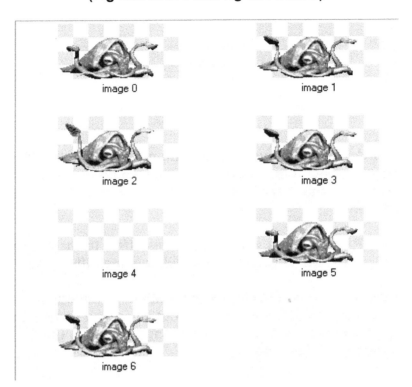

Observing figure 306 and Fig 307 would definitely give you a clear idea about the changes which take place.

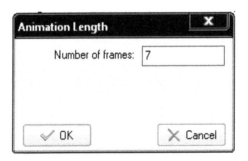

(Fig 324)

b)Stretch :- Observe the pictures given below.

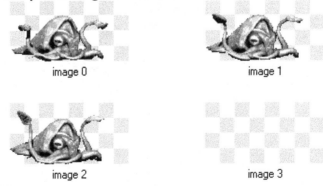

(Fig 325 , Original image)

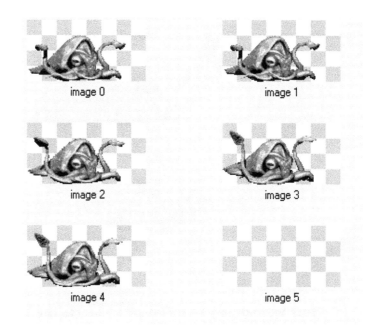

Fig 310 is shown on the previous page , the stretch value (number of frames specified was 6)

If you carefully compare and experiment with Stretch and Set Length you would come to know the difference.

c)Reverse

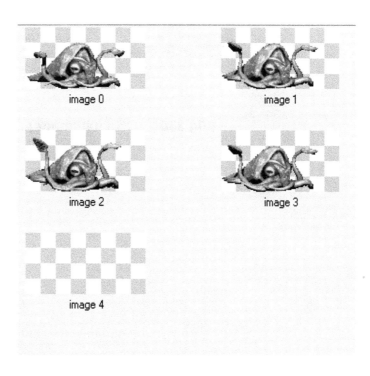

(Fig 327 , Original Image , Fig 328 (Below) after applying effect)

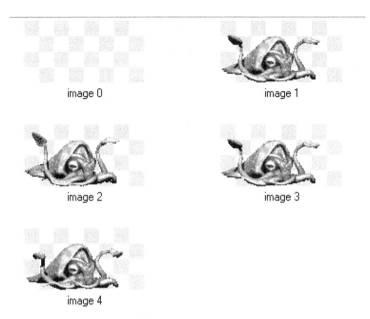

Thus we can say that Reverse inverts the sequence of the images

d)Add Reverse

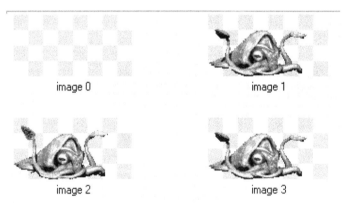

(Fig 330 , Original Image)

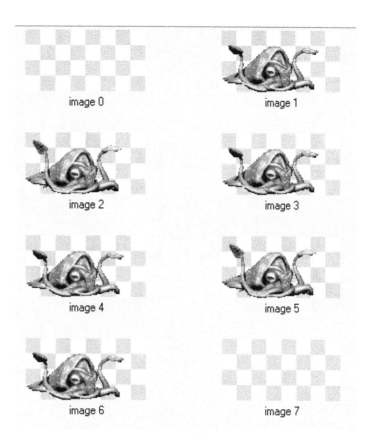

(Fig 331 , Image after applying the effect)

Thus we can say that **Add Reverse** inverts the sequence of the images and places them after the original sequence

e)Translation Sequence :- You have to specify the number of images , horizontal and vertical values , It is not possible to provide images of the changes caused due to this effect because the changes depend upon the values you enter.

Tip :- -ve horizontal value shifts the images to the left and vice-versa

2)-ve vertical value shift the images above and vice-versa

f)Rotation Sequence :- Contains 2 functions viz. 1)Clockwise and 2)Counter-Clockwise (Anticlockwise)

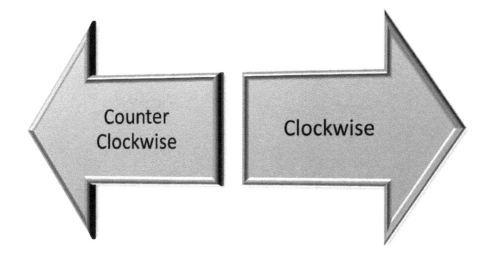

(Fig 332)

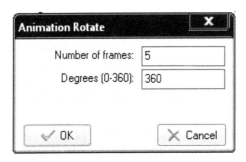

(Fig 333)

Number of Frames :- This number denotes the number of images to which this effect would be applicable

Degrees :- Degrees denote the angle of Rotation

g)Colorize :- Colorize is taught earlier , when you change the settings in this mode a dialog box would prompt asking the number of images to which the effect has to be applied.

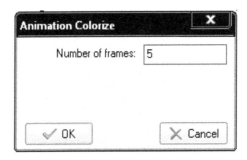

(Fig 334)

h)Fade to a color :- Let's you fade the image to a color , it is always adivisable to apply the effect to all the subimages.

i)Disappear :- The transparency of the latter images increases , when the subimages are imaged in a sequence the object seems to disappear

Note :- The quality of disappearance is directly proportional to the number of images.

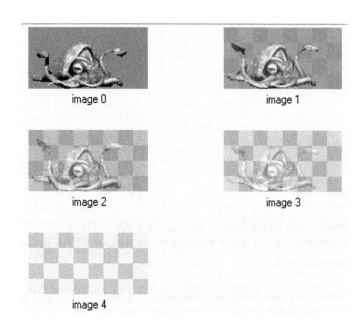

(Fig 335)

j)Shrink :- Contains 5 different functions 1)Top , 2)Bottom , 3)Left , 4)Right , 5)Centre

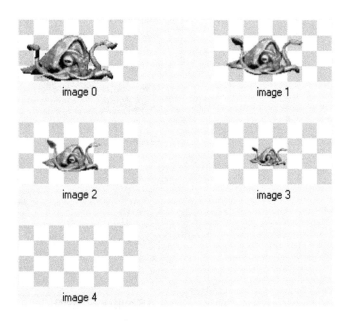

(Shrink Centre)

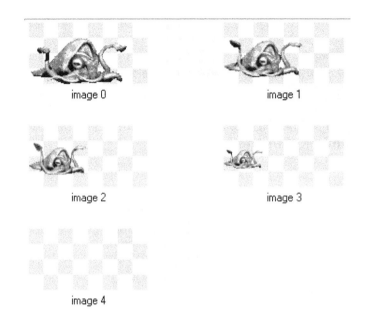

(Shrink Left)

Note :- It is possible to apply more than one effect to any of the images but is also possible to apply different effects to different images.

To apply more than one effect select the first effect after the changes are applied apply the second effect.

Experiment with them and use the immense functionality of all of them wisely to produce very powerful graphics for your games

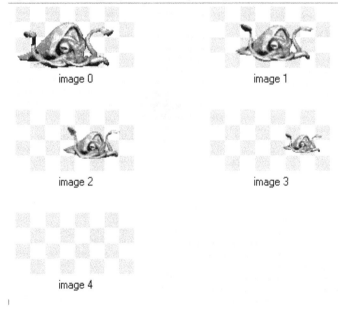

(Shrink Right)

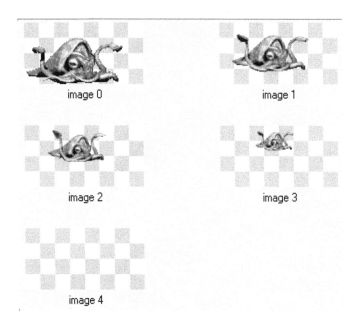

image 0

image 1

image 2

image 3

image 4

(Shrink Top)

Remember :- Earlier we have studied that it is possible to apply different effects to different subimages by changing the number of images to which the effect would be applied but this must be avoided because the overall animation may appear broken or disjoint.

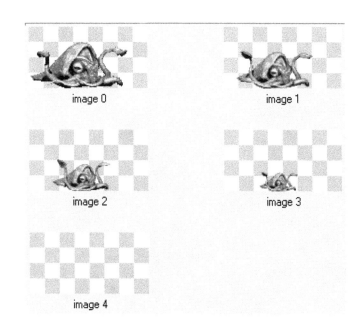

image 0

image 1

image 2

image 3

image 4

(Shrink Bottom)

k)Grow :- Contains 5 different functions 1)Top , 2)Bottom , 3)Left , 4)Right , 5)Centre

Note :- Grow is just the opposite of Shrink , study the pictures below to understand this concept

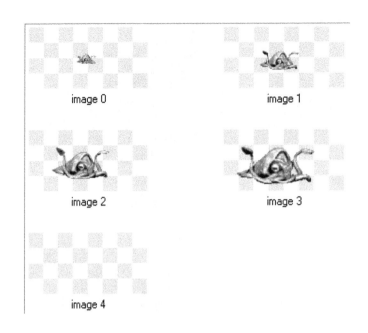

(Grow Centre)

The size of images goes on increasing gradually.

l)Flatten :- Contains 4 different functions 1)Top ,   2)Bottom ,   3)Left , 4)Right

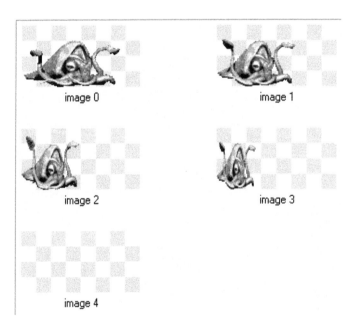

(Flatten Left)

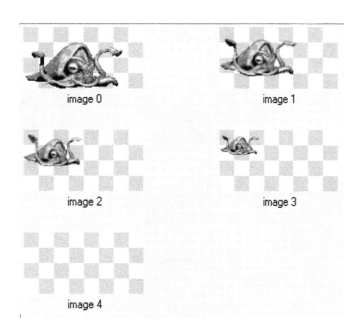

(Flatten Right)

Note :- You may apply more than two effects

(Fig 327) shows the image formed when Flatten Left is applied along with Flatten Top.

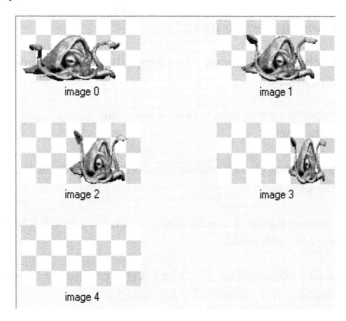

(Fig 344)

Compare Figure 327 with flatten Left and you will feel the difference , this is just a sample you can apply a combination of Shrink , Grow , Flatten Together , you just have to apply the first effect when the effect takes place apply the next one.

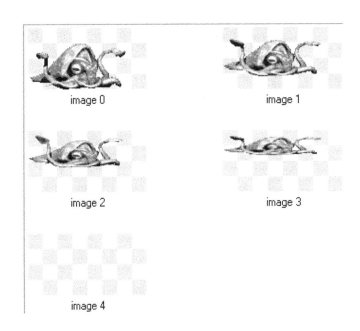

image 0   image 1

image 2   image 3

image 4

(Flatten Top)

Tip :- when all the subimages are focused together the character appears to jump

2) The character appears to bend when Flatten bottom effect is applied.

3) We feel that the character is moving away from us when we apply shrink

4) We feel that the character is coming towards us when grow is applied

5) To feel the effect check the box show preview located to the extreme left side.

(Fig 346) shown besides shows the preview column ,   you can specify any speed of your choice.

Note :- this speed would be just for viewing not for the game.

You may even change the Background and the Background color.

(Fig 347)

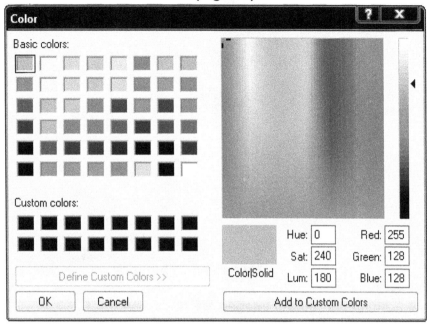

The Flatten Bottom effect is demonstrated below.(Fig 348)

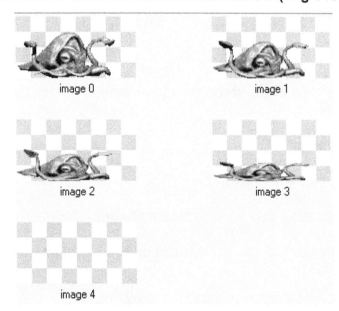

m)Raise :- Raise is just the opposite of flatten ,   Raise contains 4 functions 1)Left ,   2) Right ,   3)Top ,   4)Bottom

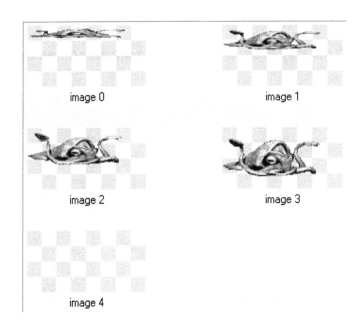

image 0   image 1

image 2   image 3

image 4

(Raise Top ,   Fig 349)

Note :- Images of all the images are not shown.

(Fig 350 ,   Doom Dragon)   (Fig 351 ,   Kraken)

n)Overlay :- To understand the effect we would use the two sprites shown above.

1)Load Kraken

2)Open Editor (Edit sprite)

3)Select Overlay and choose Doom Dragon.

Note :- The later image is imposed on the initial image.

(Fig 352 ,   Resulting Image)

Note :- we have used the combination of Kraken and doom Dragon because they have the same number of subimages.

o)Morph :- Follow the procedure to understand.

1)Load Kraken

2)Open Editor (Edit sprite)

3)Select Morph and choose Doom Dragon.

Note :- The later image is merged with the initial image

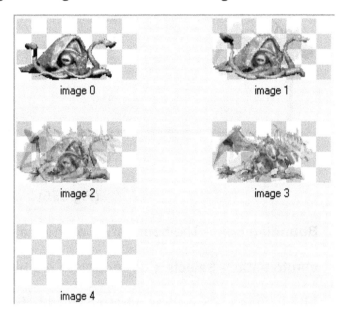

(Fig 353)

Note :- The Kraken appears to be converted into Doom Dragon.

Editing Sprites ends here Hope you enjoyed , we will now learn to modify the masks that we had studied earlier.

Modifying Masks

Load a sprite (Kraken is used in this book)

Press the button Modify Mask to open a new window which provides different tools for changing the settings involved in modifying masks

Alpha Tolerance :- this changes the bounding box settings.

The image section situated to the right show the Width , Height and the number of subimages.

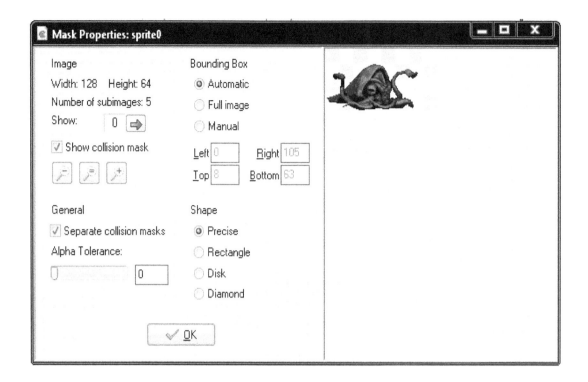

(Fig 355)

Bounding box :- The boundaries of the mask for collision.

a)automatic :- Selects a boundary on it's own

b)Full image :- Specifies a boundary which covers the entire image

c)Manual :- Let's you specify the boundaries

Shape :-   Shape of the mask for collision

a)Precise :- covers only the image

My Recommendation :- Precise lowers the chances of collisions compared to the others.

b)Rectangle :- Rectangular collision mask

c)Disk :- collision mask of the shape of a disk or an ellipse

d)Diamond :- Similar to a rhombus.

Editing backgrounds

1)Load a Background

2)Press the button Edit Background

Note :- Rest everything is the same.

Summary

In this chapter we discussed about editing sprites , the effects available (shadow effect , blur effect .....) the use of masks and modifying masks , using the screenshots provided we could even judge the way an image would appear if that particular effect was applied

You have learnt everything related to editing sprites ,   backgrounds and masks.

Chapter 7 Converting Videos

One may ask "What is the use of converting videos ?"

Answer :-Videos coded in the format .mpg , .flv and .swf cannot be played on all the computers . If you make your own videos then there is no problem because Movie maker would code your videos in the .wmv format which is easily playable on all the Windows PC's but if you want to provide a video which requires codec to be installed what would you do ?

Answer :- Convert into .wmv format .

To convert videos read further.

You must have a video converter installed to convert videos.

Note :- There are more than 50 audio/video converters available to convert audio/video   files and from among them I have selected Any Video Converter.

Reasons are

1)Cost	Free , but has a paid version , free one contains pop-ups which make purchase it.
2)Codec's supported	Almost all
3)Size	63.5 mega bytes (After Installation)

   Installing Any Video Converter (It would be referred as AVC from now on)

1)Execute the file 'avc_free_3.exe'

2)Press Next >

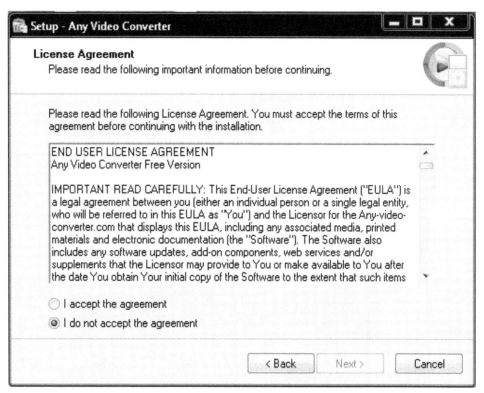

(Fig 357 , The license agreement)

2)Read the agreement and if you agree check the radio button 'I accept the agreement' , like fig 358 given below and press next

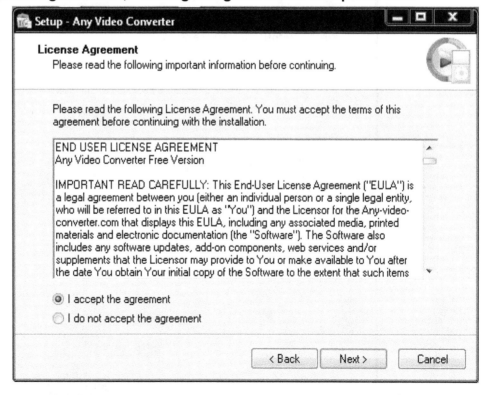

Note :- No software can be installed without accepting the agreement only GPL/GNU softwares provide that facility.

(Fig 359 , Select a location for installation and press Next >)

You may create a desktop icon for easy access like Fig 360 given below.

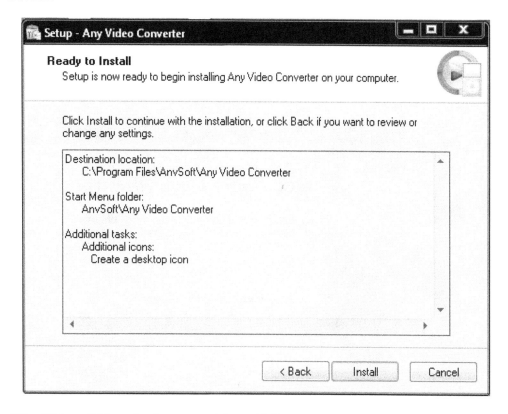

(Fig 361 , This window provides all the necessary information , if you want to change go back and change the settings.

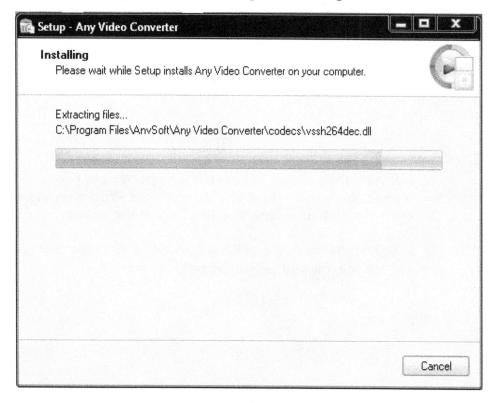

Fig 362 shown above shows the progress bar , the progress in the installation is conveyed by the progress bar.

(Fig 363)

Conversion is added because it is important to possess a bit knowledge about every field related to Game Programming and you can even merge two videos or edit a part of the video

Fig 364 given below is the main window of Any video Converter , the profiles column let you select the output format.

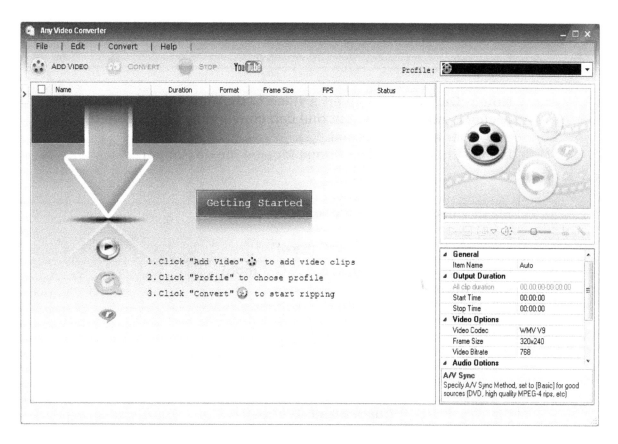

To the right hand side is a media player which can be used to play any available audio/video file before converting. Profile (above the media player) is the list of available formats you have to select any one of them. Profile are divided under 4 heads

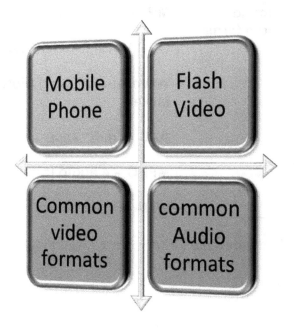

(Fig 365)

Note :- One cannot convert a video to the .3gp video format as the profile is not available but one can convert any video from the .3gp to any other available format.

Mobile Phone	Mobile Phone Mpeg-4 movie (*.mp4)
Flash video	Flash video movie (*.flv) Flash SWF (*.swf)
Common video Formats	DVD video NTSC (*.mpg) DVD video PAL(*.mpg) MPEG – I(*.mpg) MPEG – II(*.mpg) Customized AVI(*.avi) Customized WMV(*.wmv) Customized MP4(.mp4) Matroska Video(.mkv)
Common Audio format	MP3 Audio (*.mp3) OGG Vorbis Audio (*.ogg) Wave Audio(*.wav) (Format supported by Game Maker) AAC audio(*.aac) MPEG – 4 audio (*.m4a) WMA Audio(*.wma)

Add video file (File ⟶ Add video file)

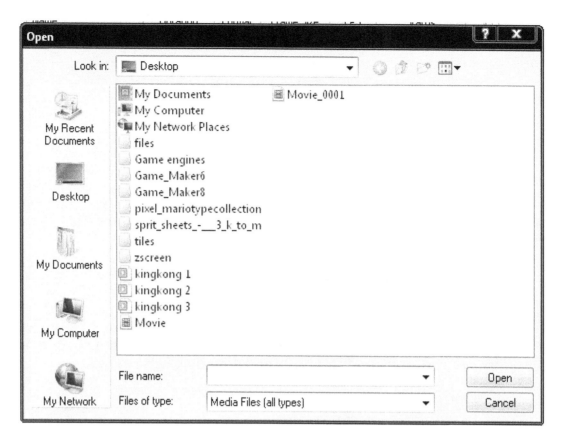

(Fig 366)

Select *.WMV from the profiles

Change the settings as specified by me ,   the settings column is below the media player

1)The item name is the location of the input

2)Don't change the start and the stop time.

3) Two video codecs are available V9 and V8 choose V9

4)Let the frame size be 640x480

5)Video bitrate be 512

The Audio codec/track and subtitles is disabled which means that it cannot be changed.

6)A/V sync is better when basic than default

Note :- We cannot afford an increase in size for quality

Factors affecting file size

1)Bitrate (Directly proportional to file size)

2)Frame Rate (Directly proportional to file size)

When all the settings are set press the covert button

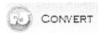

(Fig 367)

AVC would show the progress and finally show the status as completed.

Note :- It is possible but it is absolutely not recommended by me to convert a video into sound.

Tip :- It is possible to convert only a part of the video for that you must adjust the start and the stop time accordingly.

Example :-A video file is of the duration 30:00 minutes ,   you don't want to convert the entire video but the first 20 minutes so in this case your start time will be 00:00 and stop time will be 20:00.

Merging videos

Merging means combining two or more videos

Add two videos (in case of merging 2 videos you can even merge more than that) select them and right click them select 'Merge Output'

Note :- The second video would be played after the first.

After conversion a dialog would prompt (if you are using the free edition)

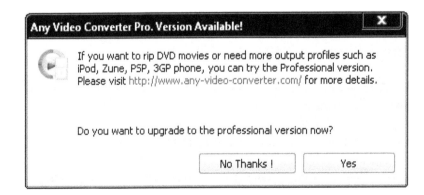

(Fig 368)

Summary

Let us recapitulate the main points we discussed

Animation is just a set of still pictures accompanied by sound , the images don't move but appear to move , we even discussed about sound formats and recording sounds at the end we learnt about merging videos

Chapter 8 Cheats and Hacks

All those who play and program games surely know that in a game cheats always exist , there are very few games in which cheat codes are not programmed. Cheats are of two types 1)Cheats programmed in the game , 2)Cheats found by the player.

One may ask ' what are cheats found out by the player ?' , these are in fact faults or imperfections in the programs of which some take advantage , for example some game used an XML file for storing settings like speed: , strength: , ability: , health: etc after each setting was a numerical value , simply increasing the value and one could experience the changes , the speed of the character his strength and health increased and it became easier to play the game" this cheat was not made by the programmer he may totally ignorant about this but one may be able to take advantage of this so this falls under the second heading.

Note :- No one would be able to change such settings of your game as Game Maker doesn't support XML.

There is one more way of cheating which includes tampering the DLL and other files but that is illegal.

Let us learn how to introduce cheats in your game.

1)Load the game space (Ctrl + O)

2)Open the Object Rocket

Note :- We are programming a cheat which would increase the score by 100

3)Add an event Keypress<F12>

4)Drag an action 'Set Score where score is 100 relatively'

Try playing your game now and feel the difference when you press F12 in the course of the game the score increases by 100

Note :- You can replace F12 with any other key and Set score can be replaced by Set Health to relatively 100 or to create more lazers run your imagination wild and take fully advantage of all the actions available and your skills taught here.

2)In the sample provided above 'F12' was our cheat code.

It is important for others to know about the cheat in your game , one is not required to announce your cheats you can add information about your games on a blog especially meant for your game or register it with cheat code database.

Cheat code database is software which stores information about cheats of PC games as well as games created for gaming consoles.

Installing Cheat Code Database

Double click the setup file

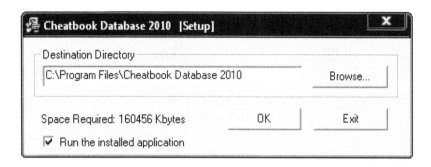

(Fig 369)

You may change the Destination folder by pressing the 'Browse...' button , when all the settings are over press OK

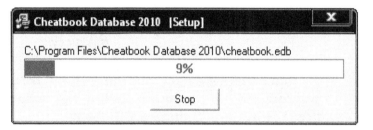

(Fig 370)

(Fig 370)shows the progress bar which denotes the progress in the installation

Reasons for using cheat Book Database

1)Free

2)Constantly updated by players all over the world

3)Provides link to various websites where discussions about games , cheats take place.

4)About more than 19000 cheats

5)Let us us submit cheat codes

(If you use this feature for submitting cheats of your games players all over the world would know about your game)

Start the cheat code database.

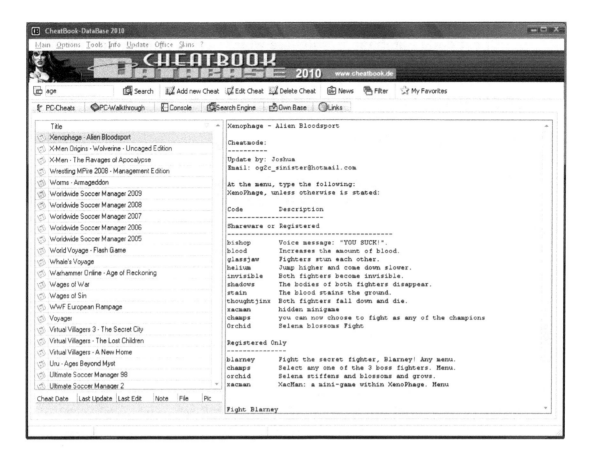

(Fig 371)

To submit a cheat select 'submit a cheat' through the 'office' menu , a window like the one shown below will appear on your screen , select the system 'Submit a PC cheat'

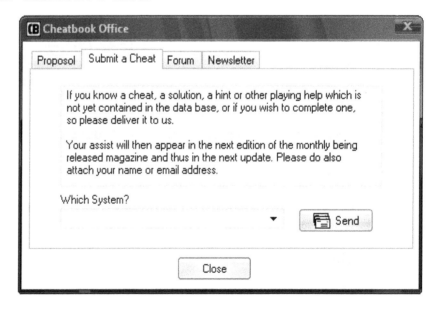

Note :- The screen shots may differ depending upon the 'Skin' selected.

After the system is selected press the button.

(Fig 374)

Fill in the details and press the send button , your cheat would be added to the database and would be available to those who update their version and also to those install a version released after the submission of your cheat.

Remember a cheat is a key or a loophole in a game through which one can increase the health , number of lives , the score , strength (of the character) and / or activate some hidden weapons and / or bonuses.

HACK

A hacker is a person who is an expert with computers and communication technology. Hacker may be a good person or a bad person. Yes , there are good hackers who help cyber police for tracking thieves.

A game made by Game Maker can be hacked to the extent of interfering with the high score (even more !!)

Note :- We are discussing this so that you may not be victimized.

Before learning this you must know a bit about the windows registry. Windows registry is a place where MS Windows and other software save information

Example :- How does Game Maker open the same folder which was opened earlier for creating sprites ? ,   the path of the folder is stored in the windows registry.

To open Registry select 'Start' ⟶ 'Run' type 'Regedit' and press Ok

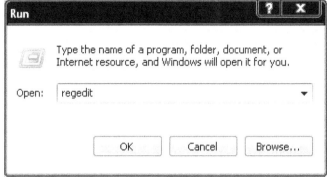

(Fig 375)

Or (In case of Windows Vista or any other later version)

'Start' ⟶ 'Search' type 'Regedit' and press Ok.

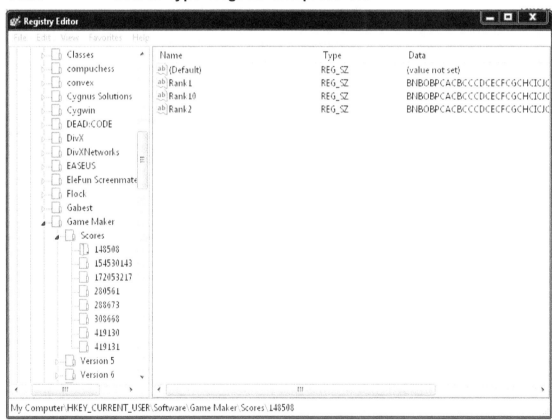

Navigate to the key My Computer \ HKEY_CURRENT_USER \ Software \ Game Maker \ Scores \ x

Where x stands for the Game Identifier ,   so if someone opens the key which you have opened you he can easily tamper with the highscore but the values are stored in the form of a hash value which makes it a bit secure.

Before saving Game Maker converts it in the form 'BCGDEFRTHJ' which is meaningless for a human but the x value (Game Identifier) is expressed in the numerical form so some one may copy the Game Identifier and create a new game with the same identifier and the new scores would replace the old ones! Or if someone deletes the entire key your scores are lost.

It may be possible by coincidence that two programmers produce games with the same identifier ,   both the games (if present on a single PC) would overwrite their scores on one another and would never know as the Game Identifier is their only identity.

This information is not for tampering with the settings of game made by others the intention behind providing this was to make you understand the vulnerabilities of the identifier.

Other type of cheats

In some games(example :- Midtown Madness) one has to press a combination of keys(example :- Shift + Ctrl + alt + F8)for opening a window(inputbox) where one enters the cheat and then it is activated.

Even you can program such Games after reading this entire book

Summary

In this chapter we discussed about programming cheats in our game , we even installed CheatBook Database and learnt to use it , we even discussed the procedure to submit a cheat.

Chapter 9 Paths

Paths are files which stores data regarding movement of an object in a room.

Before proceeding it is necessary to understand the utility of Paths

Where paths should not be used.

(Fig 377)

In a game like the one shown above where one has to shoot at clowns for earning points paths should not be used as one easily learns the movement after playing the game 5 or more times.

Creating Paths

Press Shift + Ctrl + P

Paths are of two types open and closed

Open paths are the ones where the start and end point don't meet

Closed paths are the ones where the start and end point meet

Which means that after the object follows the path it returns to the point from where it started.

(Fig 378 Open path)

(Fig 379 Closed path)

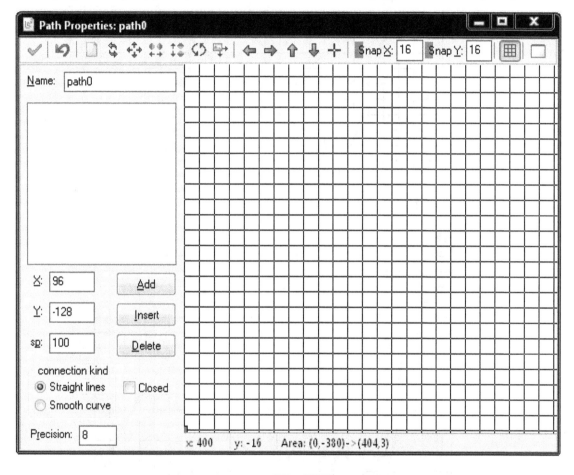

(Fig 380)

Paths are of two types 1)Straight lined and 2)Curved.

Curved are better than straight lined paths

They can be selected through the Frame 'Connection Kind' located to the left-bottom of the window as shown in Fig 380

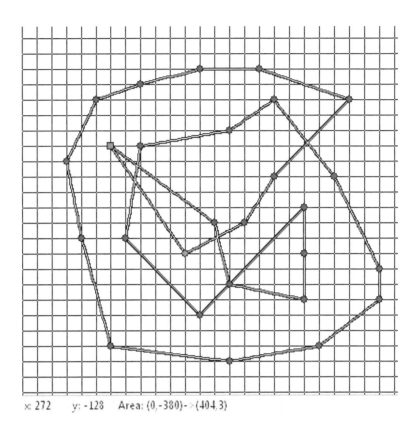

x: 272   y: -128   Area: (0,-380)->(404,3)

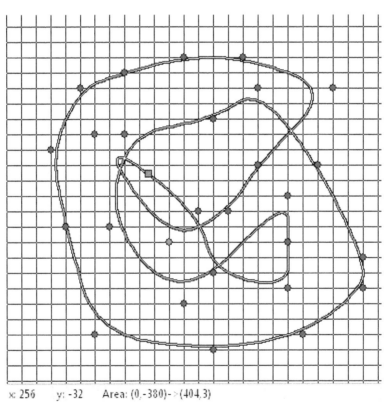

x: 256   y: -32   Area: (0,-380)->(404,3)

More about paths

1) The start is denoted by a rectangle and the end by a red circle.

2) The precision value ranges from 1 to 8

Note :- The precision value is directly proportional to the smoothness of the path.

How to add paths

1)Just click on the open space like the one shown below

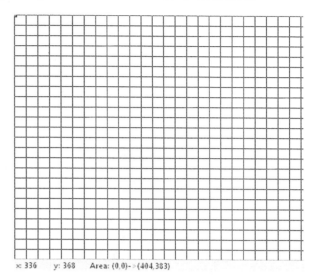

x: 336   y: 368   Area: (0,0)->(404,383)

The point clicked first is the starting point.

Starting clicking on the open space the way you want your path to be.

As soon as more regions on the area are selected the co-ordinates of the points are added to the list

(96,80)	sp: 100
(160,160)	sp: 100
(160,224)	sp: 100
(160,256)	sp: 100
(320,192)	sp: 100
(320,64)	sp: 100
(176,16)	sp: 100
(80,32)	sp: 100
(80,176)	sp: 100
(112,288)	sp: 100
(160,368)	sp: 100
(304,352)	sp: 100

(Fig 384)

The object follows these co-ordinates.

Tip :- You can add points by supply suitable co-ordinates using the add button

Note :- If you don't want a grid you can remove it by pressing the 'Grid Button'

Tip :- Sometimes we don't know the location of a co-ordinate in a room in that case you can indicate a room by pressing the button located to the extreme right.

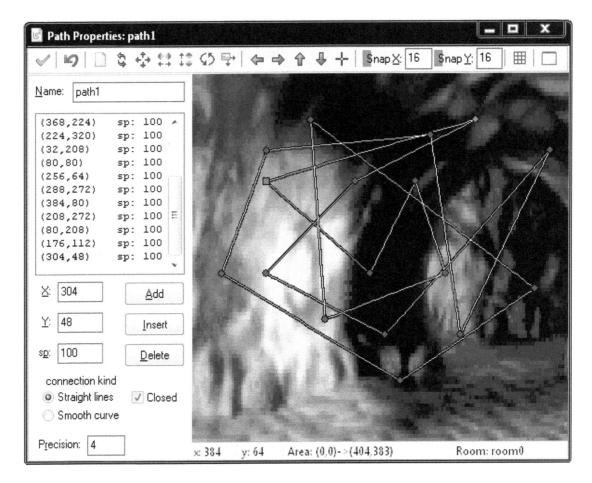

In this case it becomes easier to draw a path.

Understanding the buttons

(Fig 387)

We would proceed in the order from left to right

1)Saves the changes

2)Undo button

3)Clears the path

4)Reverses the path

Example :- The co-ordinates are (224 ,   87) (324 ,   67) (90 ,   78) after the effect is applied the order would be (90 ,   78) (324 ,   67) (224 , 87)

In other words the start becomes the end and vice-versa

5)Let us use shift the path

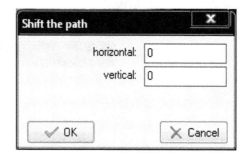

(Fig 388)

Enter suitable values.

Tip :- To remove a co-ordinate just right click on it (on the path)

6) Provides a mirror image.

7)Flips the path vertically (upside down)

(Fig 389 ,   Original Image)   (Fig 390 ,   Mirrored Horizontally)

(Fig 391 ,   Original Image)   (Fig 392 ,   Flipped vertically)

8)Rotates the path by an angle

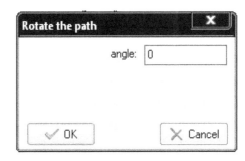

(Fig 393)

Note :- 0 and 360 wouldn't affect the image

2) If you enter a value > 360 the picture would be rotated by the difference.

9)Scaling the path Let us you change the proportion of the path

Note :- Enter the same values for maintain the aspect ratio.

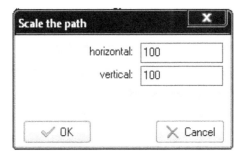

(Fig 394)

The next five buttons are not explained as they deal with shifting the path.

The actions related to Path are discussed earlier (Set Path etc) so this chapter ends here.

Summary

Let's summarize the important points discussed in this chapter

At the beginning we distinguished between an open path and a closed path we even discussed about games in which paths should not be used   then we discussed about the type of connections (straight lined and curved) and at last scaling the path

Chapter 10 Timelines

This feature is available only in the advanced mode.

Many times in games certain things are programmed to happen after a fixed period (example 5 seconds) , timelines are used during such needs , one may argue ' Why should one use timeline when one can achieve the same by using alarms ?' , it is possible but may get complicated , timelines simply the task.

Adding timelines

1)Press (Shift + Ctrl + T)

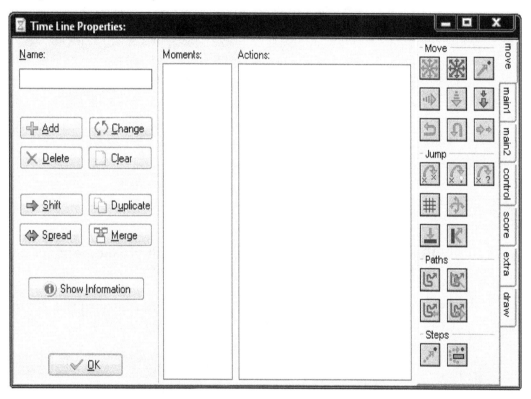

(Fig 395)

There are some buttons located to the left we will understand them first.

1)Add :- Let us you add a moment , you must mention the number of steps , the actions associated with this moment would be executed after the number of steps have elapsed.

Note :- Indicating the moment means specifying the number of steps

2) Decimals , Fractions are not allowed

3)Negative values are accepted but would never be executed.

Tip :- If you specify 7 / 8 game maker would save the input as 78

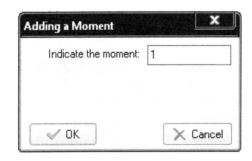

(Fig 396)

2)Change :- Let us you change the number of steps

(Fig 397)

3)Delete :- Let us you delete single or multiple moments at a time you just have to mention the start and the end

Example :- You want to delete all the moments from the 2nd moment to the 5th moment your values must be (See fig 398)

(Fig 398)

4)Clear :- Let us you delete all the moments

Tip :- Game Maker will prompt you for confirmation.

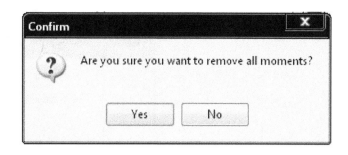

(Fig 399)

5)Shift :- Let us you shift all the moments of a group to a new one.

Example :- If you want the actions of step 0 to be executed at step 5 and the actions of step 1 to be executed at step 6 this button will help you.

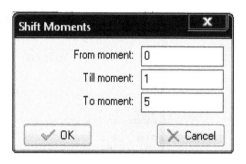

(Fig 400)

6)Duplicate :- Let us you copy individually or in a group

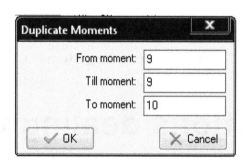

(Fig 401 , Please neglect the values)

7)Spread :- Let us you spread moments by adding steps between them or reduce the interval between them , you have to mention the start as well as the end as well as the percentage.

Tip :- To understand better experiment with different values and find out on your own.

8)Merge :- Let us you merge many moments into one , you just have to specify the initial and the final moment and all the moments in that range would be merged into a single one.

(Fig 402 ,   Please neglect the values)

9)Show information :- Gives detailed information about all the moments of the timeline.

(Fig 403)

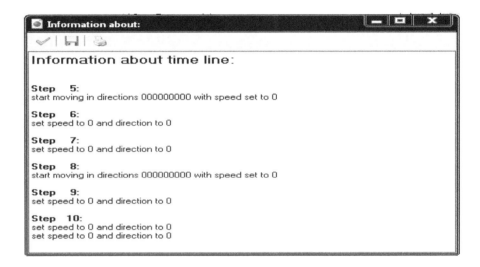

Adding actions

To add actions simply drag them the way you drag actions for an object.

Actions dealing with timelines

Earlier we have seen that for learning actions associated with timelines it is necessary to understand timelines first ,   now as we have learnt what are timelines one   can easily learn actions associated with it.

Note :- The actions associated with timelines are located in the main2 tab in the timing part.

1)Set Timeline :- Sets the timeline for a particular object ,   you have to mention the timeline and the position ,   you can also specify whether the timeline should start immediately or start again after its completed (loop)

(Fig 404)

2)Timeline position :- Let us you start the timeline from a particular point (absolutely or relatively)

Example :- If you want to skip the first 2 steps (0 and 1) the position would be 3

Explanation :- The timeline would start from step 2 ,   in other words step 0 and step 1 are skipped.

Note :- This action should be preceded by a set timeline action.

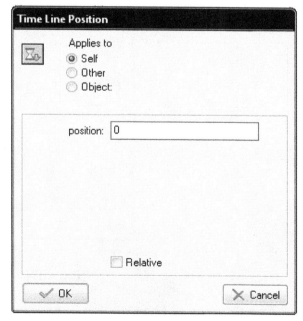

(Fig 405)

3)Timeline speed :- Let us you change the speed of the timeline (absolutely or relatively) see Fig 406 given below

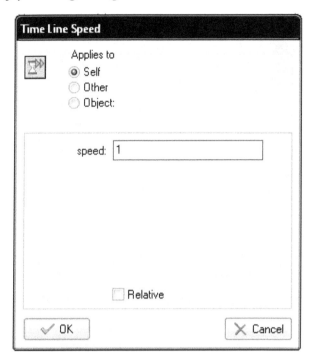

4)Start timeline :- Starts the timeline from the point where it was paused or stopped.

Tip :- It is also known as resume timeline

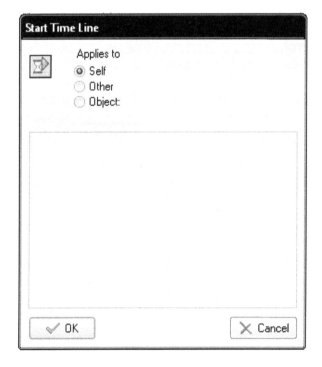

(Fig 407)

5)Pause timeline :- The timeline is paused by this action ,   Fig 408 given below

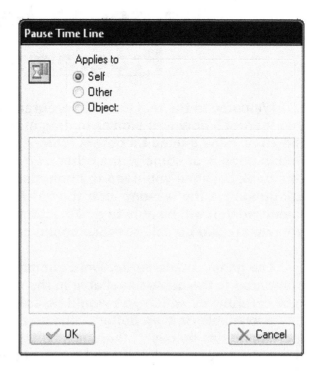

6)Stop timeline :- Stops the timeline

(Fig 409)

Note :- There is a difference between pause and stop , ' Suppose a timeline is paused at position 4 the time you resume it would start playing from the 5th position. But if you stop it would start playing from the 1st position'.

Chapter 10 ends here you have learnt everything dealing with timelines.

Chapter 11 Basics of Programming

Welcome to the real world of programming , everything which you learnt till now was similar to drag and drop. Does this mean that the knowledge gained till now is futile ? , No , everything you learn in this book is of some or the other use , this lesson is included in this book because you need to understand GML (Game Maker's Language) , the lessons after the 10th lesson are difficult but if mastered you will be able to make actions (.lib files) of your own and you would also be able to make complicated games.

The games made earlier were comparatively of a low grade compared to the games available in the market , so read the further part carefully by which you would be able to program games like the one's available or even better , the size of gaming industry is increasing day by day , there is a constant demand for professional game developers and you can be one of them if you master Game Maker.

So Let us start to learn the basics of programming

Some important definitions

1)Program :- A program is a group of instructions executed by a computer which provides us the desired output with the help of the input supplied.

2)Software :- A software is a collection of programs to accomplish a particular task

3)Algorithm :- An algorithm is a group of tasks for accomplishing a task in a limited number of steps

4)Flowchart :- A flowchart is a graphical representation of an algorithm

5)Pseudocode :- A pseudocode is a language independent code for accomplishing a task

What is a programming language?

Computers cannot understand English, Hebrew, Latin, Greek or any other language , computers can understand only binary but it is tedious and time consuming to write programs in binary so we write programs in a language similar to English for our convenience , so how does computer understand the programs written in English ? , the answer is simple , ' Imagine that you are travelling in a new land , you are enjoying there but unfortunately you are lost , you are searching some one for help and are successful but the other person cannot understand your language nor can you understand his language , whose help do you require in such times ?' a translator , similarly translators are available for communicating between humans and computers too , these translators translate the code written by you into binary so that the computer should understand.

Translators

Translators are of 2 types 1)Compilers and 2)Interpreters

1)Compilers :- A compiler compiles the code into its binary equivalent , it scAnswer the whole code before converting , if errors are found it wouldn't compile the code unless the error is rectified.

2)Interpreters :- An interpreter interprets the code line by line , if errors are found it would end the interpretation , the code is not hidden in such cases and every time the code is executed it has to be interpreted , the HTML (Hyper Text Markup Language) is the most common example of interprets (HTML is used to build web-pages and your web browser is your interpreter)

Algorithm

I believe that one can understand everything with an example s as a sample let us write an algorithm for making a phone call

1)Start your phone

2)Dial the number

3)Press the Call button

4)Talk

5)End

2)Algorithm to access the e-mail id

1)Switch on your computer

2)Switch on the modem

3)Start the web browser

4)Navigate to the web page desired

5)Enter your e-mail id

6)Enter your password

Try creating algorithm for any topic you like as an exercise.

Note :- A number is necessary for each step.

Flowchart

To understand flowcharts one must understand the symbols used in a flowchart

1)Terminal :- It is used for denoting the start and the end of a flowchart

Symbol :- ⬭

2)Flow lines :- Represent the direction of data flow

Note :- It has four symbols

a) ⟶

b) ⟵

c) ↓

d) ↑

3)Input/Outbut :- Used for input and output purposes

Symbol :-

4)Process :- Shows data processing

Symbol :-

5)Decision :- Used for condition (if x > y ,   if x = y etc)

Symbol :-

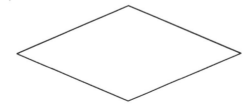

6)Connector :- Used for connecting two parts of a flowchart

Symbol :-

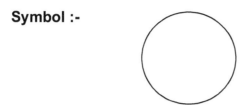

Let us make a flowchart for understanding the symbols

1)Flowchart for comparing two numbers

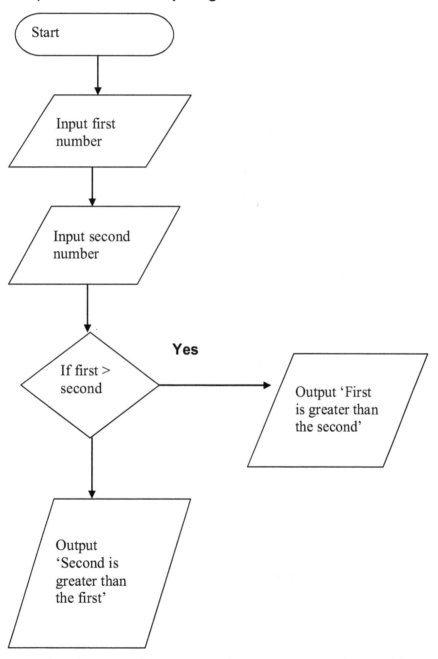

2)Flowchart for adding two numbers

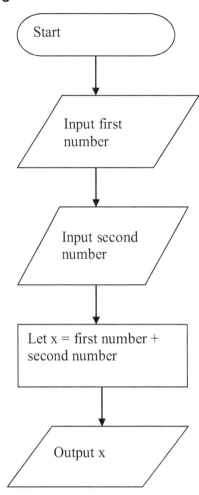

3)Flowchart of a Hello program

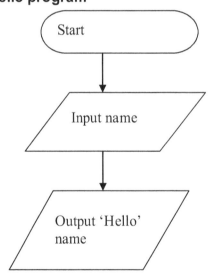

Pseudocode

As mentioned earlier (definition)pseudocode is not written in a syntax of any programming language

Pseudocode for multiplying two numbers

Display "Enter two numbers"

Input   x ,   y

Z = x * y

Output Z

Tip :- One can omit the 4th line by changing the 3rd line (the result would not change) the third line should be Output x * y !!! ,   one should take care of these small things and try his/her level best to reduce the size of code without affecting the result.

Let us understand the terms frequently used in programming.

Variables

Variables are actually a part of mathematics

$2x = 8$ means that 2 multiplied by x is equal to 8 so x = 4 (8/2)

Observe the input box of the 3rd flowchart

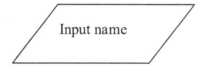

Input name

here the variable is 'name' .

Similarly observe the output box of the 3rd flowchart

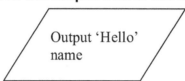

Output 'Hello'
name

Hello is placed in commas whereas name is not ,   if we write Output 'Hello name' the computer would display 'Hello name' each time irrespective of the name but as we haven't inserted name in the commas the programming language understands that name is used as a variable

Variables are of many types(example :- string ,   boolean , integer) in many of the programming languages they have to be declared before use ,   in some others one doesn't have to declare them before use ,   the available types of variables and the way they are declared differs from language to language.

For example in C++ language an integer is declared as

Int x

Whereas in VB an integer is declared as

Dim x as integer

The result is the same but there is a difference of coding.

Tip :- This difference is known as the syntax

Note :- Syntax is different for different languages

My way of defining syntax is ' Syntax is the grammar of a programming language'

Why are variables divided into many types?

Because each type of variable is designed to store different type of data , for example integer is used to store numerical value , string is used to store letters , words , phrases , sentences , Boolean is used to store values like true or false.

Don't worry the information provided above was just to increase your knowledge , Game Maker is different from other language , the point where it differs is you don't have to declare variables for their use.

Statements

A statement is used to state something , for example if you want to store the value '4' in a variable 'num' the statement would be num = 4

Operators

Operators are divided into 4 classes

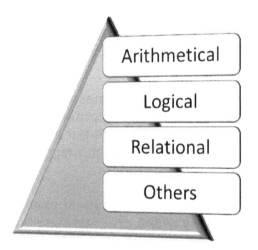

I)Arithmetical operators

Arithmetical operators are + , - , * , / , mod

Note :- Mod is for modulus

Expressions

Expressions are a combination two or more operators , one such expression is given below

X = 2 + 5 * 4

Does it mean add 2 and 5 and then multiply by 4 which would be equal to 28 ? , No it means add 2 to the product of 5 and 4 which would become 22.

II)Logical operators

Logical operators are and , or . The symbol used for and is andand and for or is ||

III)Relational operators

These operators are used for comparison like 4 < 5 , if we write 4 > 5 , it would return false

Let n1 = 5 and let n2 = 7

Operators	Meaning
n1 < n2	Would return true as 5 is less than 7
n2 > n1	Would return true as 7 is greater than 5
n2 >= n1	This operation would return true if the first number is greater than or equal to the second number So this one would return true
n1 <= n2	This operation would return true if the first number is smaller than or equal to the second number So this one would return true
n1 == n2 or n1 = n2	This is the equal to operator , this operation would return false as 5 is not equal to 7
n1 != n2	This is the not equal to operator , this would return true as 5 is not equal to 7

IV)Others

There are many operators included in game maker which are generally not available in many other programming languages

Name	Symbol	Usage
Xor	^^	Xors a number, generally used for encryption and cryptography

Shift left	<<	Shifts to the left
Shift right	>>	Shifts to the right

Categories in which variables are divided

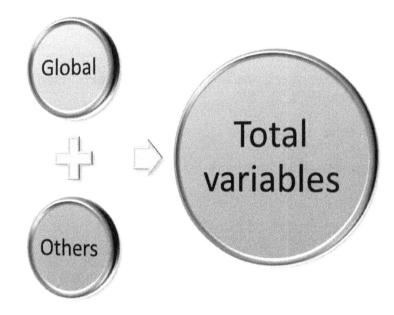

(Fig 411)

The difference between global and other variables is explained in a distinguish between form

Factor	Global	Others (Local Variables)
Available to	All instances	Instances in which they are declared
Memory consumed	More	Less
Processing required	More	Less
Name conflict	May occur	Doesn't occur
Speed	Less	More

Some important terms

Name conflict :- If you declare a variable 'x' as global , you cannot declare a new variable 'x' in any instance , doing so may result in an error , if you declare 'x' in an instance you may declare a new variable 'x' in any other instance.

Why do global variables require more processing and consume more memory ?

Global variables are available to all the instance irrespective of whether it's being used in that instance or not , hence they require more processing and memory.

Declaring global variables

Suppose you want to declare the variables speed(value = 8) , time (value = 2) as global you would declare them as

globalvar speed , time;

speed = 8

time = 2

But there is a catch over here , you cannot declare speed as global as it's an in-built variable , so variables are reserved they are known as inbuilt variables.

Note :- a semicolon ' ;' must be added at the end otherwise globalvar wouldn't recognize the end of the statement

Tip :- If you declare 'x' as global in object a , and you want to call that variable from object b , then both these objects (a and b) should exist in a room and object a should be added first.

Calling global variables from other objects (here we will display the result of speed / time)

var x ;

x = global.speed / global.time

show_message(x)

Note :- Here we want the message box to show a message which would be a value , here x is a variable so we don't have to insert x in double inverted commas , I have shown the resulting output on the next page

If x is not inserted in inverted commas

Output is :-

Else

Output is :-

Case Sensitivity

Case sensitivity means that it would treat 'game' , 'Game' and 'GAME' differently , game maker is case sensitive so you have to take a lot of care while coding.

Suppose two balls collide and you want to reduce the speed of the other one by 2 what would you do , there are two ways to do

1st way , drag the action 'Move Fixed' let the speed be a negative value relatively , 2nd way write the following piece of code

other.speed = other.speed – 2

the above piece of code would do the same.

Note :- -2 was just an example one can even write -7 , -9 , -12 but if the initial speed is 10 and one writes other.speed = other.speed – 12 then the object would move in the opposite direction with a speed of 2 (12 – 10)

One may ask 'Why should one learn coding when one can achieve the same by using actions?' , the Answer to this is quite simple , the features available due to actions are limited and one can create his own actions if he/her learns coding.

The previous code was to reduce the speed of the other object but what if one wants to reduce it's own speed ? , the code would be

self.speed = self.speed – 2

The previous code was to reduce the speed of the self but what if one wants to reduce the speed of all the instances ? , the code would be

all.speed = all.speed -2

These codes would reduce the speed of all the instances of a particular object but what if one wants to change the speed of a particular instance ? , in this case you can reduce the speed using the id , each instance in a room has a unique identification , the identification of the first object is 100001 , the second one would be 100002 and it would go on increasing , when one wants to address variables of a particular instance one has to use this unique identification.

How to find out the id of any particular instance ?

Just hover the mouse on a particular instance. Observe the Fig 414 given below

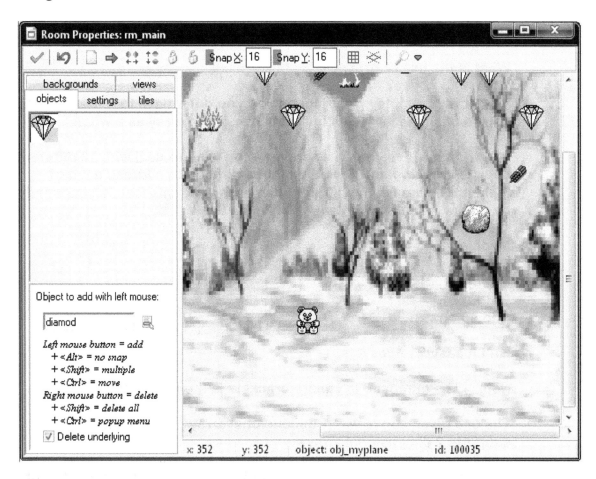

Observe the status bar (located at the bottom) the id shown(id:100035) is of the teddy bear.

Note :- he mouse is actually hovered but it can be seen as this a screenshot

So if I want to make the teddy invisible , my code would be

(100035).visible = 0

Explanation :- The id has to be inserted in brackets (Reason :- GML syntax)

2)Visible = 0 means visibility = false , visible = 1 means visibility = true

Note :- Even if the object is invisible it exists

So if I want to reduce the speed of the teddy by 5 my code would be

(100035).speed = (100035).speed – 5

Note :- This would not affect the speeds of other teddy's.

Arrays

Definition :- An array is a group of variables having similar data type .

What is the use of Arrays ?

Arrays simplify programming as you don't have to remember the names of all the variables but the name of the array as a whole.

Let me give you an example :- You wish to deal with 12 different objects in your game ,   wouldn't it be difficult to address each of them if they are having different names ? ,   so this task is simplified by arrays ,   you can write it as

Myobject [0] = monster;

Myobject[1] = hero;

And so on…………..

Isn't it easy ? ,   yes it is.

Note :- The number 0 in square brackets is the index number.

The one given above was 1 dimensional array ,   Game Maker even supports 2 dimensional arrays

Note:- In a 2 dimensional array the index number contains 2 different numbers separated by a comma

Observe the table given below for ease in understanding

Hero
Wall
Arrow
Gun
Friend
1st enemy
2nd enemy
3rd enemy
Bike
Car

Plane
Final enemy

The objects in the table above represent one dimensional array , here Myobject[0] is Hero , Myobject[1] is wall and so on , observe the table given below for understanding 2 dimensional arrays

Vehicle	Enemy
Bike	1st Enemy
Car	2nd Enemy
Plane	3rd Enemy

Here Myobject [0 , 0] is Bike , Myobject [0 , 1] is 1st enemy , Myobject [2 , 0] is Car and so on……….

Conditions

In some of the games the level of difficulty goes on increasing as the scores increase in such cases condition are used , for example :- you want the player to go the next room if he/she scores 200 or more points then your code would be

{

If score >= 200 then room = room + 1

}

Explanation

The code checks the score , if the score is greater than or equal to 200 the player goes to the next room.

2nd example

Suppose you want to create an instance of an object named monster at (160, 140) if the score is greater than or equal to 500 your code would be

{

If score >= 500

X = instance_create(160 , 140 , monster)

}

Explanation

Instance_create is used to create an instance , 160 is the x value , 140 is the y value and monster is the name of the object

Tip :- It is a good practice to write the code in curved brackets {   }

3rd example

Suppose you want to write a code which compares the speed of object car whose id is (100025) to 8 , your code would be

```
{

if (100025).speed > 8 then

show_message("Speed is greater than 8")

if (100025).speed = 8 then

show_message("Speed is equal to 8")

if (100025).speed < 8 then

show_message("Speed is less than 8")

}
```

Note :- show_message displays a message (explained earlier)

The Else statement

Suppose you want to check whether the speed is equal to 8 , your code would be

```
{

if (100025).speed != 8 then

show_message("Speed is not equal to 8")

else

show_message("Speed is equal to 8")

}
```

Explanantion :- This code checks whether the speed is not equal to 8 , if it is not equal to 8 the first message is shown otherwise the 2nd message is shown , the commands succeeding the else statement are executed if the condition is not fulfilled.

Tip :- There are many ways of obtaining a solution in programming , I mean that this code can also be written as

```
{

if (100025).speed = 8 then
```

show_message("Speed is equal to 8")

else

show_message("Speed is not equal to 8")

}

Try experimenting with both the pieces of code , you must get the same result.

Loops

Note :- This is different from the one learnt earlier

Loops are of three types

a)While loop

b)Do while loop

c)For loop

While Loop

The statements in this loop are executed till a certain condition is fulfilled

For example :- You want to display 'Hi' 3 times will you write ?

```
{
show_message("Hi")

show_message("Hi")

show_message("Hi")

}
```

I would like writing the code given below

```
{
i = 0

while ( i != 3 )

    {
    show_message("Hi")
    i = i + 1
```

```
        }

}
```

The 2nd code uses the while loop

Note :- Though the output is the same isn't it convenient to write the second one ? , Suppose you want to display it 100 times will you write show_message hundred times or just change the expression from i != 3 to i != 100.

Explanation

i = 0 sets the value of the variable i to 0 , while (i != 3) means that the code inside the curved brackets (known as block) would be executed till the value of i is not equal to 3 , as we all know show_message displays message and the statement i = i + 1 increases the value of i (also known as incrementing) by 1.

Message Number	Value of i
1	0
2	1
3	2

When the 1st message is displayed the value of i is 0 , when the second one is displayed the value of i is 1 and when the third one is displayed the value of i is 2 after the third message is displayed the value of i becomes 3 (because of i = i + 1) and after that the condition while(i != 3) proves false so the loop ends

Warning :- Never write the code

```
 {

i = 0

while ( i != 3 )

    {

    show_message("Hi")

    }

}
```

Reason :- Here the value of i would never increment so the message would be displayed forever ,   try your best to avoid such codes.

Experiment :- Try the code given below

```
{

repeat(3) show_message("Hi")

}
```

This is even more simpler than the while loop.

Conclusion :- From the above experiment we conclude that same output can be obtained by code written in different form.

Explanation :- repeat(3) show_message("Hi") means repeating show_message 3 times.

Do While Loop

   A do while loop is similar to while loop the only difference is that in a do .... While loop the block would be executed at least once.

```
{

i = 0

do

        {

        show_message("Hi")

        i = i + 1

        }

until( i = 3 )

}
```

Explanation :- The code in the block is executed until (i = 3) is false , when (i = 3) turns true the execution of the block is stopped.

For Loop

   A for loop is used for executing a statement or a block of code a required number of times ,   so for displaying "Hi" 3 times in a for loop our code would be

```
{

for(i = 0; i < 3; i += 1)
```

```
    {

      show_message("Hi")

    }

}
```

In this loop we don't have to write i = i + 1 because the incrementing is done by the statement i += 1.

Functions :- Functions are like statements with parameters for performing task.

Functions are of two types

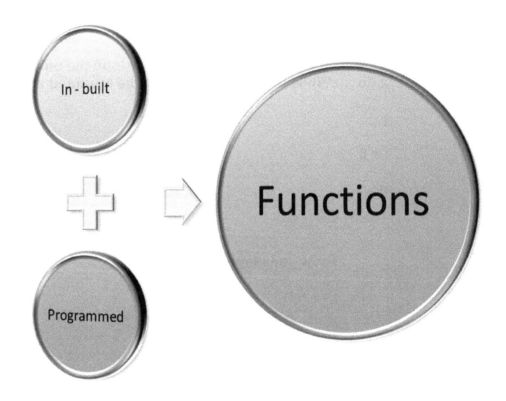

(Fig 415)

There are many in-built functions available in Game Maker which cater many of our needs,   unlike many other languages we cannot program our own functions in Game Maker but Game Maker's functionality can be extended by Dll's(Dynamic Link Libraries) and through Extension Maker which are explained later.

Blocks :- The code in curved brackets { } is known as a block , suppose you program a while loop

While(expression)

```
{

any code

}
```

Here the code in the brackets would be executed while the expression turns true. The curved brackets actually tell Game Maker that execute this code if the expression is true.

Comments

Comments actually have a negligible effect on the output , they are just placed for explaining the programming , copyright notices and / or credentials if any.

Suppose we want to add one's credentials we would write

```
// Made by Aditya Kale
```

If we want to add 2 or 3 lines more we would write it as follows

```
/* Made By Aditya Kale

Copyright 2011

Confidential code , do not copy */
```

You may even write it as

```
// Made By Aditya Kale

// Copyright 2011

// Confidential code , do not copy
```

The effect is the same

Comments are ignored by the compiler , So if you write

```
// show_message("Hello")
```

Hello would not be executed as Game Maker would assume it to be a comment and ignore it.

So anything written to the right hand side of // or anything written between /*...*/ is ignored by the compiler.

Tip :- This is similar to the C++ programming language.

Components of a programming language

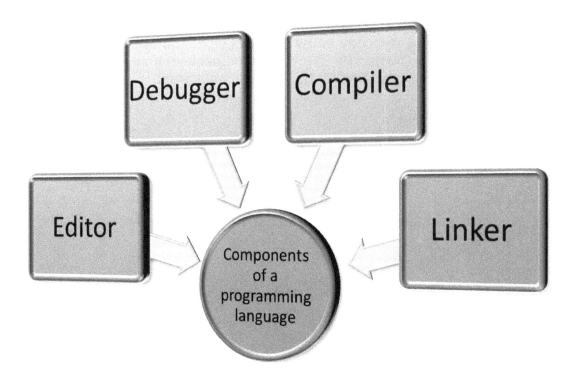

(Fig 416)

1)Editor :- The program code is written in the editor ,   the editor is like the windows notepad ,   every editor is different ,   in some languages the in built functions are given different color while in some others there is error – checking ,   the editor is a very important component but many of the languages don't provide an editor ! ,   in such languages the code is compiled through command line ,   thankfully Game Maker has it's own text editor.

2)Debugger :- This program checks the code for errors.

3)Compiler :- Compiles the program and creates the object code.

4)Linker :- The linker links all the object code files in an executable which can be executed on an computer running windows.

Note :- Unlike other languages Game Maker doesn't create .obj files this is an advantage as it would reduce the risk of the file being mistakenly deleted.

2)Game Maker directly combines everything in an executable.

Constants

Constants are like variables but their value is constant , here is a complete list of constants and their corresponding values , constants are divided into three categories

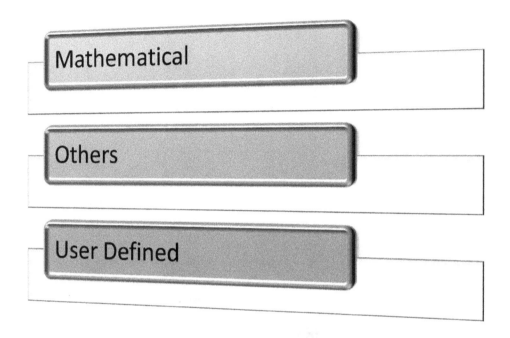

(Fig 417)

There are only 3 mathematical constants in Game Maker

Constant	Value
Pi	22 / 7 which is equal to 3.142857
true	1
false	0

All the other constants excluding the three mentioned above fall under the category of other constants , user – defined constants are defined by the programmer (you)

To define constants press Shift + Ctrl + N

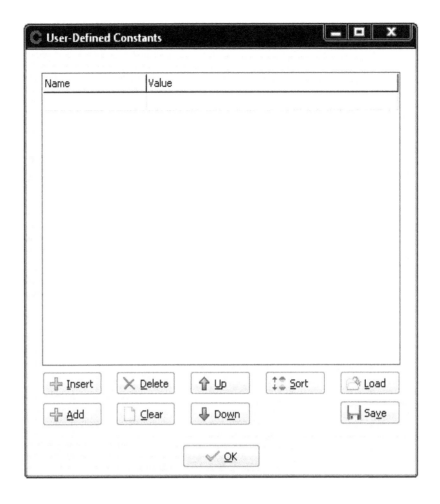

(Fig 418)

There are 10 buttons located on this window Let us learn them one –
by – one

Button	Use
1)Insert	Used for inserting a constant before the current constant
2)Add	Used for adding a constant after the current constant
3)Delete	Deletes the current constant
4)Clear	Clears the whole list Note :- Prompts for confirmation
5)Up	Suppose the 1st constant is true and the 2nd one is false where the current constant is false , after this button is pressed 1st constant would be false and the 2nd one would be true.
6)Down	Suppose the 1st constant is false and the 2nd one is true where the current constant is false , after this button is pressed 1st constant would be true and the 2nd one

	would be false.
7)Sort	Used for sorting the constants
8)Load	Loads the constant from a text file
9)Save	Saves the constants to a text file
10)Ok	Saves the constants

Tip :- The user – defined constants would be defined in the list of constants in red text

Current constant :- The constant which is clicked by the mouse becomes the current constant.

Note :- current constant is highlighted by a blue marking

2)Value may not be necessarily be a numerical value.

Summary

Let's summarize some very important points in this chapter

If you wish to apply changes to a particular instance you can use the id of that particular instance. We even discussed about arrays and types of arrays , later we learnt loops and the way of handling them , we even read a piece of code where the value of I was not at all incremented and we even discussed the disastrous effect of such code

Chapter 12 The Game Maker's Language (GML)

GML is the programming language which is built in Game Maker , GML has it's own syntax which is similar to the C++ syntax to some extent , GML has it's own editor , to open the editor press Shift + Ctrl + C

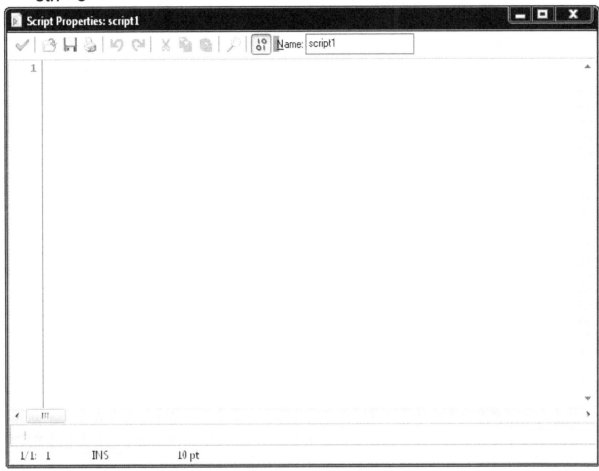

(Fig 419)

The title shows the name of the script , here the name is 'script1' , program code or the source code or code is known as a script in Game Maker.

Let us understand the toolbar

(Fig 420)

As shown in the Figure(420) there are 11 buttons available on the toolbar Let us understand each of them in the order left to right

Order	Name	Use

1)	Ok	Saves the changes Note :- Doesn't prompt for confirmation
2)	Load	Loads a saved script file Note :- Extension is .txt
3)	Save	Saves the code to a file Note :- Extension is .txt
4)	Print	Prints the code
5)	Undo	Undo the last change
6)	Redo	Redo the last undo
7)	Cut	Cuts the code and sends it to the clipboard
8)	Copy	Copies the code to the clip board
9)	Paste	Used for pasting the text on the clipboard
10)	Find / Replace	Shows the find / replace panel
11)	Check code	Checks the code for syntax errors

The find / replace panel

The find / replace panel is used to find a keyword or an text , replace can be used for replacing the word with another one.

For example :- I want to change all the Myobject to obj I would find Myobject and in the replace panel type obj and replace them.

Note :- It is possible to replace only one , you may even replace all or more than one , all the three types of replacements supported

2)This is one of the features of Game Maker , not supported by many other text editors

The two checkboxes are explained here

SR No	Name	Use
1)	Case sensitive	This checkbox would activate case sensitivity My recommendation :- Uncheck this box.
2)	Whole word only	If this checkbox is activated it would match the input given by you to each and every word and check if they tally , it wouldn't find your input if your input is a part of a word My recommendation :- Uncheck this box.

Note :- The script editor would just highlight the found words with a yellow marking ,   unlike other editors it wouldn't take you to the line or display the line number.

   The 4 buttons 1)Previous ,   2)Next ,   …….. would work only if the editor finds the word you are searching for at more than one place.

It is obvious that all the code is written in this editor.

Note :- There is one more editor ,   it is actually used as an action which is execute code (code part ,   control tab) ,   there is only difference between the 2 editors the execute code action's editor contains applies to : property

Let us learn all the functions with their parameters and their utility.

1)Functions dealing with values

   The list of functions dealing with values is given below but there are some terms used in the list which you must know

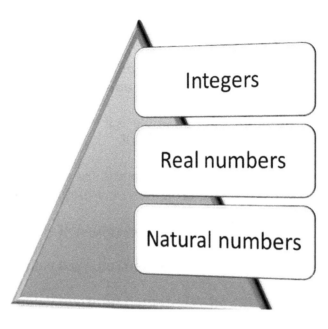

(Fig 422)

1)Integers :- Integers include all the numbers ....-2 , -1 , 0 , 1 , 2 ....

2)Real numbers :- Include numbers greater than 0 which means that they are 1 , 2 , 3 ...

3)Natural numbers :- Include numbers 0 , 1 , 2 , 3 , ...

Functions	Use
1) random(val)	Returns a value (randomly generated) in the range 0 to val. Tip :- generated number < val
2)random_range(val1 , val2)	Returns a value (generated randomly) in the range val1 to val2 Note :- generated number may be equal to val1 or val2 , which means that the range becomes val1 – 1 to val2 + 1
3)irandom(val)	Returns an integer between 0 and val Note :- The generated number may be val if val is an integer.
4)irandom_range (val1 , val2)	Returns a randomly generated real number in the range val1 – 1 to val2 + 1
5)random_set_s eed()	Sets the seeds which is used for generating random numbers
6)random_get_s eed()	Returns the present seed

7)randomize()	Sets the seed to a number which is generated randomly
8)choose(a , b , c , d , ...)	Returns any one (a , b , c , d) of them (generated randomly) Note :- Maximum 16 arguments
9)abs(val)	Returns the absolute value of val For example :- If val is 22 / 7 the absolute value would be 3.14 Tip :- abs stands for absolute
10)sign(val)	Returns a value which may be 1 , 0 or -1. If val > 0 then returned value = 1 If val = 0 then returned value = 0 If val < 0 then returned value = -1
11)round(val)	Rounds the value of val to the nearest integer For example 1)If val = 3.14 round(val) = 3 2)If val = 3.50 round(val) = 4
12)floor(val)	Rounds the value of val to the lower integer For example 1)if val = 3.14 floor(val) = 3 2)if val = 3.50 floor(val) = 3 3)if val = 3.99 floor(val) = 3 Tip :- This is known as the floor value
13)ceil(val)	Rounds the value of val to the higher integer For example 1)if val = 3.14 ceil(val) = 3 2)if val = 3.50 ceil(val) = 3 3)if val = 3.99 ceil(val) = 3 Tip :- This is known as the ceil value

14)frac(val)	Returns the value which is after the decimal For example 1)if val = 3.14 frac(val) = 0.14 2)if val = 3.1415 frac(val) = 0.14 3)if val = 3.145 frac(val) = 0.15 Tip :- This is known as the fractional part Note :- From the 2nd and the 3rd example we conclude that frac(val) would return a value only upto 2 decimals not more than that
15)sqrt(val)	Returns the square root of val Note :- val must be > 0 or val = 0 Tip :- If the above condition is not fulfilled an error would be generated as follows Cannot apply sqrt to negative number.
16)sqr(val)	Squares the value of val and returns it Tip :- In simple terms it means val multiplied by val
17)power(val1 , val2)	Returns a value = val1 to the power val2 For example power(2 , 3) would return 8 (2 * 2 * 2 = 8)
18)exp(val)	Returns a value = e * e * e val times For example exp(5) would return (e * e * e * e * e)
19)is_real(val)	If val is a real number it would return 1 meaning true else it would return 0 meaning false
20)is_string(val)	If val is a string it would return 1 meaning true else it would return 0 meaning false
21)min(val1 , val2 , val3 , ...)	Returns the minimum among (val1 , val2 , val3 , ...)
22)max(val1 , val2 , val3 , ...)	Returns the maximum among (val1 , val2 , val3 , ...)

For learning the further functions you must have a basic idea about logarithms , statistics and trigonometry

You must also know the relation between degrees and radians

I have simplified your work by eliminating the formula , you just have to remember 1 thing

Approximately 57.272727 degrees is equal to 1 radian

Logarithms

There are many functions dealing with log so I would give a basic idea to you about what is logarithm.

$\log_x c = a$ means that $c = x^a$

$\log_x c = a$ is read as logarithm of the number c with respect to the base x

Some rules

If $\log_x c = a$ hold true the conditions given below are valid

1)C should always be greater than 0 (c > 0)

2)X should be greater than 0 (x > 0) but not equal to 1

a) $\log_x a + \log_x b + \log_x c = \log_x abc$

b) $\log_x a / \log_x b = \log_b a$

c) $\log_x a^n = n\log_x a$

d) $\log_x x = 1$

Statistics

Statistics is the way of representing data in a simple and a lucid manner

Note :- We would not learn anything about group data , we would just learn about raw data because game maker doesn't support grouped data

Basics of statistics

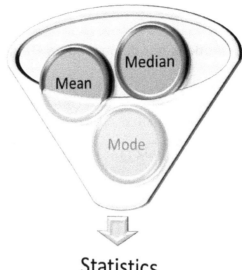

Statistics

(Fig 423)

Mean :- Mean means average.

Suppose you want to find the mean of 1 , 2 , 3 , 4 , 5 , the formula is

Sum of all terms / total terms , which means (1 + 2 + 3 + 4 + 5)/ 5 which would be equal to 15 / 5 which is equal to 3.

Median :- Median means the middle term

Suppose you want to find the median of 1 , 3 , 5 , 7 , 9 , the formula is

(Number of terms + 1)/ 2 , which means (5 + 1) / 2 which is equal to 6 / 2 = 3 but here 3 is not the median , 3 means the 3rd term which is 5 , so the median is 5

This formula doesn't work in all the cases , this formula works only if the number of terms is an odd number , if the number of terms is an even number another formula is applicable

[(number of terms) / 2 + (number of terms + 2) / 2] / 2

So if you want to find median of 1 , 3 , 5 , 7 , 9 , 11 the substitution would be

[(6) / 2 + (6 + 2) / 2] / 2 which is equal to [3 + 4] /2 which means (3rd term + 4th term) the whole divided by 2 which is equal to (5 + 7)/2 which is equal to 6 , so in this case 6 is the median.

But Game Maker follows a different formula , it would find out the average of 5 and 7 but it would return the lowest among them which is 5.

Note :- Mode is not discussed as Game Maker doesn't support it

Functions	Use
1)mean(val1 , val2 , ...)	Returns the mean Note :- Maximum 16 numbers are supported
2)Median(val1 , val2 , ...)	Returns the median Note :- Maximum 16 numbers are supported

Functions dealing with conversions

Functions	Use
1)degtorad(val)	Converts val degrees into radians Let us breakdown the function name deg to rad meaning degree to radians
2)radtodeg(val)	Converts val radians into degrees Let us breakdown the function name rad to deg meaning radians to degrees

Note :- It is assumed that you know trigonometry

Note :- Radians is the internationally accepted (SI unit) for measuring angles , Game Maker supports radians , there is a way to obtain the results in degrees which is explained later

Function	Use
1)sin(val)	Returns the sine value of angle val
2)cos(val)	Returns the cosine value of angle val
3)tan(val)	Returns the tangent value of angle val

4)arcsin(val)	First finds out the value of sin(val) and then inverts it
	For example :- If sin(val) = 7 / 8 then arcsin(val) = 8 / 7
5)arcos(val)	First finds out the value of cos(val) and then inverts it
	For example :- If cos(val) = 7 / 8 then arccos(val) = 8 / 7
6)arctan(val)	First finds out the value of tan(val) and then inverts it
	For example :- If tan(val) = 7 / 8 then arctan(val) = 8 / 7
7)arctan2(val1 , val2)	Divides actan(val1 / val2) and returns a value

A few more functions

Function	Use
1) point_distance(x1, y1, x2, y2)	Finds the distance between two points x and y having co-ordinates (x1 , y1) and (x2 , y2) respectively
2) point_direction(x1, y1, x2, y2)	Finds the direction between two points x and y having co-ordinates (x1 , y1) and (x2 , y2) respectively Note :- Measured in degrees
3) lengthdir_x(length, direction)	Finds the x –component of the vector by the specified length and direction
4) lengthdir_y(len, dir)	Finds the x –component of the vector by the specified length and direction

Functions dealing with strings

Functions	Use
1)chr(val)	Returns the character corresponding to the ascii number val For example chr(65) = A
2)ord(str)	Returns the ascii number of the first character of the string For example Ord("A box") = 65
3)real(str)	If a variable contains "5" it would treat 5 as a string , to convert this "5" into a number this function is used
4)string(val)	Converts a mathematical value into a string
5)string_format(val , total , dec)	Here val means the value , total means the total places and dec means

	decimal places
	Example
	String_format(653 , 2 , 1) = 653.0
6)string_length(str)	Returns the total number of characters in the string
	For example
	string_length("star") = 4
	but "this is a star" = 14 , one may feel that there are only 11 characters but it's wrong even the spaces are calculated while calculating the length .
7)string_pos(substr , str)	Note :- substr means sub-string
	This function finds the position of substr in the string str
	For example
	string_pos("a", "this is a star") = 9
	but in the case of
	string_pos("a", "that is a star") = 3
	there are 2 a's in this sentence that and a in such a case the first one is considered
8)string_copy(str , index , count)	Returns a string which is a part of the string provided from the start (index) to the end (count)
	For example
	string_copy("that is a star", 2 , 8) would result "hat is a"
9)string_char_at(str , index)	Returns the character at the number index in the string str
	For example
	string_char_at("that is a star", 4) = t
10)string_delete(str , index , count)	Returns a string with the part erased between index and count
	For example
	string_delete("that is a star", 2 , 5) would result "ts a star"
11)string_insert(substr , str , index)	Attaches the sub string substr to the string str at the specified index

12)string_replace(str , substr , newstr)	Replaces substring substr in the string str with newstr In this case substr is replaced by newstr only once , if you want to replace substr by newstr each time it occurs use the function String_replace_all(str , substr , newstr)
13)string_count(substr , str)	Suppose you want to calculate the number of times the word space occurs in the sentence 'This is a space where space ships land after their arrival from space' in such a case string_count is used Note :- In this case substr is 'space' and the sentence is 'This is a ....space'
14)string_lower(str)	To understand it better read the example string_lower("Rockets Are Better Than Air planes") would become "rockets are better than air planes"
15)string_upper(str)	Just the reverse of the one taught earlier
16)string_repeat(str , count)	Copies string str count times to a string
17)string_letters(str)	Thus function would return all the letters in all the words to a single word For example string_letters("I love Game programming") would become IloveGameProgramming
18)string_digits(str)	This action would extract all the digits from the string str For example string_digits("I am 15 years old") would become 15
19)string_lettersdigits(str)	This action would return all the letters and digits in the order in which they are present and would remove all the spaces For example string_lettersdigits("I am 15 years old") would become Iam15yearsold
20)clipboard_has_text()	I have explained what is clipboard earlier , this function would check whether there is text present on the clipboard
21)clipboard_get_text()	Extracts the text from the clipboard

22)clipboard_set_text(str)	Copies str to the clipboard

Now we would write code to extract text from the clipboard , this code would check whether there is text present on the clipboard or not if text is present it would show the text if not it would inform about the absence of text on the clipboard.

```
{

a = clipboard_has_text()

If ( a = 0 )

    {

    show_message("there is no text on the clipboard")

    }

    else

    {

    show_message(clipboard_get_text)

    }

}
```

Explanation :- a = clipboard_has_text() ,   if clipboard has text a would become 1 else it would become 0 ,   If (a = 0) checks whether the value of a is zero or not ,   if it is zero the statement show_message("there is no text on the clipboard") gets executed if not the statement   show_message(clipboard_get_text) , show_message(clipboard_get_text) means that it would show what so ever is present on the clipboard in the form of a message.

Functions dealing with scores and lives

Scores and lives are very important in Game Programming so there are a few functions dealing with scores they are

Function	Use

1)score	Deals with the score
	
	Suppose you want to save the score to a variable x your code would be
	
	{
	
	x = score
	
	}

	Note :- Cannot be used for changing the score
2)lives	Finds out the number of lives Note :- Cannot be used for changing the number of lives
3)health	Finds out the health Note :- The default health is 100 it doesn't change unless changed by any action.

4) show_score :- If you want to show the score in the windows caption set this property to true

show_score = true
carefully

Observe the score

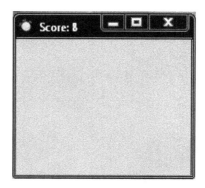

(Fig 424)

5)show_health :- Let us you show the health in the windows caption , set the show_health property to true by show_health = true

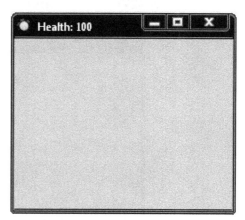

(Fig 425) ⟶

6)show_lives :- Used for displaying the number of lives , set this one to true by using the same method done earlier.

(Fig 426)

Note :- The Figures are just for illustrative purposes the values may differ.

An interesting fact

You can display the 3(lives , health and score) together just type the code

{

show_lives = true

show_score = true

show_health = true

} // Observe (Fig 427) given below

It doesn't matter whether you write show_score first of show_health first the order remains the same.

There are 3 more functions not so important

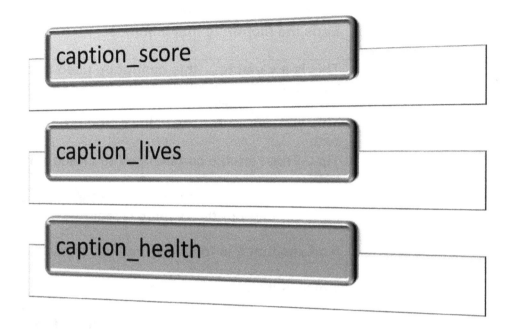

(Fig 428)

All the functions dealing with score explained earlier cannot be called functions because they don't consist of any parameters they are in fact variables.

1)caption_lives ,   2)caption_score and caption_health just return the captions for lives ,   score and health respectively.

Functions and Variables dealing with Paths

Functions / Variables	Use
1)path_start(path , speed , endaction , absolute)	Path :- The name of the path
	speed :- Path speed
	absolute :- If true the path uses the co-ordinates specified , if false a relative path is formed.
	endaction :- Means what should happen when the end is reached
	In this case 4 values are valid
	0 :- Stop the path
	1 :- Jump to and continue from the start position
	2 :- Start from the current position

	3 :- Start moving in the reverse direction
2)path_end()	Ends the motion of that instance
3)path_position	This is a variable , this cannot be used to change the position of that instance on the path , this variable can be used to just return the path position
4)path_positionp revious	This variable stores the value of the previous position of the path
5)path_speed	Tip :- This variable can be used to change the speed of the path
6)path_orientati on	Orientation means whether the instance is following the right direction or the reverse direction 0 means that it is following path as created 1 means it's following the path in the reverse order
7)path_scale	This variable deals with the scaling , 1 means the original value , 2 means it would double the path size etc
8)path_endactio n	Explained earlier , use the values specified earlier

Now that we have learnt so much about variables we would naturally like to create variables of our own

There are 2 ways of creating variables

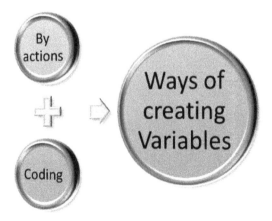

There are 3 actions which deal with variables , Navigate to the control tab variables part

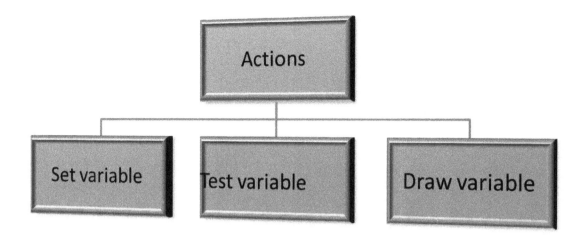

(Fig 430)

1)Set Variable :- Used for creating variables and supplying them a value

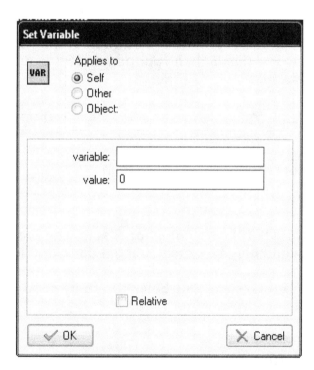

(Fig 431)

Note :- This action can also be used for changing the value of a variable already defined.

2)Test Variable :- Used for checking whether the value of a variable is equal to another value or is more than or less than another value

(Fig 432)

Suppose you want to test whether the value of the variable friction is greater than 5 than your parameters would be

variable	friction
value	5
operation	larger than

Note :- This is a conditional action so the actions succeeding this one would only be executed if the condition is true

Tip :- This can also be achieved by code

```
{

if ( friction = 5)

//code

}
```

Note :- For actions to be executed when the condition is false use the else action explained earlier

3)Draw Variable :- This action is used for drawing the variable values on the screen , you just have to specify the variable and it's location(x and y co-ordinates) relatively or absolutely

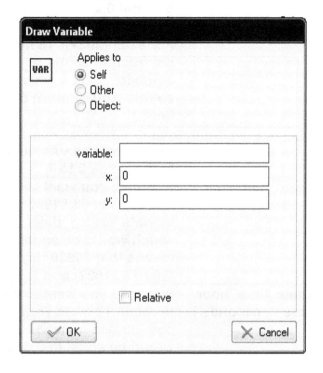

(Fig 433)

You may be knowing that there are many games who prompt users to activate them by typing an activation code after 30 days of use , how do these programs know that the trial version has expired ? , the Answer is quite simple :- These programs wisely use the functions that deal with date and time ,   Does Game Maker provide such functions ? ,   yes of course ,   so Let us understand these functions.

Functions and Variables dealing with dates and time

Functions / Variables	Use
date_current_datetime()	Returns the value corresponding to the date and time at the instant this function is executed
date_current_date()	Returns the date. Note :- This function wouldn't return the date in the (dd/mm/yyyy) format but it would return the number of days which have passed since 30 / 12 / 1899 (dd / mm / yyyyy) format For example :- If the date is 1 / 1 / 1900 then date_current_date() = 1
date_current_time	Returns the current time Note :- This function wouldn't return the value in the format (hour : minutes : seconds) but it would return a value in

	decimal 0.x
	For example :- If 18 hours have passed the fraction would be 18 / 24 which is equal to 3 / 4 which is equal to 0.75 so this would return 0.75 as the current time

Tip :- The time vAalue would always be in the range 0 to 1 |
| date_create_date(year , month ,   day) | Suppose you want to know the value of the day 19 / 08 / 1995 your syntax would be date_create_date(1995 ,   08 ,   19) which would be equal to 34930 which means that 34930 days passed between (30 / 12 / 1899) and (19 / 08 / 1995) |
| date_create_time(hour ,   minutes ,   seconds) | Suppose you want to find the value of the time 12 noon your syntax would be date_create_time(12 ,   00 ,   00) which would be equal to 0.50 (12 / 24) |
| date_create_datetime(year ,   month ,   day , hour , minute , seconds) | Suppose you want to know the value of day 19 / 08 / 1995 and time 12 noon your syntax would be

date_create_datetime (1995 ,   08 ,   19 , 12 ,   00 ,   00) which would be equal to 34930.50

34930 + 0.50 |
| date_valid_time(hour , minute ,   seconds) | Checks whether the time is valid or not

Tip :- If 1 is returned the time is valid |
| date_valid_date(year , month ,   day) | Checks whether the date is valid or not |
| date_valid_datetime (year ,   month ,   day , hour , minute , seconds) | Checks whether the date and time are valid or not |
| date_is_today(date) | Checks whether the given date is today or not

Note :- The date should be the number of days passed after 30 / 12 / 1899 |
| date_days_in_year(date) | Gives the number of days in that year |
| date_leap_year(date) | If the year indicated by the date is a leap year it would return true (1) else false (0) |
| date_time_string(time) | This function would convert the time from Game Makers format to the format supported by the system

For example |

	0.75 = 6:00:00 PM 0.5 = 12:00:00 PM
date_days_in_month(date)	This action would return the number of days in the month using the date specified by you
date_date_string(date)	This function would convert the date from Game Makers format to the format supported by the system For example 30490 = 19 / 08 / 1995
date_datetime_string(datetime)	This function would convert the date time from Game Makers format to the format supported by the system For example 34930.50 = 19/08/1995 12:00:00
date_inc_year (date , amount)	This is a bit difficult to explain so observe and try to carefully understand the example We know 34930 = 19 / 08 / 1995 so if we type date_inc_year(34930 , 1) the result would be 35296 , if you observe (35296 - 34930) = 366 , a year has 365 days but the year 1996 was a leap year so (34930 , 1) means the value of 19 / 08 /1995 + 1 year , the succeeding year was 1996 so 366 is added to 34930 So we understand that this function would add the number of years specified by you as the amount to the given date and return the final date , in other words this function would find the value of 19 / 08 / 1996 Tip :- If you specify the amount as -1 this function would find the value of 19 / 08 / 1994 Tip :- It is obvious that if you specify the amount as 0 it would find the value of 19 / 08 / 1995 which would be 34930
date_inc_month(date , amount)	This function is like the previous one but here instead of years the months would increase suppose date is 34930 and amount is 1 it would return the

	value of 19 / 09 / 1995
date_inc_date(date , amount)	This function would add the number of days specified as amount to the given date
date_inc_week(date , amount)	This function would add the number of weeks specified as amount to the given date
date_inc_hour(date , amount)	Returns a new value which would be the sum of the given date value and the number of hours (number of hours means the amount specified by you)
date_inc_minute(date , amount)	Returns a new value which would be the sum of the given date value and the number of minutes specified by you in the amount
date_inc_seconds(date , amount)	Returns a new value which would be the result of the given date and the seconds specified by you as the amount
date_get_second(date)	This function would extract the value of seconds from the given date For example 23456.7896 = 1 seconds
date_get_minute(date)	This function would extract the value of minutes from the given date 23456.7896 = 57 minutes
date_get_hour(date)	This function would extract the value of hours from the given date 23456.7896 = 1hour
date_get_day(date)	This function would find out the day(1st , 2nd etc) corresponding to the given date 23456.7896 = 20 Note :- This means 20th day of the month
date_get_week(date)	This function would find out the week in which contained the day whose date is supplied 23456.7896 = 12 Note :- This means 12th week of that particular year
date_get_month(date)	This function would extract the month from the given date 23456.7896 = 3

	Note :- This means the 3rd month (March)
date_get_year(date)	This function would extract the year from the given date 23456.7896 = 1964

Experiment :- Find out date_datetime_string(23456.7896)

Observation :- 20 / 03 / 1964 6:57:01 PM

date_get_weekday(date)	This function would extract the weekday from the given date 23456.7896 = 6 Note :- Here 6 means the 6th day of the week (Friday)
date_get_day_of_year(date)	This function would extract the nth day of the year For example 23456.7896 = 80 This means that 20 / 03 / 1964 is the 20th day of the year 1964
date_get_hour_of_year(date)	Extract the hours passed in that particular year from the date For example 23456.7896 = 1914 Means that till 23456.7896 , 1914 hours have passed in the year 1964
date_get_minute_of_year(date)	Extracts the minutes passed in that particular year For example 23456.7896 = 114897 Means that till 23456.7896 , 114897 minutes have passed in the year 1964
date_get_second_of_year(date)	Extracts the value of the seconds passed in that particular year For example 23456.7896 = 6893821

	Means that till 23456.7896 , 6893821 seconds have passed in the year 1964

Note :- Number of seconds should always be more than the number of minutes and the number of minutes should always be more than the numb
er of
hours

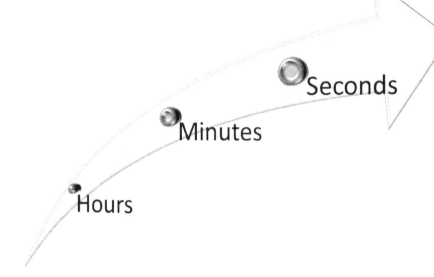

Seconds

Minutes

Hours

(Fig 434 , in an ascending order)

The functions (dealing with dates) which we are going to learn now are used for comparing 2 date values

date_compare_date(date1 , date2)	Compares the dates date1 and date2
	Results :-
	<table><tr><td>-1</td><td>date1 < date2</td></tr><tr><td>0</td><td>date1 = date2</td></tr><tr><td>1</td><td>date1 > date2</td></tr></table>
	Note :- if date1 = 19 / 08 / 1995 12:00:00 pm
	and date2 = 19 / 08 / 1995 13:00:00 pm then the result would be 0
	Reason :- This action would compare only the dates irrespective of the time

date_compare_time(date1 , date2)	This function would extract the time from both the date values and compare them Note :- The results are same as the previous one
date_compare_dateti me(date1 , date2)	This action would first compare the dates , if the dates are equal it would compare the time and then find out the greater one Let us check what would be the result if date1 = 19 / 08 / 1995 12:00:00 pm and date2 = 19 / 08 / 1995 13:00:00 pm then the result would be -1 Note :- The date functions comparing dates ends here
date_date_of(date)	This function would only return the date part of the value 'date' irrespective of the time
date_time_of(date)	This function would return only the time part irrespective of the date
date_second_span(date1 , date2)	This function would return the difference of seconds between the two dates
date_minute_span(date1 , date2)	This function would return the difference of minutes between the two dates
date_hour_span(date1 , date2)	This function would return the difference of hour between the two dates
date_day_span(date1 , date2)	This function would return the difference of days between the two dates
date_week_span(date1 , date2)	This function would return the difference of week between the two dates
date_month_span(date1 , date2)	This function would return the difference of months between the two dates
date_year_span(date1 , date2)	This function would return the difference of years between the two dates

The functions and variables dealing with date and time end here

Before proceeding I would recommend you to observe Fig 029 once again

Now we are going to learn some not so necessary function but they are of use in some cases ,   but to learn them you must know about errors so let's learn

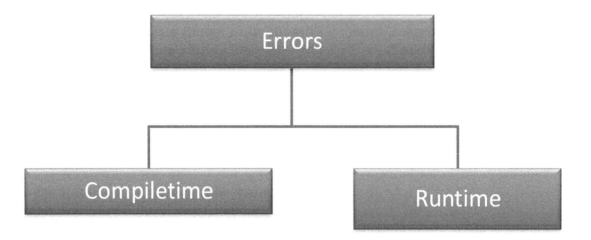

Errors and Error Handling

Errors are of two types(Fig 435)

Majority of the computer users feel the if errors occur it's the programmers fault but that's not true in all the cases , the result of an error may be the user's fault , For example let's say your program needs the file prog.config and a user of your program delete's it by mistake your program would encounter an error even though it's not your fault , 2nd example :- In a calculator suppose you type A + B the calculator would encounter an error as numerical values are expected , 3rd example :- Suppose the minimum requirement of your program is Windows XP and someone tries to install it on a Windows 98 machine an error would be generated immediately.

Errors cannot be eradicated completely but they can be minimized to a great extent if the programmer has the required skills and if the language which he uses for programming provides functions which would help tackle errors

The errors discussed earlier were run time errors , now we are going to discuss about compile time errors.

Compile time errors are flaws , faults and shortcomings in the program code , For example if you type

show_message(Made by Aditya Kale)

An error would be encountered because there is no such variable like Made by Aditya Kale , If we want to show it as a text we must insert the words Made by Aditya Kale in inverted commas

Generally compilation process is interrupted when compile time errors are encountered but that's not the case for Game Maker , Game Maker would let you compile the code even if there are errors , and during execution if that statement(containing error) is executed Game Maker would treat the error as run time error

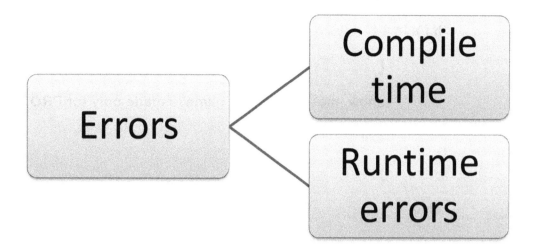

(Fig 436)

So in other words there are no compile time errors for Game Maker , Observe Fig 070 as an example of how errors encountered in Game Maker.

Note :- Gamers generally avoid playing the games which end abruptly due to errors.

Functions dealing with errors

Functions / Variables	Use
error_occured	Returns 1 if an error has occurred else 0 Tip:- Check the spellings properly while typing the code else an error would generate due to your spelling mistake
error_last	Returns a string containing the latest error message

Imagine a scenario where you have made your game in the pro version but some one opens the file using the lite edition , it would encounter an error if you have programmed a feature not available in the lite edition , what would happen ?.

It's obvious that Game Maker would encounter an error

It may be totally impossible to eradicate errors but errors can be minimized , you may be wondering the ways of minimizing errors , observe the code given on the next page

```
{

a = gamemaker_pro

If ( a != 1 )

        {

        show_message( "This game is made only for PRO edition")

        exit

        }

else

        {

        // other code of the program

        }

}
```

Tip :- You can even replace gamemaker_pro by gamemaker_registered ,   but there is no such thing like gamemaker_lite or gamemaker_unregistered

   In many of the platform games(For example :- Super Mario Bros) the player comes down automatically after a jump ,   it doesn't remain there till the game ends it has to come down after a short while ,   this is done by a variable which is known as gravity in Game Maker ,   You may have observed one more thing that underwater the speed reduces in such games ,   does the speed really reduce ? ,   No the friction increases ,   so we feel that the speed is reduced ,   Friction can be defined as a force obstructing the motion of any body ,   in Game Maker the variable that deals with friction is also friction

Suppose you want to increase the friction by 5 of an object named obj_character your code would be

obj_character.friction = obj_character.friction + 5

Note :- obj_character.friction = 5 would simply set the friction to 5 but obj_character.friction + 5 would actually increase the friction by 5

and what if you want to increase the gravity by 5 ,   simple :- replace friction by gravity

Note :- Increasing the friction would decrease the gravity as the friction would also reduce the downward fall of the object

Note :- This gravity would pull an object downwards ,   but what if you want to object to be pulled upwards

Answer :- Set the gravity to a negative value

But what if you want the gravity to be pulling towards the right , your code would be

gravity_direction = 0

Many a times in Games you have to check about collision , for example Super Mario Bros. When the Mario is in the air the game checks whether there are any collisions , if there is a collision with an object similar to a floor the Mario stands on it , if there is a collision with a monster the health reduces and it eventually dies (number of lives reduces by 1) and if the position is collision free (without any collisions) the instance falls due to gravitational force , now I am going to introduce you to some functions for handling collisions

1)collision_point(x , y , obj , prec , notme) :- This function checks whether there is any collision of object obj with any other object at the position (x , y) , prec means precise collision checking , notme means that even if one instance collides with other instance of the same object the function would return no-collision.

Note :- Prec works for only for objects with sprites having precise collision checking set to true(Observe Fig 437 given below)

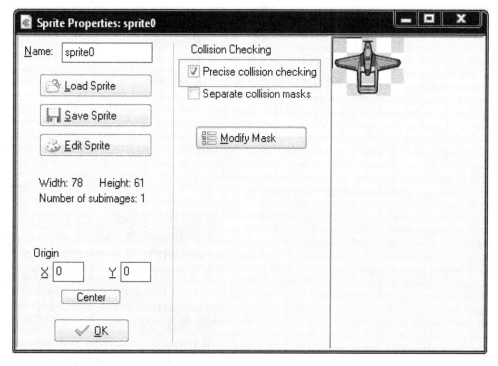

2)collision_rectangle(x1 , y1 , x2 , y2 , obj , prec , notme) :- This function is used to check the collision of an object obj with the rectangle having co-ordinates (x1 , y1 , x2 , y2)

3)collision_circle(x1 , y1 , radius , obj , prec , notme) :- This function checks whether there is any collision between an object obj and a circle with it's centre at (x1 , y1) and of the given radius

4)collision_ellipse(x1 , y1 , x2 , y2 , obj , prec , notme) :- This function checks whether there is a collision between an ellipse of co-ordinates (x1 , y1 , x2 , y2) and an object obj

5)collision_line(x1 , y1 , x2 , y2 , obj , prec , notme) :- This function checks whether there is a collision between a line and an object obj , (x1 , y1) are the co-ordinates of the start of the line and (x2 , y2) are the co-ordinates of the end of the line

```
_____

   (x1 , y1)                                    (x2 , y2)
```

(Fig 438)

The minimum requirement of any game made by Game Maker is a room , when you try to play a game without any room the message prompts

(Fig 439)

So there are naturally some functions as well as variables made for managing rooms

Functions / Variables	Use
1)room	This variable stores the index value of the current room , in other the room which is displayed on the screen at that instant Tip :- This is not a read-only variable (variable which can be read but nothing can be written in that variable) so you can use this variable to jump to a new room !!! , but still you are advised to use the Function / Variable number 4 provided in this table
2)room_last	This variables stores the index value of the last room present in the game
3)room_first	This variable stores the index value of the first room present in the game
4)room_goto(numb)	This function is used for jumping to a room whose index is numb
5)room_goto_next()	Used for going to the next room Note :- Would encounter an error if the current room is the last room !!!

6)room_goto_previous()	Used for going to the previous room Note :- Would encounter an error if the current room is the first one
7)room_restart()	Restarts the current room
8)room_previous_numb()	This function would return the index number of the room before the current room Note:- The index number of the first room is considered to be 0 so if you are in the first room and this function is executed , this function would return the number -1
9)room_next_numb()	Returns the index number of the room after the current room.
10)room_width	Returns the width of the room Note :- Read-only variable cannot be used to change the width of the room
11)room_height	Returns the height of the room Note :- Read-only variable cannot be used to change the height of the room
12)room_caption	This variable stores the caption of the room For example :- In Fig 426 the caption is 'Lives : 3'

So what do we conclude from the two variables 10th and 11th   :- There are no functions or variables to change the dimensions of the room

room_persistent :- Returns whether the room is persistent

Persistent means that if you return to a room again it would start from the position where you left earlier ,   the earlier positions of objects are saved

How to create a persistent room ?

Open any room (Shift + Ctrl + R)

Navigate to the settings tab

Check the box persistent

(Fig 440)

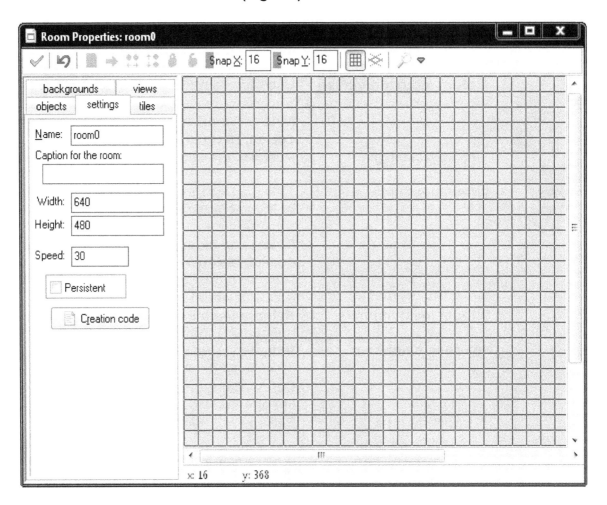

When you move from one room to another the transition (special effect) plays an important role Game Maker provides some functions for dealing with transitions

Game Maker creates 21 inbuilt transition effects

Suppose you want to go to the next room with effect number 7 your code would be

room_goto_next()

transition_kind = 7

Suppose you want to check whether transition number 29 exists , your code would be

transition_exists(29) , you can even change the time taken for the transition by transition_steps = value.

Note :- The number of steps are directly proportional to the time taken

General Functions

General functions are a completely different set of functions to deal with the game as a whole

Functions	Use
1)game_end()	This functions abruptly ends the game Note :- Many confuse between exit and game_end , exit means the control exits from the block or the code , exit doesn't end the game , game_end ends the game !!!
2)game_restart()	Restarts the game
3)game_save(filename)	Saves the game to a file whose path is filename For example You want to save the game to a file 'C:\mygame.sav' , your code would be game_save("C:\mygame.sav")
4)game_load(filename)	Opens an earlier saved game For example You want to open the file 'C:\mygame.sav' , your code would be game_load("C:\mygame.sav")
5)set_program_priority(priority)	This is a very useful function , this function sets the priority of the program , the priority range ranges from -3 to 3 , 0 is normal , more the priority more the cpu time given to this program. Note:- Priority of level 3 would affect other programs like Anti viruses
6)set_application_title(title)	Every program is shown in the taskbar when it's running , the taskbar shows the icon of the program as well as some text following the icon , that text can be changed by this function

Timing plays a very important role in Games , Game Maker supports functions dealing with timings , here is a list of few functions and variables supported by Game Maker

Functions / Variables	Use
room_speed	This variable stores the value of the speed of the room Tip :- This variable can be used to change the room_speed
sleep(millisec)	sleeps for the number of milliseconds you specify

	Note :- Sleep means the game freezes
current_second	Returns the current second according to the time saved on the system
current_minute	Returns the current minute according to the system time For example :- If system time is 5:24 this variable would return 24 Note :- If the actually time is 7:30 but according to your system time is 7:45 don't expect Game Maker to return 30 , Game Maker would return 45
current_hour	Returns the current hour according to the time saved on the system
current_day	Returns the current day (1 , 2 , 3 , ……. number of days in that month)
current _weekday	Returns the current day , 1 stands for the first day of the week (Sunday) and 7 stands for the last day (Saturday)
current_month	This variable stores the value of the current month (1 = January , 2 = February , ……………. , 12 = December
current_year	Stores the value of the current year
current_time	Stores the value of the milliseconds passed from the time the system started
fps	fps stands for Frames Per Second , more the FPS greater the effect Tip :- FPS = Speed of the room

Many a times in Games you deal with global variables , managing global variables requires a lot of time and efforts , Game Maker helps you reduce your work by supporting many functions some of them are given below

Functions / Variables	Use
variable_local_exists(name)	Checks whether the local variable name exists in the game or not 1 = exists 0 = not exists Note :- name is a parameter which stands for the name of the variable
variable_global_exists(name)	Checks whether the global variable name exists or not For example :- You want to check

	whether a global variable 'bonus' exists or not code:- variable_global_exists(bonus)
variable_local_get(name)	Returns the value of the local variable name
variable_local_array_get(name , ind)	This function returns the value of the variable with index number ind in a local array name
variable_local_array2_get(name , ind1 , ind2)	This function is similar to the previous one , there is only one difference , the previous function was for 1 – dimensional array and this one is for 2 – dimensional array
variable_global_get(name)	Returns the value of the global variable name
variable_global_array_get(name , ind)	This function returns the value of the variable with index number ind in a local array name
variable_global_array2_get(name , ind1 , ind2)	This function is similar to the previous one , there is only one difference , the previous function was for 1 – dimensional array and this one is for 2 – dimensional array
variable_local_set(name , value)	Note :- This function is not for creating a variable , this is only for assigning a new value to the local variable name For example :- If you want to assign the value 5 to a local variable points you code would be variable_local_set(points , 5)
variable_local_array_set(name , ind , value)	Suppose you want to change the value of point[11] to 5 , your code would be variable_local_array_set(point , 11 , 5)
variable_local_array2_set(name , ind1 , ind2 , value)	This function would set the given value to the 2-dimensional array name with index ind1 , ind2
variable_global_set(name , value)	This functions sets the value of the global variable name to the given value
variable_global_array_set(name , ind , value)	Sets the value of the global variable name at index ind to the given value

Timelines :- We have learned about timelines and actions dealing with timelines , now we are proceeding to learn variables to deal with timelines

Variables	Use
timeline_looping	Use this variable to set the looping to true or false
timeline_running	Stores information whether timeline is running , stopped or paused
timeline_speed	This variable stores the speed of the timeline , 1 is the normal speed of the timeline
timeline_position	Use this variable for changing the position of the timeline
timeline_index	Timelines associated with each instances contain unique identification known as the index.

Some functions dealing with movement of the objects

Functions	Use
move_random (hsnap , vsnap)	Similar to action jump to a random position
move_wrap(hor , vert , margin)	This function works like the action wrap screen
move_snap(h snap , vsnap)	Used for snapping the instance
move_toward s_point(x , y , speed)	This function is similar to the action step towards , the instance moves towards the point with co-ordinated (x , y) at the given speed
move_bounce _all(advanced)	This function makes the instance bounce after collision with all the objects
move_bounce _solid(advanc ed)	Bounces against only solid objects
move_contact _solid(dir , maxdist)	Moves the instance in the specified direction 'dir' , you may even specify the maximum distance Note :- Would stop after collision with a solid object
move_contact _all(dir , maxdist)	Same as the previous one , but would stop after collision with all the objects (whether they are solid or not)
place_free(x , y)	Checks whether the point (x , y) is position free or not. Tip :- Position free means that no other object is at the point (x , y) Note :- This function would consider only solid objects , if you want to consider all the objects use place_empty (x , y) instead of this one
place_meeting (x , y , obj)	Checks whether it meets object obj at the position (x , y).

	Tip :- If you want to consider a particular instance , replace obj by the instance id
place_snapped(hsnap , vsnap)	Checks whether the instance is aligned to the grid
position_meeting(x , y , obj)	Checks whether it's meeting object obj at (x , y)
position_empty(x , y)	Returns whether the position is occupied by any other instance or not
distance_to_object(obj)	Calculates the distance between the instance in which this command is executed and the instance of object obj which is nearest to it Note :- The other object should contain a sprite and / or a mask
distance_to_point(x , y)	Calculates the distance between the instance and the point (x , y)
move_outside_solid(dir , maxdist)	Moves the instance in a given direction (provided there is a collision at the position) till it collides with a solid object
move_outside_all(dir , maxdist)	This time not only solids but all objects are considered

We saw that most of the functions are not required as there are actions which suit our needs , so why are going to learn them ? , Because if you master GML and all it's functions you can create actions of your own!!!! , you will definitely be able to create your own actions , extension packages if you read this book completely

Functions dealing with creation and destruction of instances

Functions	Use
instance_destroy()	Destroys the current instance Note :- Instance_create is skipped as it's explained earlier
instance_copy(performevent)	Copies the current instance , performevent means that whether the events be executed for the copy . Tip :- This function would return the id of the copied instance
instance_change(obj , performevents)	Changes the instances to an instance of object obj Tip :- The id would remain the same even after transformation
position_destroy(x , y)	Destroys all the objects at the position (x , y)

position_change(x , y , obj , performevents)	Changes all the instances at point (x , y) to object obj

One may ask ' What is the use of position_destroy ?' , Suppose in a games there are bombs , when you press the trigger the bomb must blast , when the bomb blasts all the nearby objects must be eliminated. In such cases position_destroy(x , y) is used

Note :- In some cases you can use the keywords all , self , other

A few variables

Variables	Use
persistent	Stores the value , whether the object is persistent or not
solid	Stores the value whether the instance is solid
mask_index	The index of the mask

Note :- Values are always in the form 0 or 1 , 0 stands for false and 1 for true , there is no may be or may not be in such cases

A few read-only variables (variables whose values cannot be changed)

Variables	Use
id	This variable stores the value of the unique identification assigned to each instance Reason for being read-only :- Reducing the complexity , one may assign it the value already being used by other instance
object_index	This variable stores the value of the object whose instance this is
instance_count	This variable stores the value of the number of instances in the room Note :- Number of instance present when this command was executed
instance_id	Id of the instance in which this command executed

Other functions dealing with instances

Functions	Use

instance_find(obj , n)	This function would return the id of the instance numbered (n + 1) Note :- (n + 1) because the first instances id = 0
instance_exists(obj)	Returns whether any instance of object obj exists or not Tip :- One can write id in the obj parameter Tip :- Here the use of keyword all is allowed
instance_position(x , y , obj)	This function would return the identity of the object obj at the point whise co-ordinates are (x , y)
instance_number(obj)	Returns the number of instances of object obj For example You want to find out the number of monsters and save them in a variable mon , your code would be mon = instance_number(monster)
instance_nearext(x , y , obj)	This function would find out the instance of object obj nearest to the point (x , y) and then return it's id
instance_furthest(x , y , obj)	This function would find out the instance of object obj which is furthest to the point (x , y) and then return it's id Note :- If there is only instance of object obj the instance_nearest = furthest
instance_place(x , y , obj)	Suppose you want the id of an instance of type obj which meets the current instance at (x , y) you will use this function

Deactivating Instances

Deactivating instances saves a lot of processing power and memory (RAM) , but it is also important to activate them , if there is a co-ordination between two objects and if one of them is de-activated the co-ordination would spoil , deactivated instances cannot be seen (they aren't visible) and if persistent they are not carried to the next room , so one must take care when deactivating instances.

For example the function instance_deactivate_object(notme) , if we supplied the value of 0 to the parameter notme and when this command was executed we see the background and hear the music , one cannot do nothing else , even able to end the game , so please make sure that you set the notme parameter to 1 and always remember to write the functions of activating instances in the same object in which the function for deactivating is written.

Functions	Use
instance_deactivate_object(obj)	Use this function to deactivate all the instances of object obj in the room , if you want to deactivate a particular instance specify the id instead of the object
instance_activate_object(obj)	Use this function to activate all the instances of object obj in the room , if you want to activate a particular instance specify the id instead of the object
instance_deactivate_all (notme)	Use this function to deactivate all the instances of all the objects in the room , If you want to deactivate all the other instances excluding the one which execute the command you can set the notme parameter to true instance_deactivate_object(1)
instance_activate_all()	Use this function to activate all the instances of all the objects in the room Note :- The instance executing this command must be active , a deactivated instance cannot activate others
instance_deactivate_region(left, top, width, height, inside, notme)	This function deactivates all the instances in the region whose boundaries you specify if inside is 1 , if inside is 0 This function deactivates all the instances outside the region whose boundaries you specify
instance_activate_region(left, top, width, height, inside)	This function is completely the opposite of the previous one

Event handling

Games created by Game Maker are composed of many events belonging to different objects , the functions explained here would help you to perform events using code

To generate event the code is

event_perform(type , numb) , we know that there are 12 types of events they are represented by adding 'ev_' before the event name , For example :- event create is written as ev_create , trigger as ev_trigger and so on , sometimes there are more than one event of the same kind , for example there are many types of other event , in that case the numb parameter comes into action , for example :- you want to execute the event other(game_end) your code would be

{

event_perform(ev_other ,   ev_game_end)

}

Here ev_game_end is the constant ,   but in the case of keyboard and mouse it's known as keycode ,   because keyboards and mouse are made up of keys

These keycodes are known as virtual keycodes as the keys are not pressed on the keyboard ,   the keys are pressed virtually ,   given below is the list of such keycodes

Keycode	Key
vk_left	The left arrow
vk_right	The right arrow
vk_up	The up arrow
vk_down	The down arrow
vk_alt	The alt key Note :- On a standard keyboard there are 2 alt keys , the right one is represented by vk_ralt and the left one by vk_lalt
vk_control	The ctrl key Note :- On a standard keyboard there are 2 control keys , the right one is represented by vk_rcontrol and the left one by vk_lcontrol
vk_delete	The delete key
vk_end	The end key
vk_escape	The escape key 'Esc'
vk_enter	The enter key
vk_space	The space key
vk_shift	The shift key Note :- On a standard keyboard there are 2 shift keys , the right one is represented by vk_rshift and the left one by vk_lshift

vk_backspace	The backspace key
vk_tab	The tab key
vk_home	The home key
vk_insert	The insert key
vk_nokey	If a key is not pressed
vk_anykey	If an of the available keys is pressed What's the use of anykey Many a times in Games we can press any key to start a paused game in such cases this keycode comes in action
vk_pageup	The page up key
vk_pagedown	The page down key
vk_pause	The pause key Note :- The pause and the break keys are the same
vk_printscreen	The print screen key Note :- The print screen and the SYS Rq are the same
vk_f1 , vk_f2 ……. , vk_f11 , vk_f12	The keys F1 to F12
vk_multiply	The multiply key (*)
vk_divide	The division key (/)
vk_add	The addition key ('+' plus)
vk_subtract	The subtract key (- minus)
vk_decimal	The decimal key (.)
vk_numpad0……vk_numpad9	The numpad keys 0 to 9

These were the keycodes of keyboard ,   similarly there are keycodes for mouse and joystick they are

Keycodes for mouse

Global keycodes

ev_global_left_button
ev_global_right_button
ev_global_middle_button
ev_global_left_press
ev_global_right_press
ev_global_middle_press
ev_global_left_release
ev_global_right_release
ev_global_middle_release

Keycodes for buttons

ev_left_button
ev_right_button
ev_middle_button
ev_no_button

Keycodes for press events

ev_left_press
ev_right_press
ev_middle_press

Keycodes for release event

ev_left_release
ev_right_release
ev_middle_release

Keycodes dealing with wheels

ev_mouse_wheel_up
ev_mouse_wheel_down

Others

ev_mouse_enter
ev_mouse_leave

The mouse enter event occurs when the mouse is hovered on a particular instance , the mouse leave event occurs when the mouse leaves the instance , It is recommended to avoid the middle button as it's available only on old mouse

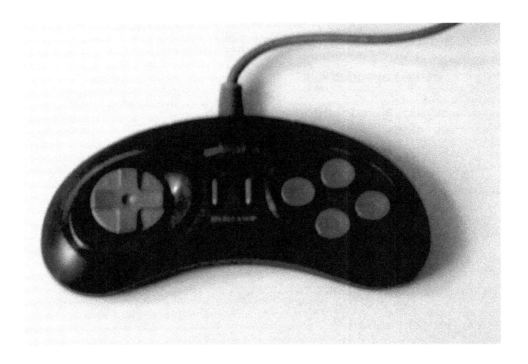

(Fig 441 ,   Only for illustrative purposes)

Note :- It is assumed that all the drivers ,   settings etc to use joysticks are applied

Keycodes for Joysticks

Keycodes for navigational buttons

ev_joystick1_left
ev_joystick1_right
ev_joystick1_up
ev_joystick1_down

Other buttons

ev_joystick1_button1
ev_joystick1_button2
ev_joystick1_button3
ev_joystick1_button4
ev_joystick1_button5
ev_joystick1_button6
ev_joystick1_button7
ev_joystick1_button8

Keycodes for 2nd joystick (Offline Multiplayer Games)

ev_joystick2_left
ev_joystick2_right
ev_joystick2_up
ev_joystick2_down

Other Buttons

ev_joystick2_button1
ev_joystick2_button2
ev_joystick2_button3
ev_joystick2_button4
ev_joystick2_button5
ev_joystick2_button6
ev_joystick2_button7
ev_joystick2_button8

The constants for other event (ev_other)

Game

ev_game_start
ev_game_end
ev_outside
ev_boundary

Room

ev_room_start
ev_room_end

Health and Lives

ev_no_more_lives
ev_no_more_health

Others

ev_animation_end
ev_end_of_path
ev_close_button

User Defined

ev_user0
ev_user1
ev_user2
ev_user3
ev_user4
ev_user5
ev_user6
ev_user7
ev_user8
ev_user9
ev_user10
ev_user11
ev_user12
ev_user13
ev_user14
ev_user15

The constants for step event

Constants	Meaning
ev_step_normal	Step normal
ev_step_begin	Step begin
ev_step_end	Step end

A few read only variables

event_type	This variable contains the value of the type of the event being executed
event_number	This variable contains the value of the number of the event being executed
event_action	This variable contains the list number of the event being executed For example If 2nd event is being executed , this variable would store the value 1 because 0 is the 1st event and so on............
event_object	Stores the value of the object for which the current event is executed

Variables don't return values they store values , functions return values

User response

In Games user response plays a great role , User has to respond every movement in games , the characters don't move automatically they have to be moved by pressing the right keys , the user can respond in 3 ways

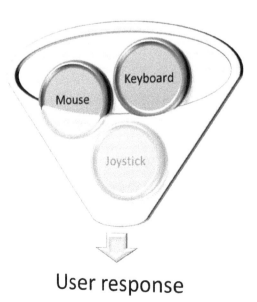

User response

Tip :- There are many more ways of expressing user response , For example :- Guns installed with cameras which find out where the person has shot the bullet commonly used in Games where ducks are killed and the user scores points depending on the ducks killed , there are videogames available in which you insert a coin and play a game , in such games there are steering wheels , gears and even brakes , The Kinect sensor of the Xbox 360 is one more such example , when the person playing the game jumps the character jumps too !!! , in some mobile phones the game can be played by tilting the mobile and by user input through touch screens and in more advanced cases (virtual reality) the character moves the same way the player moves and so on.... , Game Maker supports only the 3 mentioned in Fig 442 So let's get back to our topic

Keyboard is the most commonly used device so we would discuss keyboard first then comes the mouse and joystick comes the last

Do you know ? :- There are more than 36 types of Game Controllers

Functions dealing with user response through Keyboard

Functions	Use
keyboard_check(key)	This functions returns the Answer in true or false , if the key is pressed true is returned if not false is returned
keyboard_check_pressed(key)	This is similar to the previous one , this checks a pressed key
keyboard_check_released(key)	Checks a released key
keyboard_check_direct(key)	This function directly checks and confirms through the keyboard , this doesn't depend whether the application has focus or doesn't have focus

Virtual keyboard :- Virtual keyboard means keycodes are generated virtually which means that the user doesn't have to type the keys for performing the corresponding event , suppose you want to execute the event associated with the event key_press(left) your code would be

{

keyboard_key_press(vk_left)

}

The effect of the user pressing the left key and the command is the same

Note :- You can replace vk_left by any other keycode

suppose you want to execute the event associated with the event key_release(left) your code would be

{

keyboard_key_release(vk_left)

}

A few useful variables

Variables	Use
keyboard_lastkey	This variable stores the value of the key pressed the last. Note :- The values are set according to the keycodes
keyboard_key	Stores the value of the keycode pressed at that instant
keyboard_lastchar	Stores the value of the last key pressed Note :- There is a difference between the the 1st variable and this one , this variable would save the value in the form of characters
keyboard_string	Stores the values of all the keys typed till now , the alphabets in the string are in the order in which they are pressed

Note :- Game Maker provides functions through which you can check whether num lock is on or off they are

keyboard_get_numlock	Returns whether the numlock is on or off
keyboard_set_numlock(on or off)	Can be used to change the numlock to on or off

Key Mapping

Sometimes you wish two different keys to perform the same actions , in such cases key mapping is used

Use of key mapping :- You don't have to write the actions for the different key again

Functions dealing with Key Mapping

Functions	Use

keyboard_set_map(key1, key2)	Suppose you want to map the keys vk_left and vk_numpad4 your code would be
	
	{
	
	keyboard_set_map(vk_left, vk_numpad4)
	
	}
	
	Now if numpad 4 is pressed the event of the button left is executed

keyboard_unset_map()	Cancels key mapping
keyboard_get_map(key)	This function would return the key mapping with the specified key

The Mouse

A few variables

Variables	Use
mouse_lastbutton	Stores the value of the last button pressed on the mouse
mouse_button	Stores the values of the buttons of the mouse pressed at that instant

Values of mouse buttons

1)mb_left :- The left mouse button

2)mb_right :- The right mouse button

3)mb_middle :- The middle mouse button

4)mb_none :- If any of the mouse buttons is not pressed

5)mb_any :- If any of the button is pressed

Read only variables

Variables	Use
mouse_x	Stores the value of the x co-ordinate of the mouse in the room
mouse_y	Stores the values of the y co-ordinate of the mouse in the room

Suppose you want to move object 'car' to the place where mouse is positioned your code would be

```
{

car.x = mouse_x

car.y = mouse_y

}
```

Functions dealing with mouse wheel

Function	Use
mouse_wheel_up()	Returns true if the mouse wheel was moved up after last step
mouse_wheel_down()	Returns true if the mouse wheel was moved down after last step

Other Functions

Functions	Use
mouse_check_button_pressed(value)	Returns true if the mouse button value was pressed after last step Note :- The values are given on the previous page
mouse_check_button_released(value)	Returns true if the mouse button value was released after last step Note :- The values are given on the previous page
mouse_check_button(value)	Returns whether the button value is presently pressed
mouse_wait()	Waits till the user presses any button on the mouse Note :- This can be used to pause a game and then start it by pressing any of the buttons on the mouse
mouse_clear(value)	Clears the status of the button whose value is supplied

A variable

cursor_sprite :- Used to change the sprite of the cursor.

Example – There is a popular game that revolves around sailors sailing for adventures   in that Game the mouse cursor was replaced by an hook used by sailors , a small change that induced a dramatic effect. The variable mentioned above can be used for such purposes ,even the order of their arrangement plays a very important role

Note :- Game Maker supports a maximum of two joysticks.

2)Joysticks are given identifications ("id's") , the id of a joystick can be 1 or 2.

3)Remember the earlier note as id is a parameter in many functions

4)Point of view directions :- The smart art below shows the directions

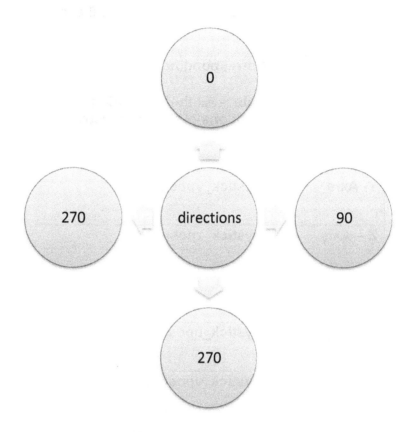

(Fig 443)

Note :- Remember to provide values in degrees

Functions	Use
joystick_axes(id) id = 1 or 2	This function returns the number of axes supported by the joystick whose id is given Suppose you want to find the number of axes of joystick 2 and store it in a variable joy, your code would be joy = joystick_axes(2)
joystick_name(id)	Returns the name of the joystick whose id has been given
joystick_exists(id)	Checks whether a joystick with the given id exists or not Tip :- This is useful for reducing errors

joystick_buttons(id)	Returns the number of buttons on the joystick whose id has been given
joystick_has_pov(id)	Checks whether the joystick has point of view capabilities
joystick_check_button (id , number)	Checks whether the button corresponding to the given number of the joystick whose id is provided is pressed

Game Maker supports Joysticks upto 6 axes they are given below

Axis	Corresponding Function Note :- All these functions return the positions of their respective axes	Number
X – Axis	joystick_xpos(id)	1st Axis
Y- Axis	joystick_ypos(id)	2nd Axis
Z – Axis	joystick_zpos(id)	3rd Axis
Rudder	joystick_rpos(id)	4th Axis
u – position	joystick_upos(id)	5th Axis
v – position	joystick_vpos(id)	6th Axis

joystick_pov(id) :- Returns the point of view of the joystick whose id is provided

Note :- This function must succeed the function ' joystick_has_pov(id) ' , here's an example

{

a = joystick_has_pov(id)// Here id can be replaced by 1 or 2

if (a = 1)

    {

    x = joystick_pov(id) //This id must be similar to the previous one

    }

Else

    {

```
        exit

    }

}
```

The Figure given below shows the numpad value corresponding to a given direction

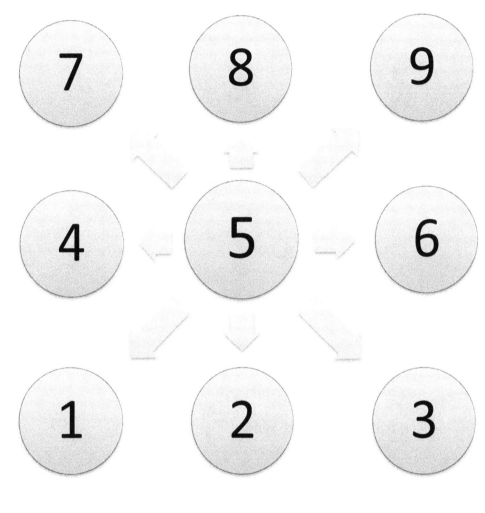

(Fig 444)

What is the use of Fig 444 ? ,   you will understand now

joystick_direction(id) :- This function returns the keycodes of numpad values depending upon the direction of the joystick

Let's write some code for moving an object ball using numpad

co_ord_num = 5

if (keyboard_check(vk_numpad4))

{

ball.x -= co_ord_num;

```
}
if ( keyboard_check(vk_numpad2))
{
ball.y += co_ord_num;
}
if ( keyboard_check(vk_numpad8))
{
ball.y -= co_ord_num;
}
if ( keyboard_check(vk_numpad6))
{
ball.x += co_ord_num;
}
if ( keyboard_check(vk_numpad1))
{
ball.x -= co_ord_num;
ball.y += co_ord_num;
}
if ( keyboard_check(vk_numpad7))
{
ball.y -= co_ord_num;
ball.x -= co_ord_num;
}
if ( keyboard_check(vk_numpad9))
{
ball.y -= co_ord_num;
ball.x += co_ord_num;
```

```
}

if ( keyboard_check(vk_numpad3))

{

ball.x += co_ord_num;

ball.y += co_ord_num;

}
```

Explanation :- co_ord_num = 5 is a variable made by me ,   this is a value in units ,   suppose you change this to 10 your ball would move by twice the length ,   if you change it to 2.5 your ball would move by half the length and so on…

Reason for using a variable :- If you want to change the value you would have to replace the old one with the new one ,   but in this case you can simply change the value of the variable and the new value would be applicable everywhere the variable is used

Note :- This code should be included only in the step event or else it wouldn't be of any use ,   if you wish to download the source file mail me at n160165@yahoo.com

Now we are going to write code for movement using the arrow buttons

```
co_ord_num = 5

if ( keyboard_check(vk_left) )

{

ball.x -= co_ord_num;

}

if ( keyboard_check(vk_down))

{

ball.y += co_ord_num;

}

if ( keyboard_check(vk_up))

{

ball.y -= co_ord_num;

}
```

```
if ( keyboard_check(vk_right))

{

ball.x += co_ord_num;

}
```

if you want the ball to move by arrows as well as the numpad just combine both the codes and it's done

Now we would do certain changes to the game we created last time ('Space') , we would program the game to fire lazers if any of the buttons on the mouse is pressed.

Perform the tasks given below

1)Open the game

2)Open the object rocket

3)Add an event step

4)Drag the action execute code (code part , control tab)

An editor would appear like the one given below(Fig 445)

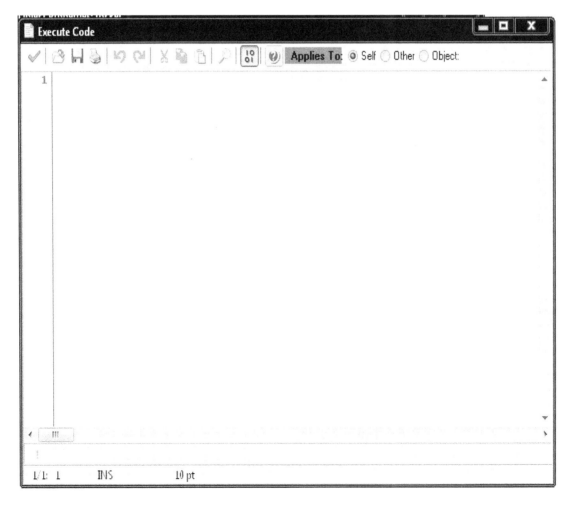

The code provided here as well as the code provided earlier must be written in this window !!!

5)Write the given code

```
if ( mouse_check_button(mb_right))

{

event_perform(ev_keypress, vk_space)

}

if ( mouse_check_button(mb_left))

{

event_perform(ev_keypress, vk_space)

}

if ( mouse_check_button(mb_middle))

{

event_perform(ev_keypress, vk_space)

}
```

Save the code

But !!! , think for a while , is there any better way to achieve the same result ? , If you are unable to answer it is recommended that you revisit the previous pages again and then proceed , if you can, compare your answer with this one

```
if ( mouse_check_button(mb_any))

{

event_perform(ev_keypress, vk_space)

}
```

if you have a better way to achieve the same result with a different piece of code which is even more effective than this one you may challenge me and send your code to me through e-mail

This was one more example to prove that programs can be written in many different ways

One may ask to differentiate between execute code and execute script , the reason of using a variable co_ord_num instead of a numerical value , if you execute code using the action it's fine but if you are executing the same code it's advisable to use a script and call it using the action 'Execute Script'

Note :- Like 2 sides of the same coin both possess + and - points

Note :- Execute Script is located In the code part in the control tab

Sometimes the values of the variables of the same code need to be changed for use with different objects ,   in that case you can use arguments ,   arguments are like variables ,   you can change their values through the action itself.

Note :- You can change a maximum of 5 arguments through Execute Script not more than that

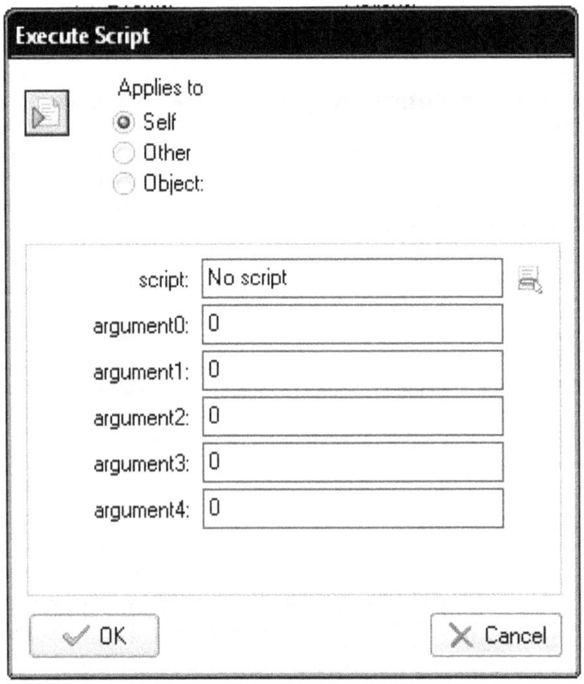

Execute Script

Applies to
- ⦿ Self
- ◯ Other
- ◯ Object:

script:	No script
argument0:	0
argument1:	0
argument2:	0
argument3:	0
argument4:	0

✓ OK   ✗ Cancel

(Fig 446)

Now we are going to learn a few read-only and other variables about sprites

Variables	Use
sprite_height	This variable stores the value of the height of the sprite
sprite_width	This variable stores the value of the width of the sprite
image_number	This variable stores the value of the number of subimages for the sprite used
visible	The visible property of the sprite if visible = 1 then the visibility is activated

	else deactivated , this is not a read-only variable but can be changed
sprite_index	This variable stores the value of the index of the sprite

If this variable is used for an object and if the object is not having any sprite then -1 is returned

1st sprite is given the value 0 , but this doesn't mean 2nd = 1 and so on , the number of subimages is also one of the factors affecting the index |
| image_alpha | This variable stores the alpha value of the image , this value should lie between 0 and 1 , the default value for any image is 1. |
| image_blend | Used for blending the colors of the sprite , suppose you wish to blend the image of object car with yellow your code would be

image_blend = c_yellow

Note :- This code should be executed in the object 0

Note :- c_yellow is a constant whose value is 65535 , there are a few more constants which deal with colors they are

c_aqua
c_black
c_blue
c_dkgray
c_fuchsia
c_gray
c_green
c_lime
c_ltgray
c_maroon
c_navy
c_olive
c_orange
c_purple
c_red
c_silver
c_teal
c_white
c_yellow

In all 19 different constants dealing with 19 different colors with 19 unique values |
| depth | Stores the depth value

Tip :- Can be changed !!! |

image_speed	This variable stores the value of the speed at which subimages of a single image are shown Recommendation:- Don't use this variable because if you use this increase the value of this variable for a sprite possessing more than 1 subimage the subimages may be seem to be disjoint and if you reduce the value the user playing the game would feel as if the game is running slowly Result :- Chaos
xscale and yscale	The variables for scaling
image_angle	Moves the image through a particular angle

Do you remember 'bounding box' , here are a few read only variables

bbox_right	Stores the value of the co-ordinates of the right side of the bounding box of the image in the room
bbox_left	Stores the value of the co-ordinates of the left side of the bounding box of the image in the room
bbox_top	Stores the value of the co-ordinates of the upper most side of the bounding box of the image in the room
bbox_bottom	Stores the value of the co-ordinates of the lower most side of the bounding box of the image in the room

Now we would use the knowledge gained now and modify our game , we would add a functionality in our game such that if 'r' is pressed red color would be blended with the rocket and if 'y' is pressed yellow color would be blended with the rocket

So follow the procedure given below

1)Open the game space

2)Open the object 'Rocket'

3)Add event key_press 'R'

4)Add event key_press 'Y'

5)Open the event created in step 3

6)Drag the action execute code

7)Type the code

image_blend = c_red

8)Save the code

9)Open the event created in step 4

10) Drag the action execute code

11)Type the highlighted code image_blend = c_yellow

Try pressing 'r' or 'y' during the game and feel the difference

Now we would improve the graphics of the game

Follow this procedure

1)Open the object 'UFO_simple'

2)In the create event drag action 'execute code'

3)Type the code

image_alpha = 0.495

Note :- If you feel that the user may be uncomfortable with the value you may let the user decide the alpha value , just replace the above code by

image_alpha = get_string("Enter alpha value for transparency between 0 to 1 , where 0 is completely transparent and 1 is completely opaque", "")

Explanation :- Function used :- get_string

Use :- Receiving text from the user

1st parameter = "Enter alpha value for transparency between 0 to 1 , where 0 is completely transparent and 1 is completely opaque"

Use :- Displays the message to the user

In short :- This function would prompt an input box like the one given below

(Fig 447) ———→

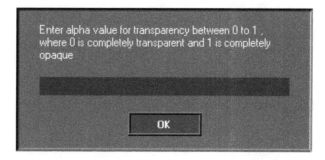

One may wonder what is the second parameter for ? , the second parameter is for the default value , suppose you change the value to 0

image_alpha = get_string("Enter alpha value for transparency between 0 to 1 , where 0 is completely transparent and 1 is completely opaque", "0")

In this case the window which would appear would be

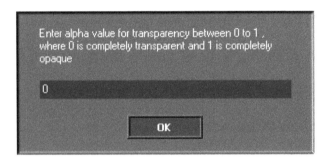

(Fig 448)

Note :- 0 would be automatically displayed with the box

2) Many a times the user accepts the value provided as default and if he accepts the value he wouldn't be able to see the UFO's at all which would result into chaos so it's advisable to use 0.5 as default values

3)Suppose the number of UFO's in the room is 3 this box would be displayed 3 times , once for each one , but this has an advantage and a disadvantage

Can you guess ? , read the next page if you cannot

Advantage	Disadvantage
The user can specify unique values for all the 3 different UFO's	The user has to enter values thrice which would be irritating/frustrating depending upon the user

Note :- Game Make even supports variables and functions for backgrounds

Tip :- A list of all the functions as well as all the constants is available in Game Maker

List name	Command
Functions (in-built)	Located in the script menu

Variables (in-built)	Located in the script menu

Variables dealing with background

background_alpha :- The alpha value of the background

background_blend :- Used for blending colors , just like blending images

background_color :- The color of the background

background_foreground :- The color of the foreground

background_height :- (Read – only) Background Height

background_hspeed :- The horizontal speed (hspeed)

background_htiled :- Horizontal tiling

background_index :- Vertical tiling

background_showcolor :- A Boolean value

background_visible :- A Boolean value to handle visibility

background_vspeed :- Vertical speed

background_vtiled:- Vertical tiling

background_width :- (Read – only) Background width

background_x :- X co-ordinate of the background

background_xscale

background_y ——————— Scaling

background_yscale :- Y co-ordinate

Observe the Figure given on the next page

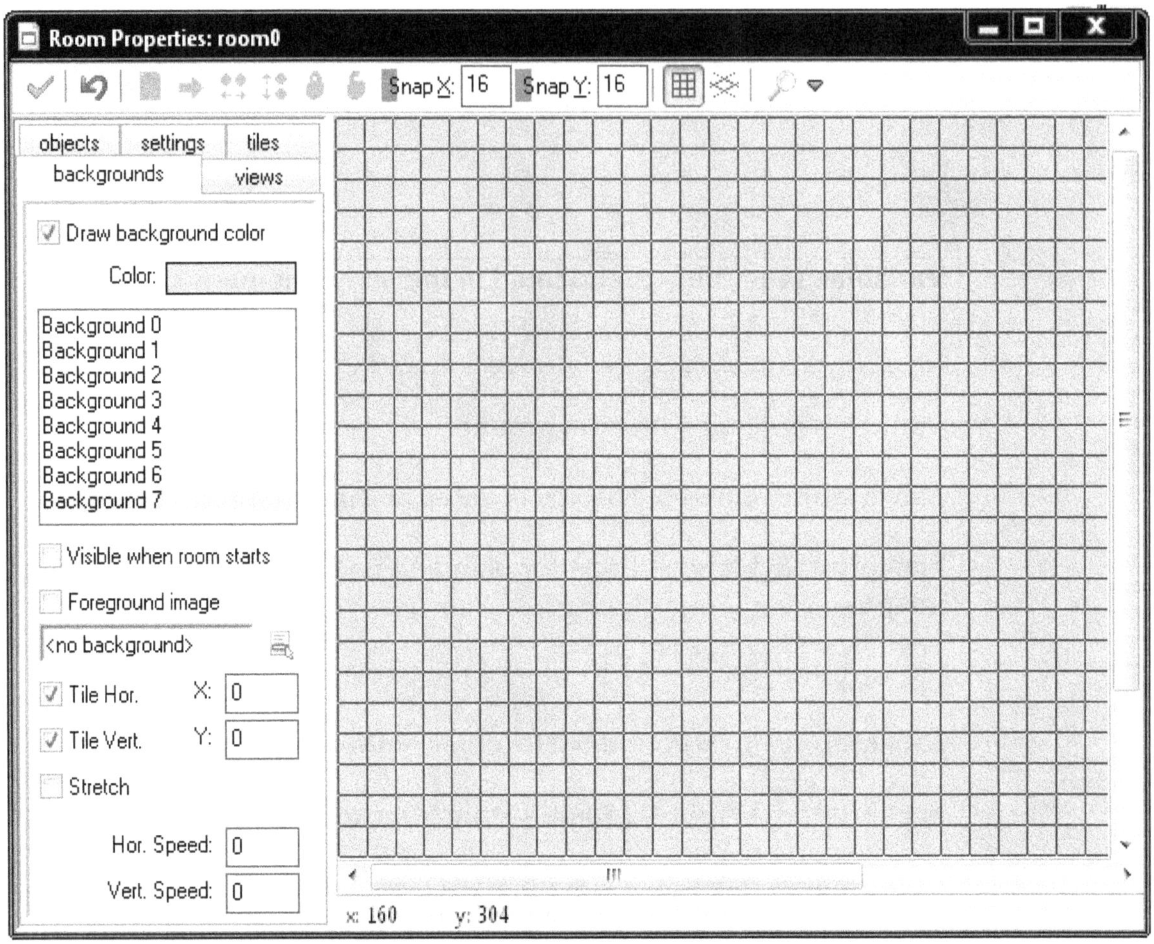

(Fig 449)

It can be clearly observed that a room supports 8 backgrounds (0 to 7) so while providing values the values must be in the range 0 to 7

Dealing with Compact Discs (Only for PRO users)
1)cd_close_door()

Closes the CD drive

cd_init :- Init stands for initialize it's a good practice to call this functions before others

cd_length :- This function calculates the length of all tracks(in milliseconds) in the Cd

and returns their value

cd_number :- This function returns the number of music files on the CD

cd_open_door :- Opens the CD drive

Note :- some computers may contain 2 disc drives this one is applicable only to the 1st one

cd_pause :- Pauses the CD

cd_paused :- Checks whether the CD is paused or it's playing

cd_play (first ,   last):- Starts playing the CD in the order of the range supplied

cd_playing :- Checks whether the CD is paused or it's playing

cd_position :- Checks the position of the CD and returns the value

cd_present :- Checks whether a CD is present in the drive or absent

cd_resume:- Continues playing a paused or stopped CD

cd_set_position(position) :- Changes the position to the given position

cd_set_track_position(position) :- Changes the position of the current track

cd_stop :- Stops a CD

cd_track :- Calculates and then returns the number of tracks

cd_track_length(track number) :- Calculates and returns the length of the track

cd_track_position(position) :- Sets the position of the current track to the given position

Here are a Few functions about receiving user response

show_question(string) :- Shows the question provided by you (string) ,   the user has to select between 2 options yes or no ,   if yes 1 is returned else 0 is returned

Suppose we type show_question("Are you enjoying")

the question would appear in a window with 2 buttons yes or no

(Fig 450)

Note :- It may seem silly but it's advised to place a question mark at the end as small small things do matter get_string(string , default) :- Requests the user for entering a string (Example :- Player Name) , string is the message shown (Example :- Enter your name) , default is the default value (Example :- Aditya)

your code would be

{

get_string("Enter your name" , " Aditya")

}

(Fig 451)

if you don't want a default value change it to " " example

get_string("Enter your name" , " ")

get_integer(string , default) :- Similar to the previous one but there is a difference , this function returns the value (supplied by the user) in the form of an integer and the earlier one used to supply the values in the form of string

Here are a few functions which would affect the appearance of the message boxes

suppose you want to change the background of the input box (Fig 451) with a background 'peak' your code would be

Note :- A background whose name is peak must exist in the given game

{

message_background(peak)

get_string("Enter your name" , " Aditya")

}

This one would appear as

(Fig 452)

where the background was

(Fig 453)

Note :- If you type the code

{

message_background(peak)

get_string("Enter your name" ,   " Aditya")

get_integer("Enter any numerical value", "")

}

In this case the new background would be applicable to the get_string as well as get_integer

message_button(sprite) :- Used for changing the sprites of the buttons of the message box

Suppose you want the change the button to (Fig 454) ,   where the name of the sprite is spr_wall your code would be

{

message_button(spr_wall)

get_string("Enter your name" ,   " Aditya")

}

it would look like (Fig 455 given besides)

Tip :- If there are 2 or more buttons the new sprite would be applicable to all the buttons

(Fig 456)

message_alpha(alpha value) :- You can add transparency effect to the messages using this function

example :- message_alpha(0.5) would make the message box partially transparent

Note :- You must be wise enough , you must never make the mistake of writing 0.5 in commas

2)Alpha values must be in the range 0 to 1 including 0 and 1

if you type

{

message_alpha(0.5)

get_string("Enter your name" , " Aditya")

}

the window would appear as follows

(Fig 457)

Note :- This is not a matter of darkness , this dialog box looks dark because the background is dark and it's infact partially merged with the background

message_mouse_color(color) :- When the mouse hovers on the buttons of the dialog box the font color changes to the given color

(A list of available colors is already provided to you in the section image_blend)

message_input_color :- let us demonstrate this one with the help of Fig 458

your code

{

message_input_color(c_yellow)

get_string("Enter your name" ,   " Aditya")

}

Result

(Fig 458)

message_caption(show ,   string(caption)) :- Let us you give a sort of Heading to the message

Example

{

message_caption(1, "Pop - Up sample")

get_string("Enter your name",   "Aditya")

}

Result

(Fig 459)

Note :- The show parameter should always be 1 else there's no use in writing this line as the caption would not be shown at all

There are many more functions and variables but they are not so important like the ones discussed earlier therefore they are not explained here ,   if I try to explain all of them they would cost me approximately 300 more pages of this book

Summary

Let us recapitulate some points discussed in this chapter

At the beginning we learnt about the process of creating variables (one must note that when one uses actions for creating variables he indirectly uses code for creating variables) then we discussed about many of the available functions of Game Maker

Chapter 13 Triggers

Triggers :- Triggers are files which can be used as events which are executed after a certain condition is fulfilled

Note :- Triggers are available only for PRO users (PAID edition)

How to Define Triggers ?

1)Open the Game

2)Open any object

3)Add event

(Fig 460)

4)Press Trigger

5)An option would be available Add/Modify triggers

6)Press that option

7)A window would appear which would help you Add or Modify triggers

There is always a doubt :- What can be the condition ? , the condition can be anything , 1)The user presses a combination of Keys , 2) The number of Monsters are less than a specific value , 3) The number of monsters are more than a specific value , 4) The score has crossed a certain limit , 5) The user has gained bonuses more than a particular value etc .... , this list can be contain infinite possibilities so let's stop over here

(

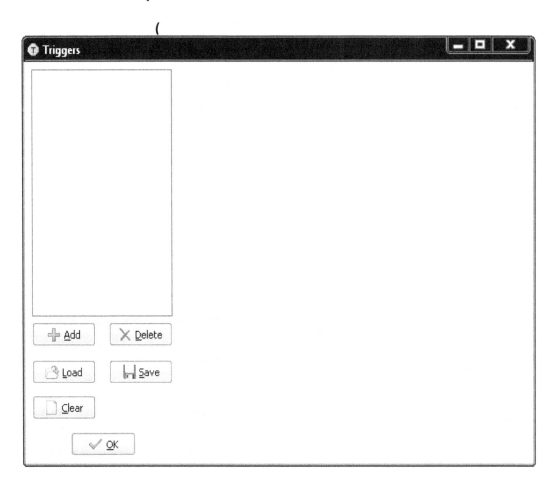

Initially there are no triggers we have to create one

We would create a trigger in such a way that if the number of objects monster is less than 3 then 1 more monster is created

1)Press the ADD button

2)Name it check monsters

(A name column is displayed when you create a new trigger)

3)Type the code given below in the condition box

{

 return instance_number(monster) < 3

}

Let the moment of checking be 'Begin of Step'

Note :- There is a difference between Delete and Clear , Delete deletes one at a time , clear clears the entire list

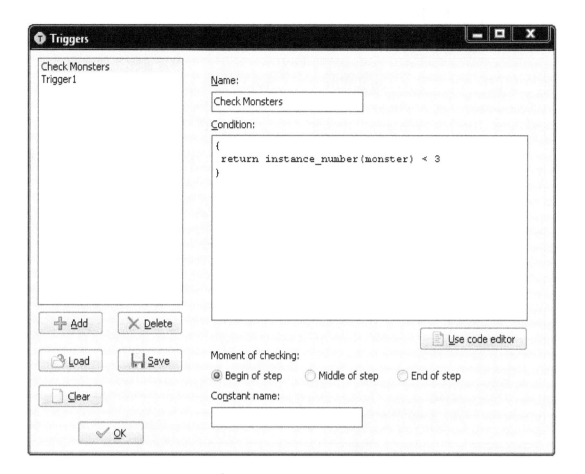

(Fig 462)

Press the Ok Button

Now follow the procedure given below

1)Open the object which has a main role

2)Add the event Trigger 'Check Monster'

3)Drag action for creating instance of object Monster at any position of your choice

4)Save the object

Note :- This was a very short condition , conditions can be big enough in such cases use the code editor instead

Moment of Checking

Sr No	Name	Use
1)	Begin Step	The trigger is executed at the beginning of the Step
2)	Middle of Step	The trigger is executed before the beginning and the ending of the step
3)	End Step	Trigger is executed at the ending of the step

Chapter 14 Particles

Particles are used for creating various types of effects , effects are very essential in a game to attract players and get players addicted to it , dealing with particles is a very complex task so there's no problem if you don't understand it even after reading the entire chapter , you would have to go through this entire lesson at least twice to understand particles effectively

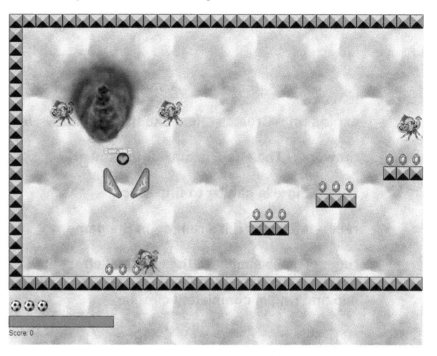

(Fig 463 and 464)

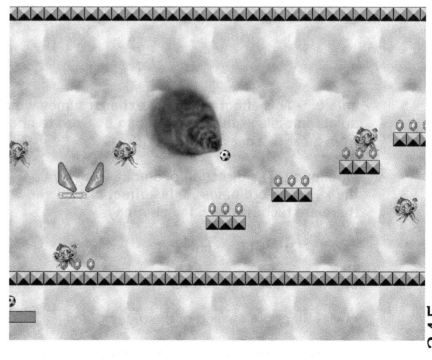

The effect shown in both the pictures was explosion effect of the color red (c_red) ,   The other available effects are

cloud :- creates clouds of the specified color ,   the darkness of the cloud goes on incresing as time passes

ellipse :- Creates elliptical rings of the given color

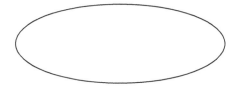

(Fig 465 ,   A sample of an elliptical figure)

explosion :- Creates effect like the one shown in Fig 463 and Fig 464

firework :- The effect is similar to fireworks

flare :- Flare is similar to fire effect

rain :- It feels as if it's raining in the game

ring :- This is similar to the elliptical effect but there is a difference between elliptical shape and ring shape ,   elliptical is the one like Fig 465 and ring is completely circular

(Fig 466)

smoke :- This effect is like the exhaust fumes which are released from an automobile ,   this function can be used to show fumes released from a car in a car game

smokeup :- The direction of smoke is always upward irrespective of the x ,   y co-ordinates ,   this effect can be shown in places where there are factories with tall chimneys

snow :- Resembles snow fall

spark :- Resembles sparks

star :- Stars are formed of the given color

Note :- You must never create yellow color smoke ,   black color rain , white color explosion ,   red or yellow color clouds ,   Game Maker would let you create them but you must never use the effect and color combination given here as they never exists in the nature , your game must look realistic

screen shots of all the effects are reproduced below

(Fig 467 Cloud)   **(Fig 468 Ellipse)**

(Fig 469 [Below] Shows fireworks)

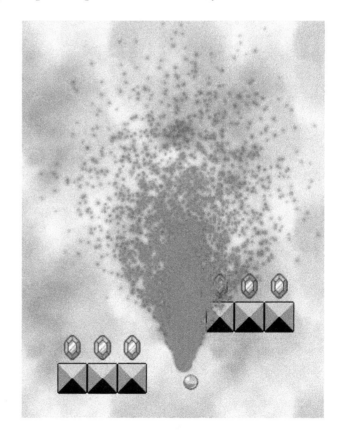

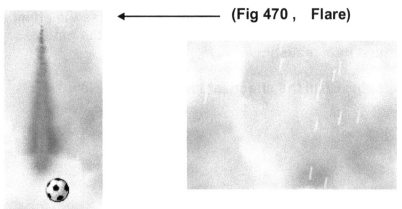

(Fig 470 , Flare)

(Fig 471 , Rain)

Note :- The size of all these effects is adjustable and is completely dependant upon you

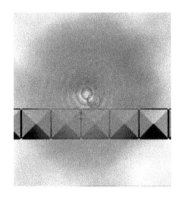

(Fig 472 , Ring)

(Fig 473 , Sparks)

(Fig 474 , Smoke)

(Fig 475 , Star)

Here are some functions which would help you create particles

Function	Use
effect_clear()	Clears all the effects Note :- From now on clear means that the settings are cleared rest all remains the same , after the settings are cleared default values are set for them
effect_create_above(type , x , y , size , color)	This function creates an effect of the specified type , type of effects are explained earlier , (x , y) are the co-ordinates , size is the size of the effect which must be in the range 0 to 2 and the last parameter is the color of the effect Example For creating an explosion effect_create_above(ef_explosion , x , y , size , color) To specify the type write ef_ and then the effect name
effect_create_below(type , x , y , size , color)	Similar to the previous one but this one would create the effect below the other objects whereas the earlier one would create the effect above the other object Note :- above and below works for objects in the range -10000 to 10000

These were just the simple ones particles is a huge and complex topic

Particles :- Effects are composed upon many particles , you can create a new type of particle by the function

{

part_type_create()

}

this function would return a value known as the index this index a parameter for other functions , the other functions are

part_type_clear(index)	Clears the particle of the given index
part_type_destroy(index)	Destroys the particle of the given index

part_type_exists(index)	Returns a Boolean value (True / False , True = 1 and False = 0)

Observe Fig 475 , the shape of the particle is like a star , similarly the shape of the particle can be anything else , you can even use a sprite as the shape of the particle and you may provide a suitable alpha value for creating to such sprites , there are 15 in-built shapes they are

pt_shape_circle
pt_shape_cloud
pt_shape_disk
pt_shape_explosion
pt_shape_flare
pt_shape_line
pt_shape_pixel
pt_shape_ring
pt_shape_smoke
pt_shape_snow
pt_shape_spark
pt_shape_sphere
pt_shape_square
pt_shape_star

(These are all constants)

To use a sprite for creating particles use the function

part_type_sprite(index , sprite name , animation , stretch , random)

there's no need to explain what's index and sprite name

Parameter	Type	Information
animation	Boolean	If 1 the sprite is animated , provided that the number of subimages > 1 Else it's not animated
stretch	Boolean	If 1 the image would be stretched else it would appear in it's regular size
random	Boolean	If 1 any of the subimages is selected at random

part_type_shape(index , shape) :- Used for specifying the shape of a given particle

(Shape must be one of the constants mentioned earlier)

The size of the particle plays a very important role , the function for dealing with sprite size is

part_type_size(index , size_minimum , size_maximum , size_increase , size_wiggle)

Here you have to mention the minimum and the maximum value , the amount by which the size must increase after every step and the wiggle value

Scaling is the next factor , scaling can be adjusted by

part_type_scale(index , x-scale , y-scale) :- You just have to specify the index and the X and Y scaling

Orientation is the 3rd important factor affecting the particle effect , orientation can be set by

part_type_orientation(index , angle_minimum , angle_maximum , angle_increase , angle_wiggle , angle_relative)

You have to specify the minimum angle , maximum angle , increase in the angle , wiggle angle and the relative angle

Time Span

The time span for which a particle exists is also very important , this time span is known as it's life(Life of the particle) there are a few functions dealing with the life span of a particle , the units for measuring particle lives is the number of steps , the particle exists only till the completion of it's life , this completion of his life is known as death of the particle , this is similar to the life and death cycles of the HumAnswer , particles can even give birth to other particles , how it's done is explained over here

Functions dealing with life and death
part_type_life(index , life_minimum , life_maximum) Used for specifying the total life of the particle , you just have to enter the minimum as well as maximum life

part_type_step(index , step_number , step_type) Used for creating new particles you just have to indicate the number of particles and their type to be created in individual steps

part_type_death(index , death_number , death_type) This function is also used for creating particles but there is one difference between the previous one and this one , this one would create new particles only when the old one dies

Colors

Colors are very important in particles , the features offered by Game Maker are so advanced that you can even specify more than 1 colors for a particle.

Functions dealing with colors

part_type_color1(index, color1) This Function can be used for using only 1 color with the particle

part_type_color2(index, color1, color2) This Function can be used for using 2 colors with the particle

For example if you specify red and yellow

The particle would be red in color but as time progresses it would go on becoming yellow in color

part_type_color3(index, color1, color2, color3) This Function can be used for using 3 colors with the particle

part_type_color_hsv(index, hminimum, hmaximum, sminimum, smaximum, vminimum, vmaximum) HSV stands for Hue, Sat and Lum respectively the mimumum values and the Maximum values must be in the range 0 to 255

part_type_color_mix(index, color1, color2) If you use this function the resultant color of the particle would be a randomly selected mixture of the 2 specified colors

part_type_color_rgb(index, rminimum, rmaximum, gminimum, gmaximum, bminimum, bmaximum) RGB stands for Red, Green and Blue respectively the mimumum and maximum values must be in the range of 0 to 255

Colors are not enough for particles they must also be a bit transparent and must smoothly blend into the background

The Functions for Handling this are

part_type_alpha1(index, value) :- Sets the alpha value for the particle with the given index

Note :- This value must be in the range 0 to 1 where 0 is completely transparent and 1 is completely opaque

part_type_alpha2(index, val1, val2) :- The alpha value would be randomly selected from the range val1 to val2

part_type_alpha3(index, val1, val2, val3) :- Similar to the previous one but here there are 3 values

Blend

part_type_blend(index, additive_blend) :- This feature is used for blending, Additive is a type of blending or giving better effects, additive is a Boolean value and therefore if you want to set it to true set this parameter to 0 else 1

If the enemies remain standstill would you like to play the game ? , you would probably like to play the game only when the other objects are moving , similarly you wouldn't like if the particles are standstill , one would like them to be in continuous motion , the motion of the particles can be set by the following functions

part_type_gravity(index , gravity_amount, gravity_direction) This function sets the gravity for a particle whose index and direction is specified , you have to enter the amount of gravity which must affect the particle (Example :- 2)

part_type_speed(index, speed_minimum , speed_maximum , speed_increase , speed_wiggle) Use this function to specify the speed of the particle , you just have to enter the index , the minimum and the maximum speed of the particle , and the amount by which the speed must increase you can even set the wiggle parameter

part_type_direction(index , direction_minimum , direction_maximum , direction_increase , direction_wiggle) This function is used for setting the direction of the particle , you just have to specify the index , the minimum and the maximum direction for deviation , the increase in the direction and the wiggle parameter , study the given note properly

Note :- The direction should always be in degrees in the range 0 to 359

For particles to run part systems must be created , in other words

"Particles exist only if part systems exist"

To create a part system execute the code

part_system_create() :- This function would return an index value , this index value must be used as a parameter for other functions

part_system_exists(index) :- This function returns a Boolean value depending upon whether the particle system of the given index exists or not

part_system_destroy(index) :- This function destroys the particle system of the given index (Use the earlier function to check whether a particle system of the given index exists or not , program in such a way that if it exists then only this function would be executed)

Depth is very important while dealing with particles so to adjust the depth use the function

part_system_depth(index , depth)

part_system_position(index , x , y) :- Used for changing the position of the point where the particles are drawn part_system_clear(index) :- Clears the particle system of the given index

part_system_draw_order(index , oldtonew) Used for changing the order in which the particle system draws the particles. When oldtonew is a Boolean parameter which if set true draws the old systems before the new ones.

Game Maker supports a feature known as automatic updating , if set true the particles are updated automatically

The function supporting automatic update is

part_system_automatic_update(index , automatic)

To set it to true type

{

part_system_automatic_update(part system index , 1)

}

If you want to set it to false you may replace 1 by 0 and to update manually use the function

part_system_update(index)

This is an example of what you can achieve if all the functions associated with particles are wisely used

(Fig 476)

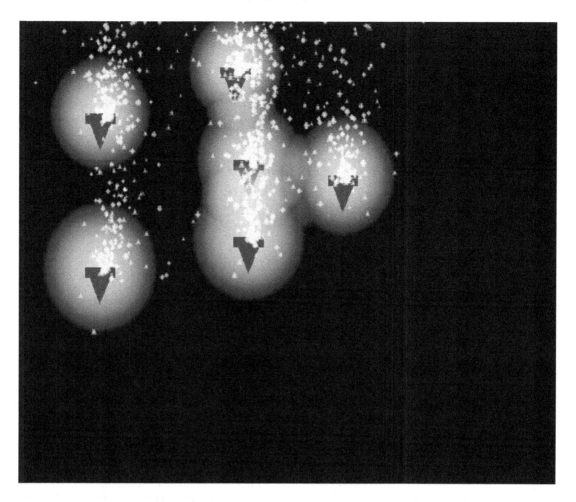

Drawing is a very essential aspect which may be set to be handled automatically or manually ,   to update automatically use the function

part_system_automatic_draw(index ,   automatic) :- Automatic may be 1 or 0

To draw manually use the function

part_system_drawit(index)

As particles can be handled by particle systems there must be some functions to handle particles in a system ,   there are such functions , they are

part_particles_create(index ,   x ,   y ,   particle type ,   number of particles) This function is used for creating particles at the position (x ,   y) ,   you have to mention all the parameters stated here

Note :- Here the index refers to the index of the particle system

part_particles_create_color(index ,   x ,   y ,   parttype ,   color , number) This is similar to the earlier one but here you may also define the color of the particles part_particles_clear(index) This functions clears all the particles in the system whose index is specified

part_particles_count(index) This functions is used for counting the number of particles in the given system

Have you ever tried to understand the phenomenon of light ? , light is always emitted by a luminous body , similarly particles are emitted , here the luminous body is known as the emitter.

Emitters work only upto a certain region (specified by you) , this region can be specified by the co-ordinates

Co-ordinates
x-minimum
x-maximum
y-minimum
y-maximum
If you observe one thing the region has a range of x and y values
The x values are in the range x-minimum to x-maximum and the y values are in the range y-minimum to y-maximum

The shape of the region can be an ellipse , a line , a diamond or a rectangle , they are represented by the following values respectively

Values
ps_shape_ellipse
ps_shape_line
ps_shape_diamond
ps_shape_rectangle

The way the particles are distributed also matters , they can be distributed by the following values ps_distr_linear :- Stands for linear distribution , in other words equal distribution throughout

ps_distr_gaussian :- Stands for guassian distribution , guassian means crowded at the centre

ps_distr_invgaussian :- Stands for opposite of guassian distribution

The following functions deal with particle emitters

Note :- Here particle system stands for the index of the particle system

part_emitter_create(particle system) :- Used for creating a particle emitter in the given particle system , this function would then return the index of the particle emitter

part_emitter_exists(particle system , index) :- Checks whether an emitter exists of the given index in the given particle system

part_emitter_clear(particle system , index) :- Clears the emitter of the given index in the given particle emitter

part_emitter_destroy(particle system , index) :- Destroys the emitter of the given index in the given particle system

But what if one wants to destroy all the emitters in a given particle system , in that case use the function

part_emitter_destroy_all(particle system)

part_emitter_region(particle_system , index , xminimum , xmaximum , yminimum , ymaximum , shape , distribution) :- Used for creating a region and the distribution for the particle

part_emitter_burst(part_system , index , part_type , number of particles) Creates all the at once from the emitter

part_emitter_stream(part_system , index , part_type , number of particles) Creates particles in the form of a stream in steps

Just like the creation of particles the destruction of particles also plays a very important role , if you don't destroy particles they would go on and on and would never end , they would be active even if not required in that case destructors are used for destroying them

Like Emitters destroyers work upto a certain region , the co-ordinates of the region is specified by

Co-ordinates
x-minimum

x-maximum
y-minimum
y-maximum
If you observe one thing the region has a range of x and y values The x values are in the range x-minimum to x-maximum and the y values are in the range y-minimum to y-maximum

The region may have the following shapes

Values
ps_shape_ellipse
ps_shape_diamond
ps_shape_rectangle

Even here the particle system stands for the index of the particle system

part_destroyer_create(particle system) This function would create a new destroyer in the particle system whose index is given , this function would return the index generated of the destroyer

part_destroyer_exists(particle system , index) Checks whether the destroyer of the given index exists in the given particle system

part_destroyer_destroy(particle system , index) :- Even destroyers should also be destroyed , this function would help you destroy the destroyer of the given index in the given particle system

Note :- This function must be used after the previous one to make sure that an error is not encountered

part_destroyer_destroy_all(particle system) Used for destroying all the particle systems

part_destroyer_clear(particle system , index) Clears the destroyer of the given index in the given particle system part_destroyer_region(particle system, index, xminimum, xmaximum, yminimum, ymaximum, shape) Used for creating a region for the destroyer

Have you observed the phenomenon of a magnet ?, a magnet attracts magnetic substances to itself, even our earth is a magnet which pulls us to itself similarly the particles must be attracted in some cases, here the substance which attracts exists virtually and is known as the Attractor

There are 3 types of Attractors

ps_force_constant :- This constant means that the force remains constant throughout, it doesn't change with distance, time, location etc

ps_force_quadratic :- Means that the force grows quadratically

ps_force_linear :- The growth in the force is linear

If additive is set to true the force is added to the speed as well as the direction

The following functions deal with attractors

part_attractor_create(particle system) Used for creating a new attractor in the given particle system, this function would return the index of the attractor which would be created

part_attractor_exists(ps, ind) Checks whether the attractor of the given index exists in the given particle system

part_attractor_position(particle system, index, x, y) The particle is set to the position whose x and y co-ordinates are x and y respectively

part_attractor_destroy(particle system, index) Used for destroying an attractor of the given index in the given particle system

Note :- Before destroying it must be checked whether the attractor of the given index exists or not

part_attractor_destroy_all(particle system) Used for destroying all the attractors in the given particle system

part_attractor_clear(particle system, index) Clears the attractor of the given index in the given particle system

part_attractor_force(particle system, index, force, distance, kind, aditive)

The parameters are explained over here

Parameter	Explanation
1)particle system	The index of the particle system
index	The index of the attractor
force	Any one of the 3 types of force (explained earlier)
distance	This is the distance upto which there is an effect of the attractor

Deflectors

Deflectors are something which repel the particles

Like Emitters deflectors too work upto a certain area this area is specified by the co-ordinates

Co-ordinates
x-minimum
x-maximum
y-minimum
y-maximum
If you observe one thing the region has a range of x and y values
The x values are in the range x-minimum to x-maximum and the y values are in the range y-minimum to y-maximum

Deflectors are of the following types

Type
Horizontal :- For deflecting the particles horizontally
Vertical :- For deflecting the particles vertically

Friction :- Friction is the frictional force which opposes the movement of the particles

Note :- Even Here the index means the index of the particle system
part_deflector_create(particle system) Used for creating deflectors in the given particle system

part_deflector_clear(particle system , index) Used for clearing the deflector of the given index in the given particle system

part_deflector_exists(particle system , index) :- Checks if the deflector of the given index exists in the given particle system

part_deflector_destroy(particle system , index) Used for destroying the deflector of the given index in the given particle system

part_deflector_destroy_all(particle system)Used for destroying all the particles in the particle index whose index has been given

part_deflector_friction(particle system , index , friction) Used for specifying the Friction of the deflector

part_deflector_region(particle system , index , xminimum , xmaximum , yminimum , ymaximum) Used for specifying the region of the deflector

part_deflector_kind(particle system , index , kind) Used for specifying the kind(Type)of Deflector

Many a times in Games it's a requirement to change certain parameters (shape , color etc) of the particles , in such cases Changers are used

Changers

Like Deflectors changers too work only upto a certain extent , this extent is specified by the area and the area is specified by the x and y co-ordinates

Co-ordinates
x-minimum
x-maximum
y-minimum
y-maximum

The shape of the deflector can be of the following types

Sr No	Shape	Value
1)	rectangle	ps_shape_rectangle
2)	ellipse	ps_shape_ellipse
3)	Diamond	ps_shape_diamond

The functions which deal with particles are

Even here particle system stands for the index of the particle system in which this changer must be created
part_changer_create(particle system)Used for creating a new changer in the given particle system

part_changer_clear(particle system , index) Used for clearing the changer of the given index in the given particle system

part_changer_exists(particle system , index) Checks whether the changer of the given index exists in the given particle system

Note :- This action must be called before destroying as it would help in eliminating the errors which may generate

part_changer_destroy(particle system , index) Used for destroying the changer of the given index in the given particle system

part_changer_destroy_all(particle system)Used for destroying all the changers in the given particle system

part_changer_kind(particle system , index , kind) Used for changing the type of change in the particle

The following constants can be used for changing the kind

Sr No	Constant	Type of change

1)	ps_change_all	Used for changing all the settings(by changing the parameters) of the particles
2)	ps_change_motion	Can be used for changing only the motion of the particle
3)	ps_change_shape	Can be used for changing only the shape of the particle

part_changer_region(particle system , index , xminimum , xmaximum , yminimum , ymaximum , shape) Used for specifying the region of the changer

part_changer_types(ps, index , original_type , new_type)Used for changing the type of the particle , original type means the type which is to be changed and new_type means the type into which the original type must be changed

Sample No :- 1

Effect :- Snow

Level:- Basic

Screenshot (Fig 477)

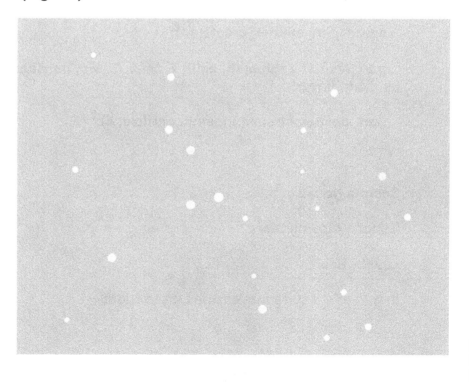

Code

```
{
  // make the particle system

  sn = part_system_create();

  // the snow particles

  particle = part_type_create();

  part_type_shape(particle, pt_shape_snow);

  part_type_size(particle, 0.1, 0.25, 0, 0);

  part_type_speed(particle, 1, 4, 0, 0);

  part_type_direction(particle, 0, 5, 0, 0);

  part_type_color1(particle, c_white);

  part_type_alpha2(particle, 1, 0.2);

  part_type_life(particle, 20, 500);

  part_type_gravity(particle, 0.24, 270);

  // create the emitter

  emit = part_emitter_create(sn);

  part_emitter_region(sn, emit, 1, 5400, 1, 490, ps_shape_rectangle,
ps_distr_linear);

  part_emitter_stream(sn, emit, particle, 4);
}
```

Sample No :- 2

Effect :- Moving Stars

Level:- Basic

In this effect stars move from Left to Right

Screenshot

(Fig 478)

Code

```
{

// make the particle system

sn = part_system_create();

// the star particles

particle = part_type_create();

part_type_shape(particle, pt_shape_star);

part_type_size(particle, 0.1, 0.4, 0, 0);

part_type_speed(particle, 2, 4, 0, 0);

part_type_direction(particle, 0, 12, 0, 0);

part_type_color2(particle, c_white , c_gray);

part_type_alpha2(particle, 1, 0.8);

part_type_life(particle, 20, 500);

part_type_gravity(particle, 0.01, 270);
```

// create the emitter

emit = part_emitter_create(sn);

part_emitter_region(sn, emit, 1, 5400, 1, 490, ps_shape_rectangle, ps_distr_linear);

part_emitter_stream(sn, emit, particle, 4);

}

Sample No :- 3

Effect :- Sparks

Level:- Basic

Screenshot

(Fig 479)

The 2 colors selected are red and yellow

Code

{

  // make the particle system

  sn = part_system_create();

```
// the snow particles

particle = part_type_create();

part_type_shape(particle, pt_shape_spark);

part_type_size(particle, 1, 5, 0, 0);

part_type_speed(particle, 2, 4, 0, 0);

part_type_direction(particle, 0, 12, 0, 0);

part_type_color2(particle, c_yellow , c_red);

part_type_alpha2(particle, 1, 0.5);

part_type_life(particle, 20, 500);

part_type_gravity(particle, 0.01, 270);

// create the emitter

emit = part_emitter_create(sn);

part_emitter_region(sn, emit, 1, 5400, 1, 490, ps_shape_rectangle,
ps_distr_linear);

part_emitter_stream(sn, emit, particle, 4);

}
```

Chapter 15 Registry and File management

Introduction to Registry

We have learnt how to open the registry editor earlier, suppose you have VLC media player installed on your system , whenever you open a .mp3 file , VLC media player opens it for you , how does windows know that the file with a particular extension(.mp3 in this case should be opened by VLC , the answer to this question is quite simple :- through the windows registry , when you install a particular software (VLC in this case) the setup creates registry entries which modify the windows registry , it is recommended that you don't create games which would create suspicious changes as they would trigger the anti-viruses installed on the end users system , and there are many in this world who are frightened by such alarms and whenever antivirus triggers they directly delete the file , this would prevent users from playing your game

Caution :- Some registry entries would even prevent the system from starting up!!!

INI Files

INI files are files used by programs for saving some type of information , these types of files are now a days used by setup programs for recording the number of files created , number of files copied and their location , the purpose for using such type of file is that the file can be used during un-installation

You will learn how to deal with INI files but it is not recommended that you save any of the information of your game in the form of such files as these files are easily accessible and can be opened even by a simple text editor , the user may delete the file by chance , these type of files can be easily modified by the end user and must therefore be avoid , is there any substitute to INI files ? , yes , the windows registry is a substitute , instead of saving information in INI files you must save information in keys of the windows registry

Note :- Game Maker doesn't support the creation of INI files , INI files must be created using the notepad(save the extension as .ini) and must be included with the game

Composition of INI files

INI files are composed of something called section and keys , an ini file is categorized into sections which are categorized into keys

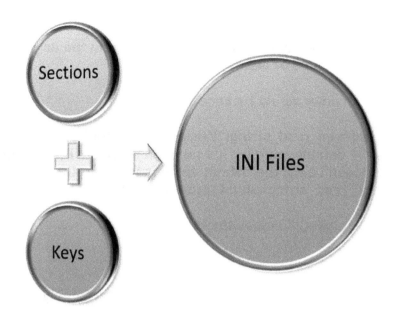

(Fig 480)

Example of an INI file

[Weapons]

Gun = 05

Knife = 12

Bullets = 09

[Movement]

Speed = 10

Friction = 0.02

Here [Weapons] is a section and Gun , Knife and Bullets are the keys in the section weapons , similarly [Movement] is a section and , speed and friction are keys in it

Tip :- INI files must be located in the same directory(folder) as the program

 Suppose the name of the above file is my.ini you would call access the value of Gun

Suppose you want to store it's value to a variable 'val' your code would be

{

ini_open("my.ini") \\ my.ini must exist in the same folder and by the same name or else

\\ an error would be encountered

val = ini_read_string("Weapons", "Gun", "") \\ The 3rd parameter is the default value \\ \\ it's not called here , if the given section or key doesn't exist the default value is \\ \\ \\ \\ returned , here ini_read_string would return the value of Gun

ini_close() \\ closes the file

}

Note :- The name of the section shouldn't be written in brackets [ ]

2)The names of the sections and keys must be returned the way they appear

3)An opened ini file must be properly closed

4)Before calling it must be checked whether the particular section and the key exists or not

5)Only one ini file can be accessed at one time

6)It is not recommended to use more than 1 ini file , if you are not using ini files and are storing the values in keys in the windows registry it's even much more better than that

To check a section the code is

ini_section_exists(section name) :- would return value 1 if it really exists else 0

To check whether a key exists

ini_key_exists(section name , key name) :- would return value 1 if it really exists else 0

Now we would improve our previous code

Observe the modified code given below

{

ini_open("my.ini")

if (ini_key_exists("Weapons" , "Gun") = 1)

{

```
        val = ini_read_string("Weapons",  "Gun" ,  "")

        ini_close()

        Else

        {

        ini_close()

        exit()

}
```

To delete section use the function

ini_section_delete(section name)

To delete a key use the code

ini_key_delete(section name ,   key name)

Suppose we want to delete the Gun key the code would be

```
{

ini_open("my.ini")

ini_key_delete("Weapons" ,   "Gun" )

}
```

but a more precise one would be

```
{

ini_open("my.ini")

if ( ini_key_exists("Weapons" ,   "Gun") = 1)

    {

    ini_key_delete("Weapons" ,   "Gun" )

    ini_close()

    }

    Else

    {

    ini_close()
```

```
     exit()

}
```

This code would check whether the given key exists if it exists it would delete it else it would just close the ini file

In some cases there is a need to obtain real values in that cases the function

ini_read_real(section name ,   key name)

Even this function would return the same value as the function ini_read_string(section name ,   key name) but there is a difference between real values and string values

If you obtain the value of the key gun from read_string it would return 05 and read_real would also return 05 but there is a difference , if you add 5 to the one obtained from read_string the Answer would be 055 but if you add 5 to the one obtained from read_real the Answer would be 10 because read_real would save the value in a variable as numerical value whereas read_string would save as a string value

Example of another INI file

[Players]

1 = Michael

2 = Rhonda

3 = Mike

4 = Max

5 = Alex

Here if you use ini_read_real("Players" ,   "1") the function would fail but ini_read_string("Players" ,   "1") would be able to return the value.

Many a times there is a need to change the values for example if you want to replace Mike by Tyson your code would be

ini_write_string("Players" ,   "3" ,   "Tyson") \\ This would change the value of the 3rd key from Mike to Tyson

In this case the key 3 in the section Players was already existing , if you want to create a new key say 6 and save it's value to Harry your code would be

ini_write_string("Players" ,   "6" ,   "Harry")

The new file would become

[Players]

1 = Michael

2 = Rhonda

3 = Mike

4 = Max

5 = Alex

6 = Harry

There is one more function ini_write_real(section name , key name , value) :- This one is used for saving a real value

The INI part ends here

Game Maker supports writing and reading information from text files (.txt) , Game Maker even let's you create folders , Game Maker even contains functions and variables to deal with disk sizes but they are not dealt with here as they are not so important and would require many more pages to explain them , at the end of this book there is a list of some variables which you may require

Registry

The registry is divided into 5 branches they are

1)HKEY_CLASSES_ROOT

2)HKEY_CURRENT_USER

3)HKEY_LOCAL_MACHINE

4)HKEY_USERS

5)HKEY_CURRENT_CONFIG

But Game Maker doesn't support the 5th one , we are left with 4 branches of the windows registry , these branches are recognized by their respective index the index is provided on the next page

Index	Branch of Registry
2	HKEY_CLASSES_ROOT
1	HKEY_LOCAL_MACHINE

3	HKEY_USERS
0	HKEY_CURRENT_USER

Before performing any of the operation it's necessary to set the root (branch) ,   this means that we must tell Game Maker the branch in which we are interested ,   this can be achieved by the function

The default root is HKEY_CURRENT_USER

registry_set_root (index of the root) :- Suppose you want to handle HKEY_USERS your code would be

```
{

registry_set_root ( 3 )

// Other code

}
```

Note :- Registry is also divided into keys

To read information from a key use the function

registry_read_string_ext(key name ,   path)

So if you want to save the root directory to a variable val your code would be

```
{

registry_set_root ( 3 )

val = registry_read_string_ext('\Volatile Environment', 'HOMEDRIVE');

}
```

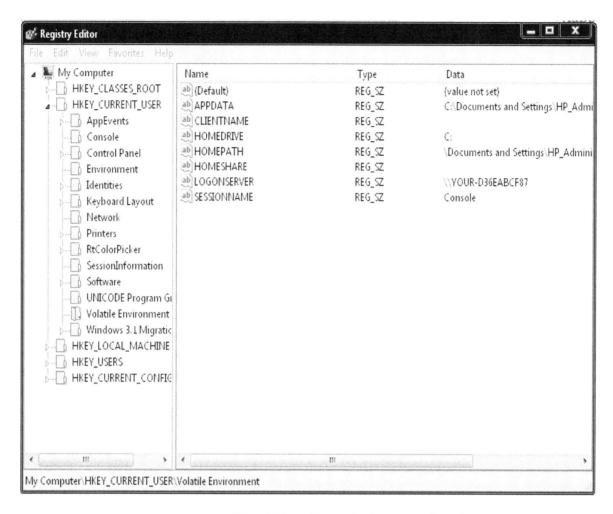

(Fig 481 ,   The windows registry)

To read a real value ,   use the code

registry_read_real_ext(key name ,   path)

To check whether a key exists use the code

registry_exists_ext(key ,   name)

To write a string value to the key

registry_write_string_ext(key name ,   path ,   string to be written)

To write a real value to a key

registry_write_real_ext(key name ,   path ,   real value to be written)

To check whether a particular path exists use the code

registry_exists(path) :- The Answer is returned in a Boolean form

To create a key use the code

registry_write_string(path ,   keyname)

To create a key having real value use the code

registry_write_real(path ,   real value)

Chapter 16 Creating Action Libraries and Extension Packages using ExtMaker

The functionality of Game Maker can be extended by using Action libraries , Extension packages and DLL's (Dynamic Linked Libraries) This functionality was included in Game Maker since version 7.0

Note :- Dll's are not covered over here because to create Dll's you must know a few programming languages which let you create Dll's like C , C ++ (pronounced as C plus plus) or Delphi , Delphi C , C , C++ or Delphi is out of the scope of this book

To create an extension pack or an action library , extension maker must be installed on your system , extension maker is available on the site

http:// www.yoyogames.com/extensions

Note :- Read the Readme File and the license agreement carefully before use

We would first learn how to create an Action Library and then we would learn how to create an extension package

Tip :- The extension of an extension pack is .gex

Note :- Official Libraries of Game Maker cannot be edited using Action Libraries

2)Extension Packages work only with the PRO edition

3)Action libraries work with both the editions (excluding the actions that deal with features available only in the PRO edition of Game Maker)

4) GML is discussed so that you can use your knowledge of GML to create your own action libraries and extension packages

Tip :- The extension of an Action Library is .lib

2)Just like every game each action library must have a unique id

3)The programmer cannot decide the unique code , the unique code is automatically generated by the Library Maker

4)The name of Library Maker is Library_Maker.exe

5)Now you can call yourself an advanced user

The Main User interface of Library Maker

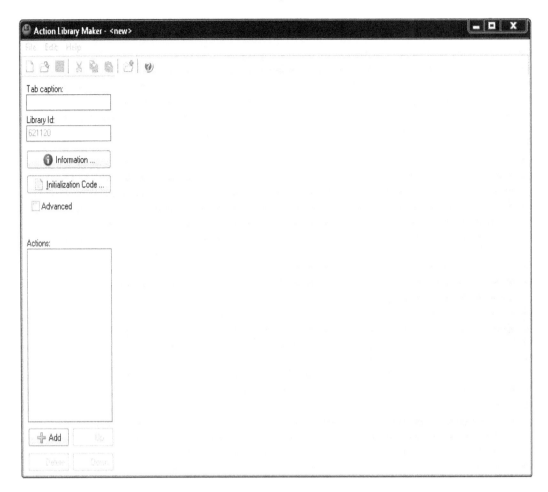

(Fig 482)

Let us understand the Menus

The File Menu

1)	New	Creates a new file Note :- It would prompt for confirmation whether the previous file must be saved or not
2)	Open	Opens an already existing library file Note :- The extension supported is .lib
3)	Save	Used for saving into .lib format
4)	Save As	Save As function
5)	Merge	Used for merge a two files

6)	Exit	Stops the Application
		Note :- Prompts for confirmation

The Edit menu is not discussed as it contains clipboard functions like Cut / Copy / Paste

To the extreme right there is a textbox located just below the label 'Tab Caption:' , in this text box you must type the name of the Tab

For example

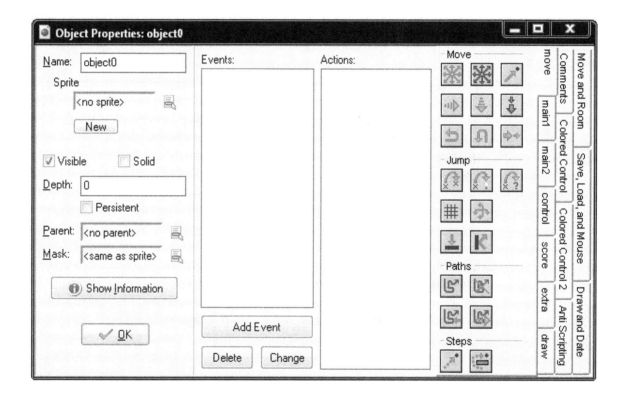

(Fig 483)

Observe the tabs , here the tab captions are 1)move , 2)main1 , 3)main2 , 4)control , 5)extra …………

Similarly if you type mylib , mylib would be shown with all these

The next textbox stores the id (identification) of the library

Note :- The id is generated automatically by Library_Maker and one is not allowed to change the library identifier

The next button Information shows General information(Authors , Version ,   Description etc)

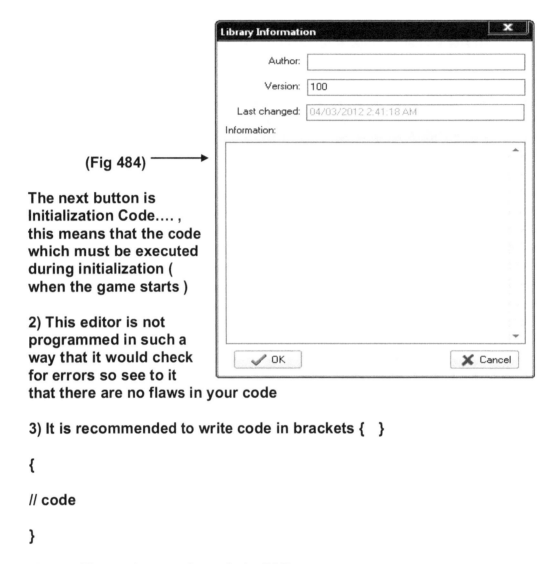

(Fig 484)

The next button is Initialization Code.... , this means that the code which must be executed during initialization (when the game starts)

2) This editor is not programmed in such a way that it would check for errors so see to it that there are no flaws in your code

3) It is recommended to write code in brackets {   }

{

// code

}

Note :- The code must be only in GML

4)If you use an action library which you have made on your own you will not be able to distribute your game as your library may not be installed on the computer of the other person

5)The above rule wouldn't apply for .exe files

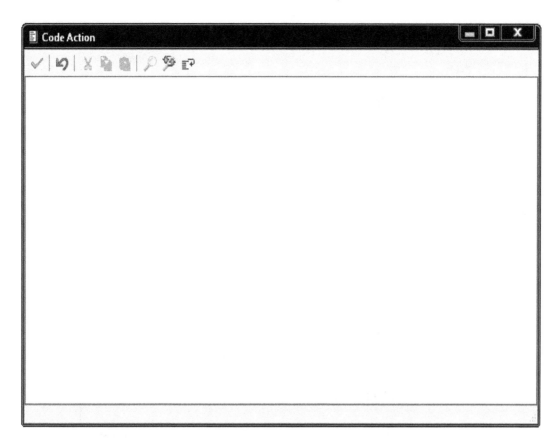

(Fig 485)

Below the button Initialization code there is a check box Advanced , if you check this box your library would be shown only in the advanced mode of Game Maker

Below the actions label listbox is located , this is a list of all the available actions

To add an action press the add button (located below)

The Delete button deletes the action

Note :- It wouldn't ask for confirmation

3)Up :- Goes to the previous action

4)Down :- Goes to the next action

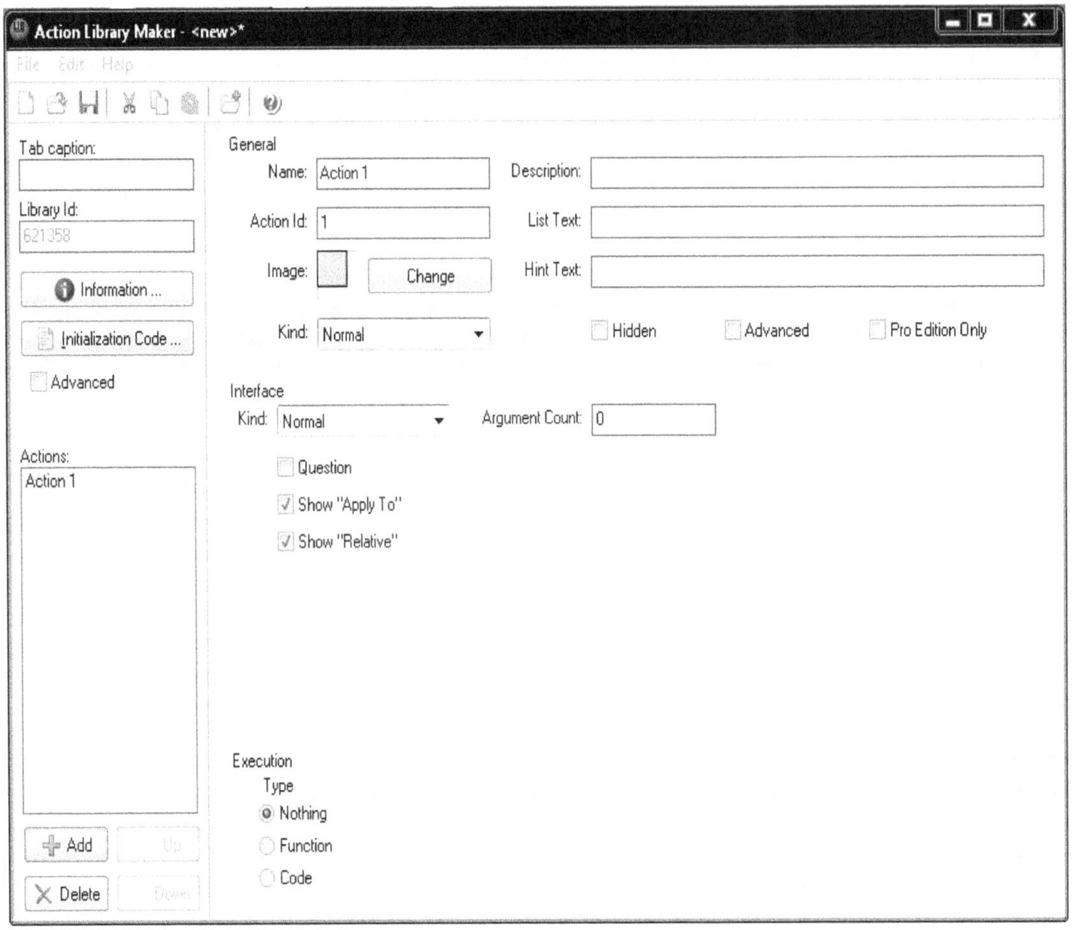

(Fig 486)

Name :- This is the name of the action

Action id :- Just like library files ,   each action has it's own id.

Note :- Each action must assigned an unique id

2)Libraries would not be created if the id's are not unique

Image :- This stores the image which is used for representing the action

Kind :- Kind stands for the kind of the action ,   there are 11 kinds (version 1.3)

Note :- We are discussing the kind located in the Frame General

Sr No	Kind	Description
1)	Normal	Stands for normal action , this kind is often used for creating actions , when you would start creating actions you would realize that you will use this kind frequently
2)	Begin Group	Denotes the beginning of the group

3)	End Group	Denotes the ending of the group
4)	Else	Works like the else statement used for coding
5)	Exit	Works like the exit statement used for coding
6)	Repeat	Works like the repeat action
7)	Variable	Used for creating variable
8)	Code	For execution of a piece of code
9)	-placeholder	Just occupies space nothing else
10)	-seperator	For separation purposes
11)	Label	For labeling purposes

Then there are 3 textboxes

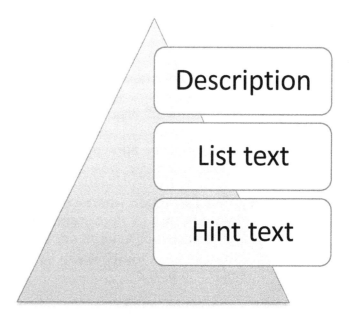

Description
:- Provides Description of the actions (similar to the function of tool tip text)

List text :- Like help in the list of all actions

Note :- In some cases there is a need to start text from a new line

2)Suppose you create a move fixed action ,   when you rest your mouse over that action the help shows the direction and the speed , it also shows whether the speed is absolute or relative , how is this achieved ?

Answer :- It's achieved by specifying certain signs and symbols , following is a list of symbols which can be used

The symbols are
:- The text succeeding this symbol is written in the next line

@FI :- Writes the complete text in italic

@FB :- Writes the complete text in bold letters

Note :-Can be used only for the list text

@N would specify whether not is checked or not

Note :- Not is shown only in questions , hence this would work only for questions

@r would specify whether it's relatively or absolutely

Now the Answer to the second note :- When you want to display an argument value the number of the argument must be written after the character @

For Exmaple :- @0 stands for the 1st argument

@1 stands for the 2nd argument and so on…………

@w is used when the applies to property is not self

Imagine a situation where you are the creator of an action library , you sell your library to a programmer who uses the Lite Edition of Game Maker and your actions contain code which is not supported by Lite Edition(or only supported in the pro edition) what would happen if he uses the action ?

Answer :- An error would be encountered , so how to avoid such errors , what are the remedial measures which must be undertaken ?

This can be achieved by checking the correct checkbox

Three checkboxes are available

(Fig 488)

1) Hidden :- Hidden is used for hiding the action , this one is like a hidden file

2)Advanced :- Would be shown only in the advanced mode

Note :- This advanced is different from the advanced explained earlier , this advanced denotes only the action and the earlier advanced denotes the whole library

3)PRO edition only :- If checked the action would be available for only the PRO edition user

By now you must have guessed the Answer to the question

We have completed the General Frame , Let us move on to the next Frame

2) Interface

This frame deals with the interface (the way the window must look) , there are 5 types (kinds)of interfaces they are

Sr No	Type Name	Description
1)	Normal	This means the normal window , majority of the actions use this window
2)	None	A window is not shown Do you know any such action without a window ? ,

		I would like to give you the example of the else action
3)	Arrows	In this type of a window 9 arrows are shown 1 corresponding to each direction with a box for speed Example :- Move Fixed
4)	Code editor	A code editor is displayed Example :- Execute code
5)	Text Editor	A text editor is shown (like windows notepad)

Then there are 3 checkboxes

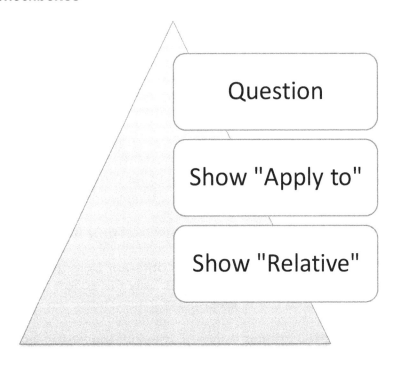

(Fig 489)

1) Question :- If you check this box , a checkbox would be shown on the window "NOT" .

Note :- Questions are a special case of the if statements , the succeeding actions are executed only if 1 (true) is returned , if Not is checked and 1 (true) is returned the succeeding actions would not be executed

2) Show Apply To :- If checked applies To is shown in the window

3) Relative :- If checked Relative box is shown

Next , there is a textbox shown 'Argument Count' before learning argument count let's understand what is an argument.

Observe Fig 490

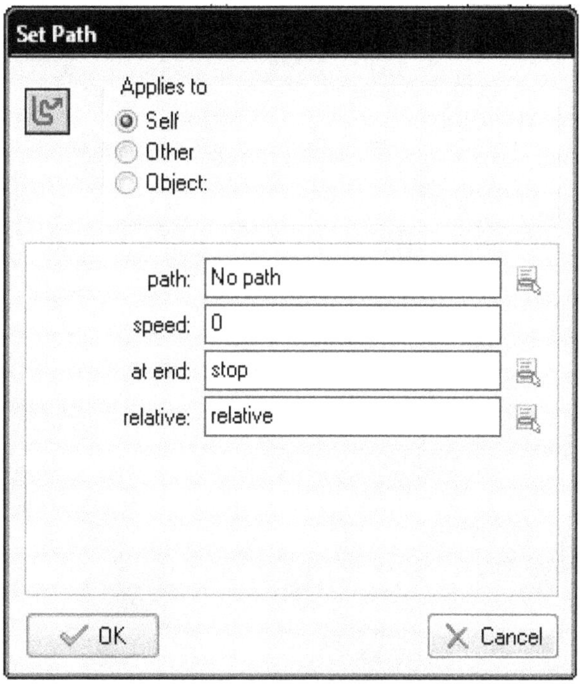

Set Path

Applies to
- ⦿ Self
- ○ Other
- ○ Object:

path: No path

speed: 0

at end: stop

relative: relative

✓ OK   ✕ Cancel

(Fig 490)

Here there are 4 Arguments

Note :- 1)path ,   2)speed ,   3)at end and relative are not arguments they are the captions for the arguments

The value supplied to each argument is stored in variable

Variable Name	Argument Number
@0	1st Argument
@1	2nd Argument and so on

Variable name of the nth term is @ (n – 1)

So if you type 2 for Argument count the following change takes place

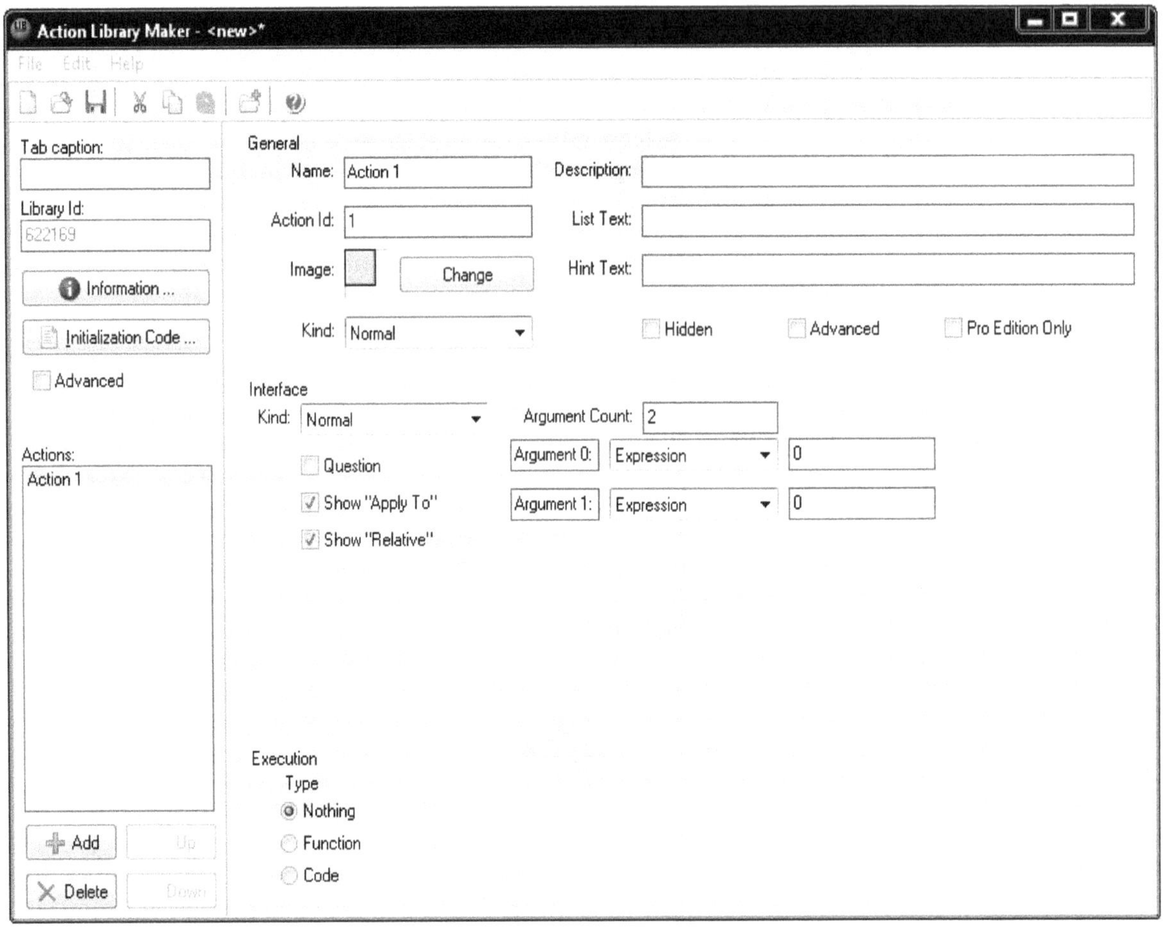

(Fig 491)

Here 6 textboxes are show in the form of a matrix , for explanation a table is given below which is similar to the arrangement of textboxes , each cell of the table corresponds to the corresponding textbox

The caption for the 1st argument	Type of expression for the 1st argument	Default value for the 1st argument
The caption for the 2nd argument	Type of expression for the 2nd argument	Default value for the 2nd argument

Expressions are of the following types

Sr No	Name	Description
1)	String	A string expression

2)	Both	This is a completely different type of expression which is difficult to define , I recommend to try and then judge whether you can use it or not
3)	Menu	A menu Note :- When you select menu a textbox is shown in this textbox the name of the menu's can be written , 2 menus can be differentiated by the symbol | , the menu's are shown from left to right
4)	Color	When you select this one the user can choose from any of the available colors
5)	Font String	I am not providing information regarding this one as it is miscellaneous and there is no need to use it
6)	After font string there are names of resources like sprites , sounds , paths	There's no need to explain this one

The last frame 'Execution'

1)Nothing :- Nothing means nothing would be executed , this one

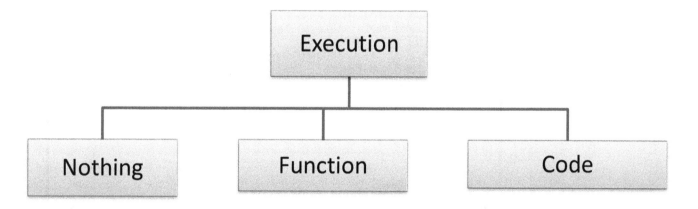

may seem funny but the action comment uses this one

2)Function :- A function of your choice is executed

3)Code :- You have to type code which would be executed

A very very very very important read-only variable

argument_relative :- Stores the value 0 or 1 depending whether relative was not checked or checked

The About Box

(Fig 493)

For creating the Library After completion save the file by pressing Ctrl + S

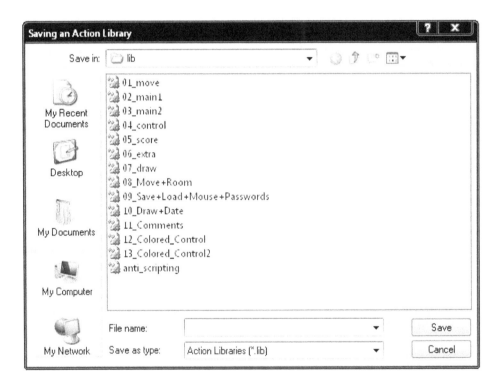

Installing Library Files

Once library files are created they must be installed on the system so that Game Maker can use them , to install library files sopy them to the Folder Lib in the Game Maker's folder

2)Restart your Game

The tab of your library would be added

Extension Packages

To create extension package execute the file Extension_Maker.exe

(Fig 495)

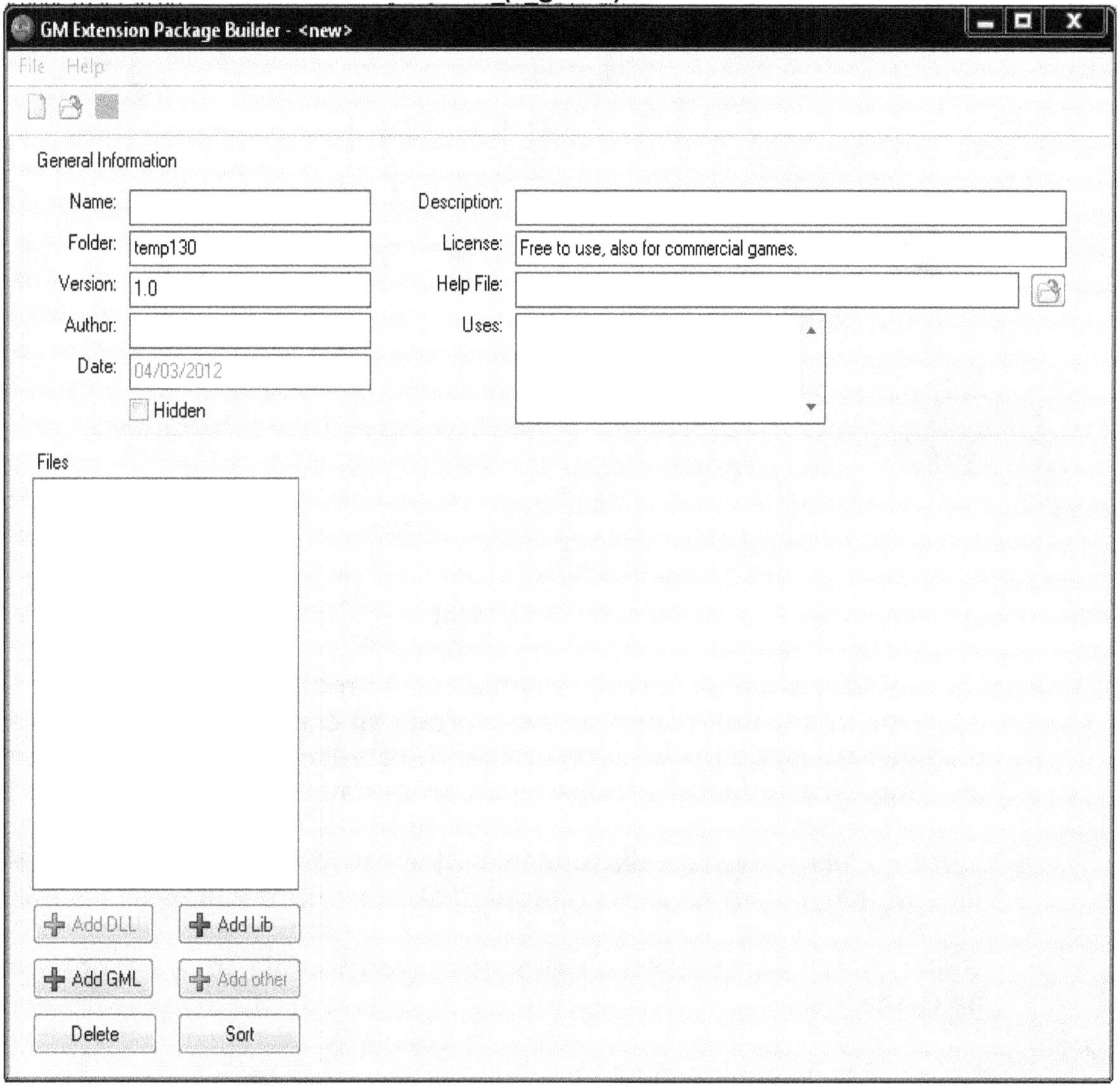

Before starting we must know the file types supported , there are 4 file types supported they are

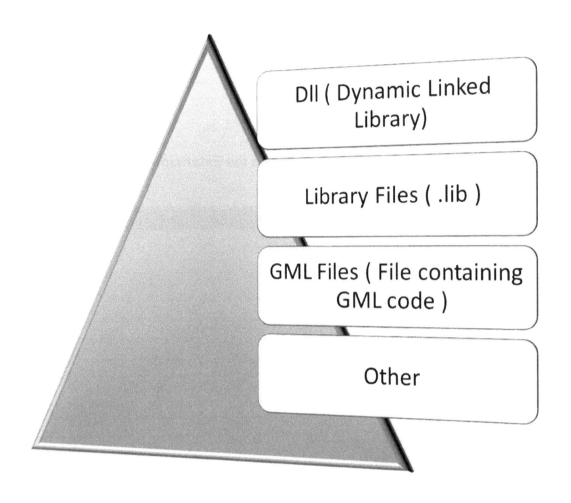

(Fig 496)

DLL :- DLL's are files containing information required by Operating Systems or any other applications , you can create DLL's on your own using a language which supports the creation of DLL's but for creating Dll's you must acquire basic programming skills

Library Files :- We have discussed a lot about library files earlier (the files which you create using Library_Maker are library files .lib)

GML :- GML (Game Maker's Language) files contain code supported by Game Maker.

Note :- The extension must be .GML

Other :- Other means any type of file excluding the ones mentioned above

Let us understand the File Menu

File Menu

1)	New	Used for creating a new file
		Note: - Before creating a new file it would prompt for confirmation

2)	Open	Used for opening a saved file Note :- .gex files are not opened , only description files .ged can be opened
3)	Save	Used for saving the extension pack
4)	Save As	Used for saving with a particular extension
5)	Build Package	Used for compiling the Data into an extension package (.gex)
6)	Exit	Closing the application

The interface is divided into 2 parts (Frames)

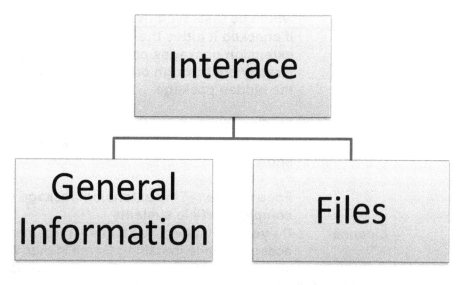

(Fig 497)

I) General Information

Name	The name of the file which would be shown when Game Maker installs the package
Folder	This stores the location of the folder where temporary files would be copied when the Game Runs Note :- In the Windows registry the location of the temporary folder is stored , Game Maker supports a variable which can be used to access the folder The variable is ' temp_directory '

Version	This stores the version of your Extension Package
	Versions must be in a format , for example the first version must be 1.0 , 2nd must be 2.0 etc , sometimes small improvements are made in such cases add 0.1 to the version number
	Example :- 1.1 , 1.2 , 2.3 etc
	It's not compulsory to follow the format given above , you can type any version number but the above format is used universally
Author	Every Book has it's Author , an extension pack is similar to a book where you are the author , you must write your name there
Date	Date means the date last changed , this cannot be changed.
	Note :- If your system follows wrong date , wrong date would be displayed over there
Hidden	If checked it hides the extension package , such extension packages cannot be used by Game Maker directly but through other extension packages which use the hidden package
	My Recommendation :- Don't use this feature
Description	Here you have to describe your extension package in short.
	For example :- This extension package can handle complex particle systems
License	Do you remember the License agreement which you accepted while installing Game Maker ? , you can license your Extension Package the way you want , you may sell your package , distribute it for free and don't forget to add a special clause for use in commercial games
	Note :- Avoid complex legal terms in your license , your license must be such that even a lay man must understand it , if your license is too huge you can write it down in the Help File
Help File	Here you have to indicate the Help file for your Game
	The Following Formats are supported
	1)(*.hlp)
	2)(*.chm)
	A Browse window would be shown as shown in the Figure given below

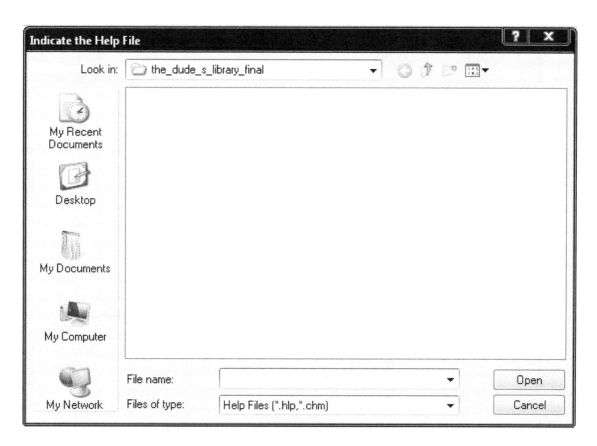

(Fig 498)

Uses :- Here you must indicate the name of other extension package if any functions are called from it

When you add a DLL or a GML script you have to provide descriptions of functions , you can add functions , sort them , remove them by the buttons provided

Name :- Means the name of the function to be used by Game Maker

External Name :- Name of the function in the file

Help Line :- A statement for help

Arguments :- A drop down list is shown where you have to indicate the number of arguments

(Fig 499)

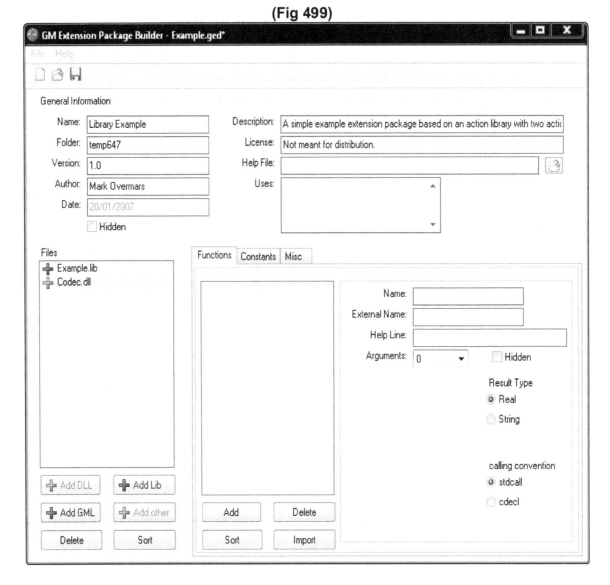

Hidden :- If checked the function is hidden

Sometimes you also have to provide whether the arguments are string or real , if more than 4 they must be of the type real else they can be string

Result Type :- Result type can be only of two types

Note :- Result type means the format in which the result must be returned

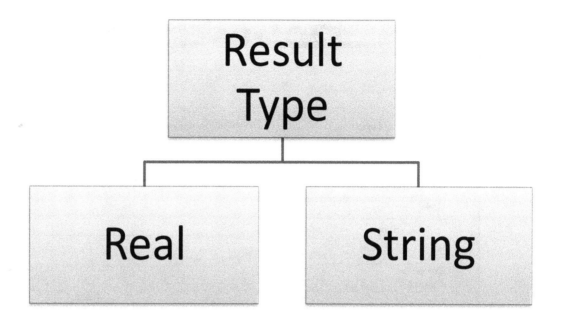

(Fig 500)

Calling Convention

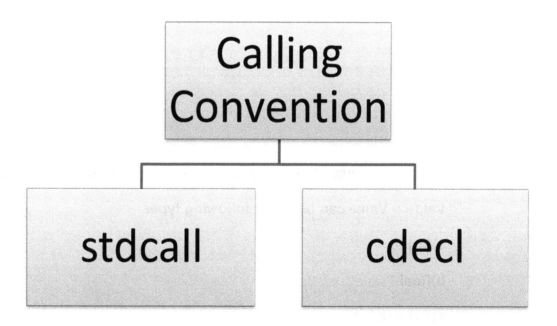

(Fig 501)

Calling convention means the convention used for calling the DLL , this has to be specified in the DLL (it means that while creating Dll's this must be specified)

For Dll's and GML's you can also specify constants through the constants tab

(Fig 502)

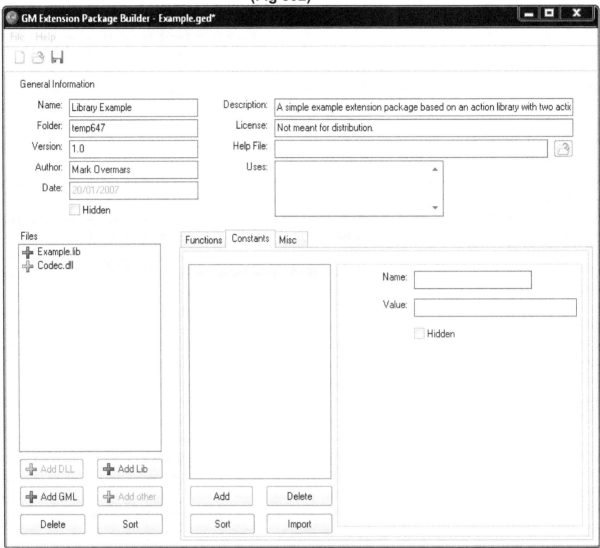

Name :- You have to specify the name to be used by Game Maker

Value :- Value can be of the following types

a)String

b)Real

c)Expression

The 3rd tab contains Miscellaneous information

It has the following fields

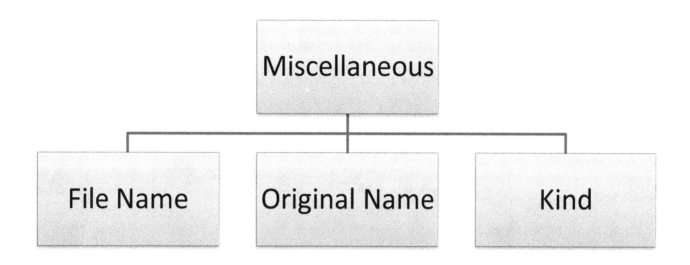

(Fig 503)

Filename :- The name of the File

Original Name :- The path (location) of the file

3)Kind :- It can be of the following types depending upon the type

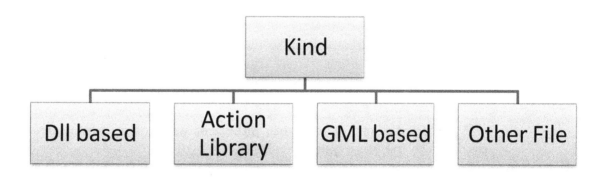

(Fig 504)

Note :- If you include a DLL ,   a GML or a Lib through others
Extension Maker would treat it as other file

In case of GML and Dll's there are two more fields

a)Initialization

b)Finalization

Initialization means a function which must be executed before the extension pack is executed

Finalization means the function which must be executed at the end

Note :- These Functions must not return any value

Building an Extension package

1)Goto the file menu and select Build Package

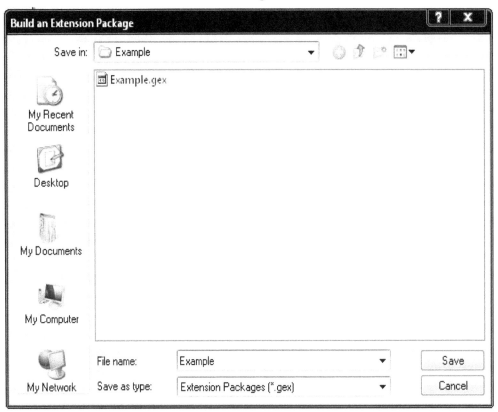

(Fig 505)

If you want others to use your packages you can submit your package to the yoyo games website

Installing an Extension Pack

To use an extension pack it must be installed on the system , installing means that Game Maker must know that a particular file with a particular extension exists ,   the method of installing is discussed later in this chapter

From the resource menu select 'Select Extension Package' or press Shift + Ctrl + E

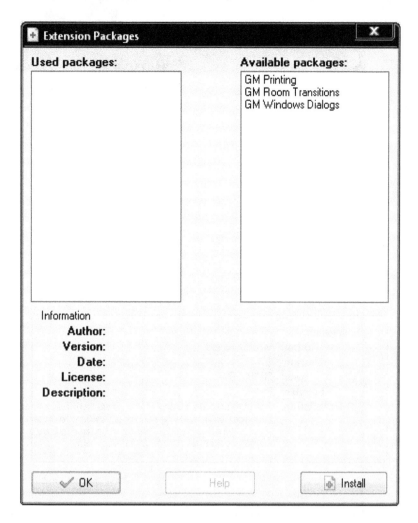

The following window would appear (Fig 506)

When you select any of the extension package the Author , Version , Date , license and Description is shown

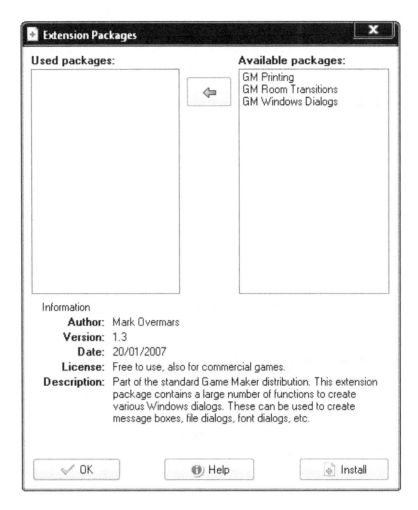

(Fig 507)

To use a package press the button with an arrow pointing ⟵ ,   for help press the 'Help' button.

Help shows the .chm or the .hlp file of the extension package which is specified during the creation of the extension package

Tip :- If you want more extension packages you can download them through the website

'http://gm.yoyogames.com/extensions.php'

Note :- Before using an extension pack you must read and understand it's license thoroughly

Note :- When you use an extension pack in your game there's absolutely no need to distribute it along with your game

Method of installing

1)Press the install button

The following window would appear

(Fig 508)

To browse for more extension packages press the install button.

Note :- Two extension packages with the same name cannot be installed , Game Maker would ask whether it shoud overwrite the previous file or not

This chapter ends over here

Chapter 17 Multiplayer Games

Now a days many of the companies who program computer games program them in such a way that users with an internet connection can log on their website and play the same game with some one maybe sitting at the other corner of this world ,   knowledge to create Multiplayer Games is the need of the hour for Game Programmers , thankfully Game Maker supports Multiplayer Game Programming

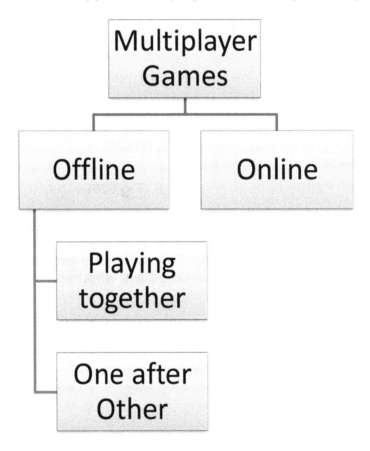

(Fig 509)

The Difference

Online	Offline
Internet required	Internet not required
The players play on different machines simultaneously	The players play on the same machines may be simultaneously or not

Examples

1)Super Contra (Players play simultaneously working as a single unit or a team)

2)Mario (Players play one after the other on the same machine)

Do you know :- Some Mobiles offer multiplayer games online without an internet connection!!! , there is only Bluetooth connectivity between the two and generally work when both the mobiles are from the same manufacturer , but even this feature has a disadvantage , the range of Bluetooth is too short (10 metres approx)

We would modify the Game Space which we made earlier and convert it into an offline multiplayer game

Follow the procedure

1)Open the game Space

2)Create one more object , rocket2 and it's sprite should be similar to the other rocket

Note :- It must be possible for the 2 players to differentiate between their rockets so we would blend the second one with red color

Now follow the procedure given

1)Add event 'Create'

2)Drag action 'Execute Code'

3)Write the code

```
{

image_blend = c_red

}
```

Copy the rest of the functions as they are and instead of left , right , up , down use numpad buttons 4 , 6 , 8 , 2 respectively and replace space by enter

now both the players can simultaneously control their rockets and work as a team such a game is called offline multiplayer game

Note :- The health and the number of lives would be common for both of them , even if one of them is damaged the overall health is reduced , you can represent the health as well as lives differently for both of them but that a bit complex and is taught later

2)You can even program the game in such a way that the second player uses a mouse or even a joystick for controlling it's rocket

3)Similarly you can even a 3rd rocket where the 3rd player uses mouse for controlling

Online Multiplayer Games

An active internet connection is needed by you and by your opponents

Note :- Due to security tools like firewalls and Anti viruses the connections are blocked your system may prompt messages as shown below

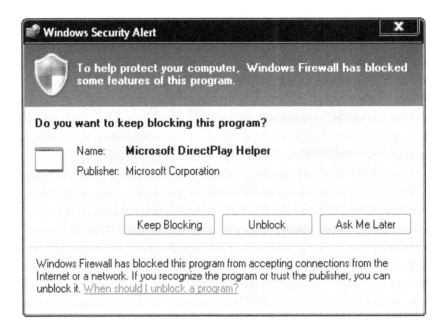

(Fig 510)

Here is a term which you must understand

Protocol :- A protocol is a set of rules followed by the network

Even our internet uses a protocol IPv4 protocol , Bluetooth devices (headsets and mobiles)use protocol like A2DP (Advanced Audio Distribution Protocol) , there are many more protocols like FTP (File TrAnswerfer Protocol) , IP (Internet Protocol) etc

Protocols are a must in any type of communication between 2 devices , without protocols the result is chaos

Note :- While programming try to make your game as simple as you can because if there is an error in connection the Game may stop working from one side or in some cases the data would never reach and may get lost

Game Maker supports 4 types of Protocols

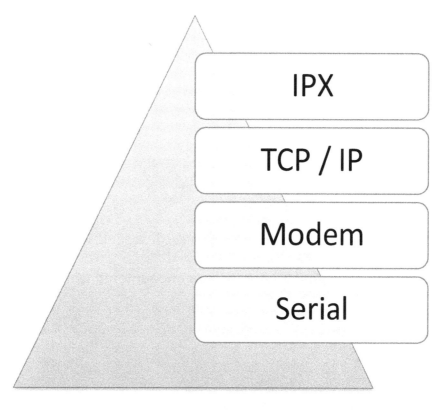

(Fig 511)

Recommendation :- Don't use the IPX protocol because you may need to install it and it may not be supported by the later versions of windows

TCP / IP :- TCP stands for Transmission Control Protocol and IP stands for Internet Protocol , this protocol is used by computers for accessing the internet , I am sure this protocol would be installed on all the systems

Modem :- Modem is a not a protocol , modem means a connection through Modulator / Demodulator , Modem is a device which can modulate and demodulate(Add the highlighted part mo + dem = modem) , If you use a modem type of connection you have to specify the phone number

Serial :- Serial means a connection through serial ports

To initialize an IPX connection the function is

{

mplay_init_ipx()

}

Code to check whether IPX connection is initialized

```
{
    if ( mplay_init_ipx())
    {
    // your code
    }
    else
    {
    show_message( " An error was encountered while initializing IPX
connection")
    }
}
```

To initialize a TCP / IP connection the code is

mplay_init_tcpip(address)

Note :- The address can be anything (name of a website or an ip address)

To initialize a modem connection

mplay_init_modem(initialization string ,   phone number) :- Here you have to provide a string for initialization and the phone number to call

Note :- An empty initialization string is allowed

To initialize a serial connection

mplay_init_serial(port_number ,   bit_rate ,   stop_bits ,   parity ,   flow of control) :- You have to specify the port number which is to be 1 to 4 ,   bit rate is the rate of bits ,   stopbits can have the following values

0 ,   1 or 2 ,   0 means stop_bits = 1 but 1 doesn't mean stop_bits = 2 it means stop_bits = 1.5 ,   2 means stop_bits = 2

Parity may contain the following values

0	0 means no parity at all
1	1 means odd parity

2	2 means even parity
3	And this one is still different from the ones mentioned above

Flow can have the following values

0 , 1 , 2 , 3 , 4

Sometimes you need your own ip address , your ip address can be found by the function

mplay_ipaddress()

This function would return your ip address

Note :- It's important to end connections

Connections can be ended by

mplay_end()

To check which type of connection your game is running use the code

{

a = mplay_connect_status()

　if(a = 0)

　{

　show_message("NO connection established")

　exit

　}

　if(a = 1)

　{

　show_message("IPX connection is being used")

　exit

　}

　if (a = 2)

　{

　show_message("TCP / IP connection is being used")

```
exit

}

if ( a = 3 )

{

show_message( " Modem connection is used")

exit

}

if ( a = 3 )

{

show_message(" Serial Port connection is being used")

exit

}

else

{

show_message("Failed to detect the type of connection")

show_message("Sorry")

exit

}

}
```

The network can be compared to a building which contains many rooms , here the rooms are known as sessions , each Game must have it's own session , you can create or join a session , each session has a session name , each game must run in a different session.

Note :- A game can interfere in the session created by other game only if both have the same identifier , so you must make sure that you assign unique id to different games and different versions of the same game.

Note :- Unlimited players cannot join the session , the maximum number of players which can join the session is decided by the programmer , you can check whether there exists any session which can accommodate players by the function mplay_session_find()

Note :- Sessions are assigned numbers ,   0 is the 1st session ,   1 is the 2nd session and so on......

Note :- Just like numbers sessions are assigned names this name is returned by the function

mplay_session_name(session number)

To join a session use the function

mplay_session_join(session number ,   player_name)

player name is the name of the person playing the game ,   you can let the user decide the player name by the code

{

a = get_string(" Enter the player name to be shown on the network" , "Player1")

mplay_session_join(session number ,   a) // you have to specify the session number

}

Here the player can decide the player name ,   the default name is player1 and I have left the session number blank as it depends on the sessions available

To create a session use the function

mplay_session_create(Session name ,   maximum players ,   player name)

Tip :- The computer which creates the session is known as the session host

Suppose if you start a session and after sometime you wish to shut down your computer what would happen to others playing your game ,   in this case you can make the other computer as the host of the session

mplay_session_mode (move)

move must be a Boolean value

To know the status of the session use the function

mplay_session_status()

This function may return 0 , 1 or 2

Value Returned	Meaning
0	Means that the player has not joined any session yet
1	The player has created a session of his own
2	The player has joined a session created by someone else

To end a session

mplay_session_end()

Note :- This would not affect other players

Communication between players is equally important in Multiplayer Games , suppose there is a game based on civilizations and there are many civilizations (let 9) these nine civilizations are further divided into 3 groups (in other words allies have been formed)

Group Number	Civilization number
1)	Civilization number 1 , 2 , 3
2)	Civilization number 4 , 5 , 6
3)	Civilization number 7 , 8 , 9

Now if civilization number 1 decides to attack group3 he must inform his fellow allies for help to fight against others , here he must send a message to the other one and at the same time civilization number 4 to 9 shouldn't receive the message, for this reason Game Maker includes mechanism for sending and receiving messages among players

Before dealing with communication between players we must know how to handle players , there are just 3 functions to deal with players they are

Note :- Each player is assigned a number 0 is the first one , 1 is the second one and so on.........

Some games work only when a fixed number of players are present , for such games a function is used which would return the total number of players

mplay_player_find()

Note :- Each player has a name and an id

The id can be found out by the code

mplay_player_id(player number)

Note :- It's obvious that you will not be able to enter the player number unless you find out the total players

To find the player name use the function   mplay_player_name(player number)

Communication (observe Fig 512 given below)

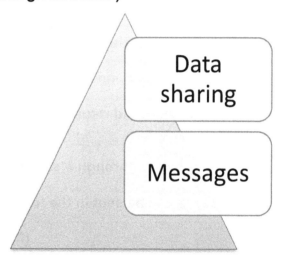

The function for sharing data is

mplay_data_write(index ,   data)

Note :- The index value should range from nil to a million

2)Data cannot be a file ,   data must be either a numeric value or a string value

Reminder :- If you wish to use numeric values don't insert the values into brackets as Game Maker would treat the numeric value as a string value

Tip :- Data is sent and received in modes ,   2 types of modes are supported

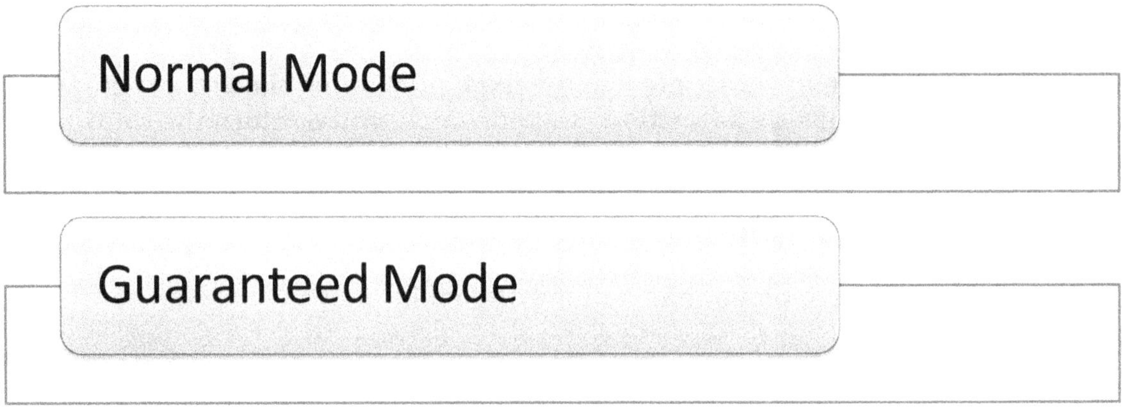

Normal Mode

Guaranteed Mode

(Fig 513)

Note :- The default mode is the normal mode

To enable guaranteed data Transmission the function is

mplay_data_mode (guaranteed)

A Boolean value must be provided for the parameter guaranteed

To read data use the function

mplay_data_read(index)

The function would return the value of the data stored in the given index

Communication through Messages

Messages can be sent in the following modes

(Fig 514)

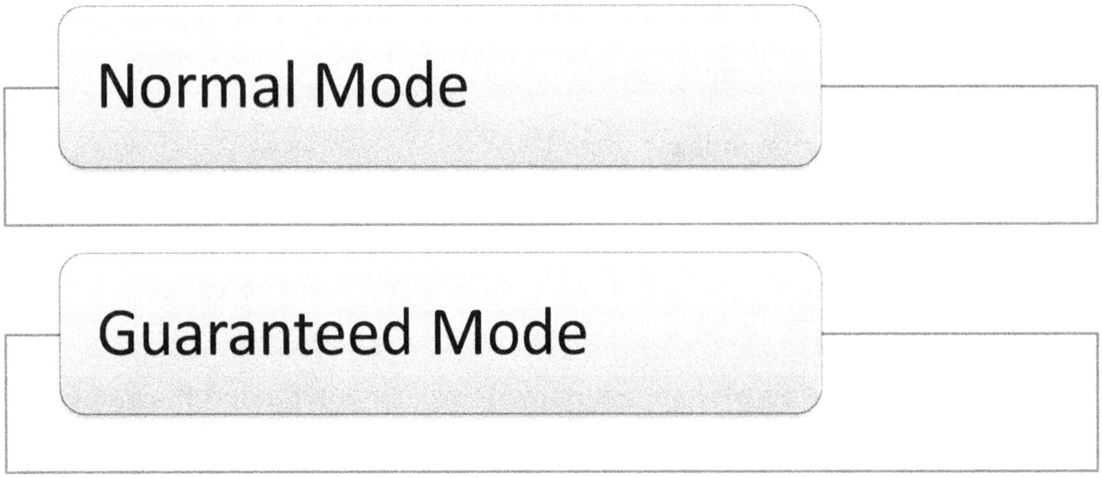

Normal Mode

Guaranteed Mode

Function to send a message in the normal mode is

mplay_message_send(player_id , message_id , message)

Note :- Player id can be replaced by player name but I recommend you to use id

2)message may be a string or a numeric value

3)Every message must have it's own id (for the reason specified below)

Suppose you have sent a message containing string value and then you send a message containing a numeric value and what if the first message doesn't reach due to some technical errors but the second message reaches , the game (played by the other player) would treat the numeric value as the string value which may or may not result into an error , so if the game is programmed in such a way that if message whose id is 2 is received treat it as a numeric value this error can be avoided , hence id's are a must.

To send a message in the guaranteed mode use the code

mplay_message_send_guaranteed(player_id , message_id , message)

This function guarantees that the player would receive the message 100%

Imagine that you are playing a game with 6 other players(whose id's are 1 , 2 , 3 , 4 , 5 and 6 respectively) and due to some unavoidable reason you wish to discontinue the game , you wish to send the message ' I resign' so would you use the code

```
{

mplay_message_send( 1 ,  1 ,  "I resign" )

mplay_message_send( 2 ,  1 ,  "I resign" )

mplay_message_send( 3 ,  1 ,  "I resign" )

mplay_message_send( 4 ,  1 ,  "I resign" )

mplay_message_send( 5 ,  1 ,  "I resign" )

mplay_message_send( 6 ,  1 ,  "I resign" )

}
```

I would recommend a better one

```
{
```

```
mplay_message_send( 0 ,   1 ,   "I resign" )
```

}

One may argue ' What will happen if the id of one of them is 0 ' , this is impossible because the id 0 would always be the one whose sending the message.

Note :- If any of the player checks his/her own id it would always be 0

The second piece of code was much better than the first one but the second piece of code would not work if you want to send messages to 8 out of 10 players

To receive a message from a player use the code

```
mplay_message_recieve( player_id or player_name )
```

Sometimes the messages from a particular player start piling up ,   if this happens you may wish to delete all the leftover messages ,   to do so use the code

```
mplay_message_clear( player_id )
```

There is a provision in Game Maker for removing messages from all the players and that provision is use 0

To count the number of messages from a particular player ,   use the code

```
mplay_message_count( player_id )
```

To count messages form all players us the code

```
mplay_message_count( 0 )
```

Game Maker has a provision for storing details of the latest message received (from any player)

To know the message the code is

```
mplay_message_value()
```

This function would return the message value

To know the identifier

```
mplay_message_id()
```

To know the player name   mplay_message_name()

  To know the player id   mplay_message_player()

This chapter ends over here , you have learnt everything about multiplayer gaming.

Chapter 18 Adjusting Views , Advanced Technique and Error Management

To know the importance of views observe the screenshots given below

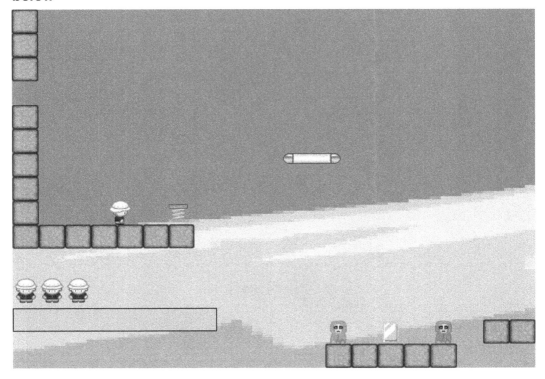

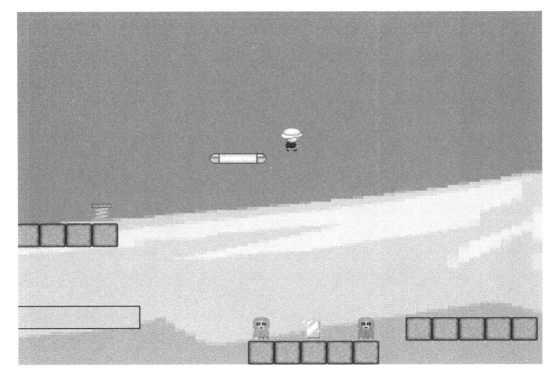

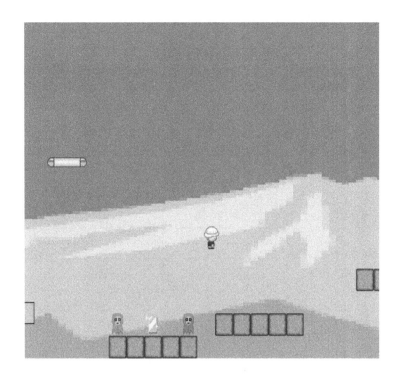

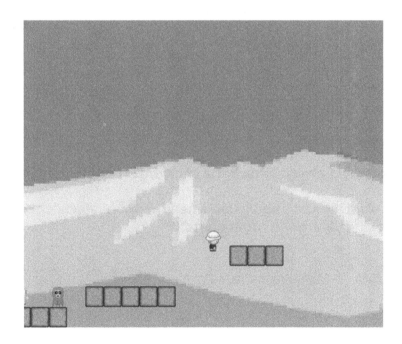

Did you observe something from the screenshots given above , if not read the observation which you should have noticed

'The static elements of the room(example :-walls) are moving in the leftward direction as the character is moving rightwards and vice-versa'

The game whose screenshots are given above is like the game Super Mario Bros such type of Games are called Platform games , here we will learn how to design the room mechanism for such games

Create a new room and open the views tab

(Fig 519)

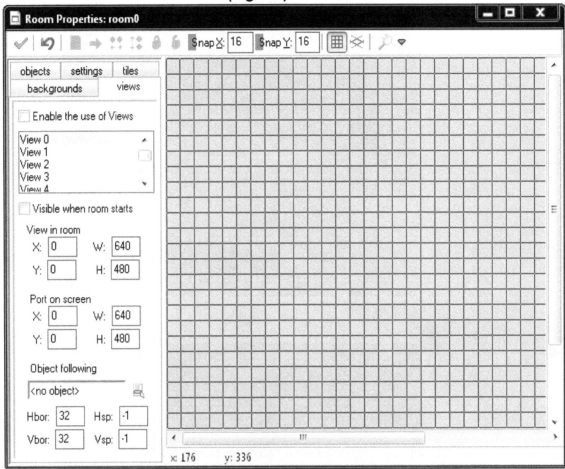

Tip :- You must always check the checkbox 'Enable the use of views'

2)If you want views to be visible when the room starts check the checkbox 'Visible when room starts'

The remaining part is divided into 3 frames

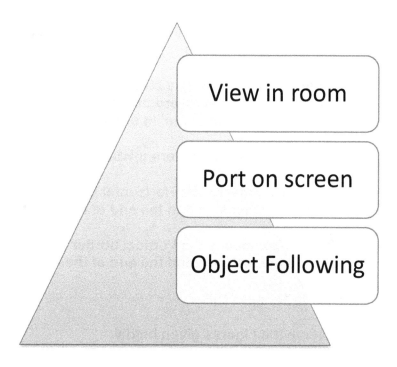

View in room

Port on screen

Object Following

(Fig 520)

1)View in Room :- Here you must specify the view for the room

Here there are 4 parameters a)X , b)Y , c)W , d)H

X and Y stand for the X and the Y co-ordinates of the topmost left hand side corner

Note the default values are (0 , 0) and I wouldn't like you to change it

W stands for the width of the view and H stands for the height of the view

Note :- If you are creating a game like the one whose screenshots were given I would recommend you to specify the height of the room as the height of the view

2)Port on Screen :- Here you have to specify the parameters for how the view should be ported on the screen

Here there are 4 parameters a)X , b)Y , c)W , d)H

X and Y stand for the X and the Y co-ordinates of the topmost left hand side corner

Note the default values are (0 , 0) and it should not be changed.

W stands for the width of the view and H stands for the height of the view

It is recommended that you use the same set of X , Y , W and H values for both of them

3)Object Following :- 'The static elements of the room(example :-walls) are moving in the leftward direction as the character is moving rightwards and vice-versa' In other words the view follows the object

Here there are 4 parameters a)HBor , b)VBor , c)HSp , d)VSp

HBor :- HBor means the Horizontal border which must be maintained between the instance and the end of the view

VBor :- VBor means the Vertical border which must be maintained between the instance and the end of the view

Why do we need this ?

Observe the Figures given below

(Fig 521)

(Fig 522)

In the Figure 521 the view changes only if the object is too close to the end of the view whereas in Figure 522 the view changes when the object is at a distance , which one would you prefer ? , people would hate your game if you choose the 1st one , you must always choose the 2nd one because in the 1st one you don't know what's ahead whereas in the second one you know about what's ahead a bit

Hence we require object following

HSp :- Stands for Horizontal component of speed

VSp :- Stands for Vertical component of speed

Other information:There are a total of 8 views (0 to 7) you may use all of them if you like

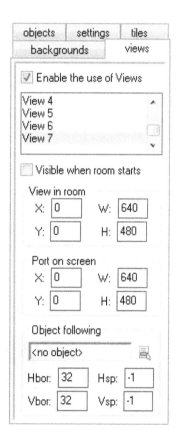

(Fig 513)

Now it's time to learn the Advanced Technique

This technique was developed to test Alarm Skills

To create an object which would move 120 steps to the left and then 120 steps to the right after completion of 240 steps it would again move 120 steps to the left , in other words it would move on the same path again and again but we have to accomplish this task without using paths , a real challenge isn't it

Follow the procedure given below

1)Create an Object

2)Name it 'm_platform'

3)Supply a suitable sprite

4)Add event Create

5)Drag Action 'Move Fixed'

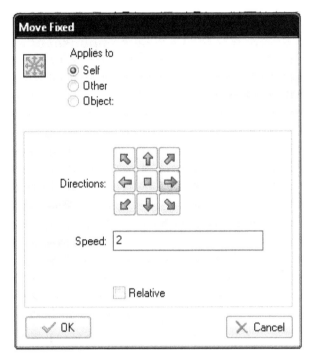

(Fig 514)

Note :- Don't chack the checkbox 'Relative'

6)Drag action 'Set Alarm'

Let it's parameters be equal to the Fig 515

(Fig 515)

7) Add Alarm Event for Alarm 0

8) Drag action Set Alarm

Let it's parameters be equal to the Fig 516

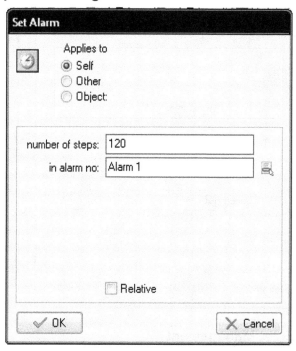

(Fig 516)

9) Drag action 'Move Fixed' let it's direction be the same and the speed be -2 absolutely (non – relatively)

10) Add Event 'Alarm1'

11) Drag action 'Move Fixed'

Let it's parameters be equal to Fig 517

12) Drag action 'Set Alarm'

Let it's parameters be equal to Fig 518

(Fig 517 and 518)

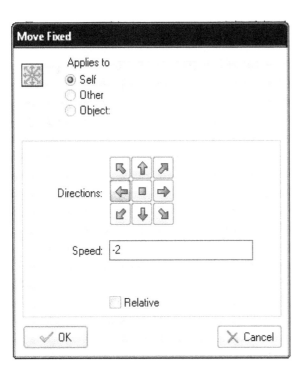

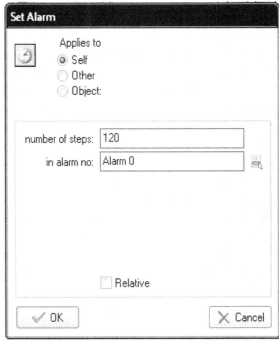

Error Management

1)Open 'Global Game Settings'

2)Navigate to the tab errors

Here 4 checkboxes are shown

1)Display Error Messages

2)Write error messages to file game_errors.log

3)Abort on all error messages

4)Treat uninitialized variables as value 0

(Fig 519)

1)If the first checkbox is checked Game Maker would display error messages ,   3 buttons would be shown (Fig 520)

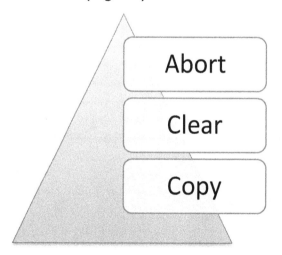

If the user presses Abort the game is aborted ,   Clear clears the message and Copy copies the message to the clipboard

Note :- It is recommended that you don't check this box because if an error encounters and the user responds by pressing 'Abort' the game would end there.

Advantage :- The player can send you the type of error encountered and the information provided by the player can be used as a valuable feedback for improving the game

It is recommended that you uncheck the 1st box because a player must not know what's happening behind the scenes. If the player knows that the Game has encountered an error there is a possibility that he may not like your game ,   2nd point :- When the error window is displayed there's no way for resuming the game

2)If you check the 2nd box the effect would be even worse because the game would write the error to a file and would just end abruptly ,   the player wouldn't even know what's happened the first one was better than this one

3)The 3rd one is even more worse than the second one because the second one at least writes the errors to a file but the 3rd one directly ends the game without displaying the error or writing it

4)The 4th one treats non initialized variables are variables possessing the value 0

Note :- If all the checkboxes are unchecked the effect would be same as checking the 3rd checkbox

This chapter ends over here

Chapter 19 3D Game Programming

Nowadays due to the evolution of technology and better graphics hardware it's possible to play 3D Games , earlier in this book it was mentioned that 3D games cannot be created, just 3D effect can be given , in this chapter we will learn how to create a 3D Game

Game Maker is limited in it's functionality when it comes to 3D effects , first of all there are no inbuilt libraries containing actions for creating 3D effects , 3D effects can be created only through GML code , to start creating 3D effects one must activate the 3D mode.

Note :- 3D mode unlike the advanced mode cannot be activated by the press of a button on the mouse

To activate 3D mode use the code

d3d_start()

If this mode gets activated the above function would return 1 else 0

To return to 2D mode use the function

d3d_end()

Note :- In the 3D mode the co-ordinate systems change!!!

There are surfaces known as Hidden Surfaces you can enable or disable them using the following function

d3d_set_hidden(activate)

To activate use

d3d_set_hidden(1)

else

d3d_set_hidden(0)

Note :- In the 3D mode depth affects the size and no 2 objects with similar depth must exist in the game

You can specify the depth by

d3d_set_depth(depth value)

Note :- If you have created a 2D game and apply 3D to it the whole game would spoil

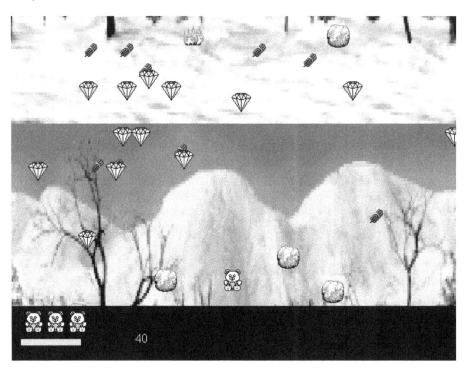

(Fig 521 , Original Game)

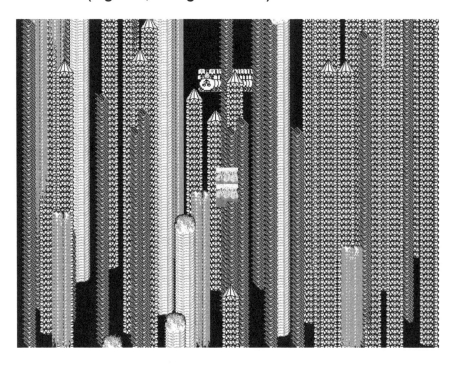

(Fig 522 , After the application of 3D mode)

Fig 522 looks like anything but a game , its best to study everything related to 3d and then activate 3d mode , if you try to experiment your skills the result would be (Fig 522)

Note :- 2 dimensional games use only two co-ordinates (x, y)

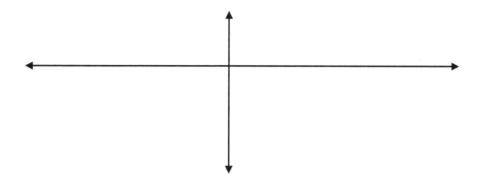

(Fig 523 , the 2 axis of co-ordinate system)

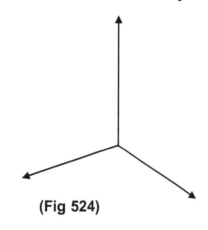

(Fig 524)

To understand Fig 524 you must observe it with a special view , when you are able to understand you will realize that it looks somewhat like one of the corners of your house

Compare fig 523 and 524 , 523 is 2 dimensional whereas 524 is 3 dimensional , 523 has 2 axis x and y whereas 524 has 3 axes x , y and z

Now you will learn the code for drawing various shapes

Note :- This code must always be dragged into the Draw event

First you must create 3D primitive

d3d_primitive_begin(type_of_primitive)

3D Primitives are of 6 types

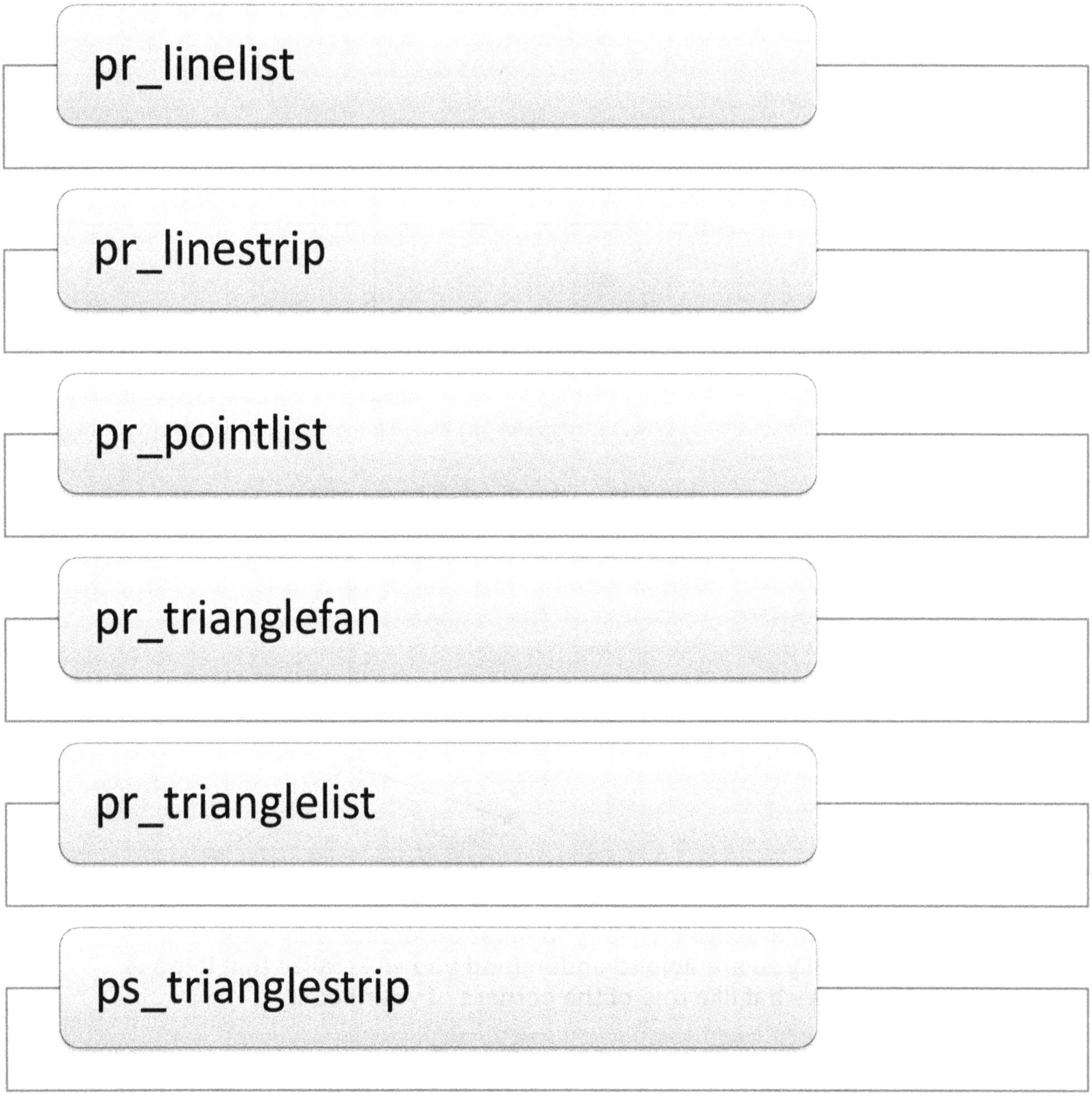

> pr_linelist

> pr_linestrip

> pr_pointlist

> pr_trianglefan

> pr_trianglelist

> ps_trianglestrip

(Fig 525)

To add a colored vertex the code is

d3d_vertex_color(x , y , z , color , alpha)

Here (x , y , z) are the co-ordinates of the points and color is the color of the point , alpha is it's alpha value

Alpha value must be in the range (0 to 255)

To add a vertex without color the code is

d3d_vertex(x , y , z)

To end the primitive the code is

d3d_primitive_end()

This function is very important , this function must be written at the end

Tip :- Functions which end contain no parameters or zero parameters

Before learning the further part you must know some advanced functions used for drawing

draw_point_color(x , y , color) :- Draws a point at the location (x , y) of the specified color

draw_line_color(x1 , y1 , x2 , y2 , color1 , color2):- Draws a line starting from the point whose location is (x1 , y1) to the point (x2 , y2) , the color of the line would be a mixture of color1 and color2 (observe Fig 526)

(Fig 526)

The above line is the result of the code draw_line_color(114, 114, 368, 288, c_red, c_white)

Note :- If you type the code draw_line_color(114, 114, 368, 288, c_white, c_red)

The result would be

(Fig 527)

Note :- Even though the color combination is the same for both the lines there is a difference between the 2 Figures

Here the line was very thin ,   sometimes there is a need for a thicker line ,   a thicker line can be obtained by the code

draw_line_width_color(x1 ,   y1 ,   x2 ,   y2 ,   width ,   color1 , color2)

Note :- You can use any value for the width

Note :- If you want the line to be painted with a single color specify the same value for color1 and color2

Just imagine , the line is perfectly horizontal or vertical and you have specified a very high width what would be the resultant figure be ?

It would no longer be a line it would form a rectangle

If you use the code

draw_line_width_color(114 ,   114 ,   368 ,   288 ,   78 ,   c_red , c_white)

The result would be

(Fig 528)

You can use such tricks to create rectangles but there is a different function made for rectangle , If you wish to draw a rectangle it is recommended to use those functions(dealing with rectangles) as they offer more parameters

To draw a rectangle

draw_rectangle_color(x1 , y1 , x2 , y2 , color1 , color2 , color3 , color4 , border)

Fig 529 given below is a rectangle

For obtaining Fig 529 the code used was

draw_rectangle_color(114, 114, 368, 288, c_white, c_red, c_yellow, c_aqua, 1)

Note :- border is a Boolean value

2)Here (x1 , y1) and (x2 , y2) are the co-ordinates of the ends of the diagonals

Note :- There is one more function for drawing rectangles

draw_rectangle(x1 , y1 , x2 , y2 , border)

It is once again repeated that codes associated with drawing must be executed through the draw event.

To draw a rounded rectangle use the code draw_roundrect_color (x1 , y1 , x2 , y2 , color1 , color2 , border)

To obtain a rectangle like

(Fig 530)

use the code

draw_roundrect_color(114, 114, 368, 288, c_white, c_aqua, 1)

There's just one difference between rectangles and rounded rectangles , rounded rectangles are curved at the edges , rectangles are not

Note :- there's no compulsion to use this code as it is you may customize the co-ordinate values and the colors as per your wish

Sometimes there's a need to draw triangles , triangles can be drawn using the code

draw_triangle_color(x1 , y1 , x2 , y2 , x3 , y3 , color1 , color2 , color3, outline)

| (Fig 531 , if border = 1) | (Fig 532 , if border = 0) |

Note :- you can draw any type of triangles equilateral , isosceles , scalene , right angled etc

The above triangle was an example of scalene triangles

Similarly you can draw circles and ovals (ellipses)

draw_circle_color(x, y , radius , color1 , color2 , outline)

In the above function x , y are the co-ordinates of the centre.

ellipse can be drawn by the function

draw_ellipse_color (x1 , y1 , x2 , y2 , color1 , color2 , border)

Let us return back to primitives

To obtain texture from a sprite

sprite_get_texture(sprite_name , subimage_number)

subimage_number is the number of a particular subimage not the sum of all the subimages

The function sprite_get_texture would return the identification of the texture , the generated id is a numerical value

Note :- Textures may not necessarily be loaded in the graphics memory to graphics memory by

texture_preload(texture_id)

suppose you want to create a texture of the sprite 'kraken' (subimage 0) and add load it's id your code would be

texture_preload(sprite_get_texture(kraken ,   0))

Sometimes it may happen that there's an acute scarcity of graphics memory ,   in such a case Game Maker would unload some textures from the memory ,   to avoid such cases you can set priority to the textures

texture_set_priority(texture_id ,   priority)

When you program advanced level games you would require the size of the textures

texture_get_height(texture_id) :- Would return the height of the texture

texture_get_width(texture_id) :- Would return the width of the textures

To start a primitive with a particular texture use the function

draw_primitive_begin_texture(kind_of_primitive ,   texture_id)

You can specify texture blending by

texture_set_blending(boolean values)

If true the texture get's blended else not

texture_set_repeat(Boolean value)

The textre co-ordinates are always in the range nil to one ,   if the value is between 0 and 1 the remaining part is skipped if it's one full texture is drawn if it's more than 1 the additional part is the repetition of the previous one , you may also specify whether to use linear interpolation or not

texture_set_interpolation(Boolean value)

If true linear interpolation is set true ,   I would recommend try using linear interpolation if you are comfortable with linear interpolation use it else discontinue using it

Blending modes

Blending modes are of 4 types

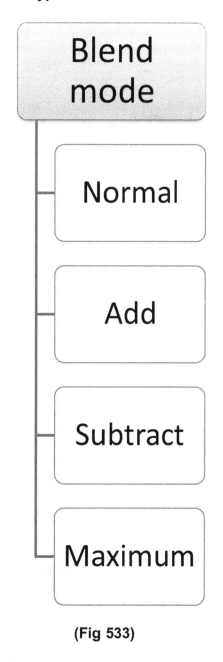

(Fig 533)

To specify the blend mode

draw_set_blend_mode(blend_mode)

Blend mode	Value (Constant to be more precise)
Normal	bm_normal

Add	bm_add
Subtract	bm_subtract
Maximum	bm_max

You have learnt the advanced functions for drawing Let us return back to 3D

d3d_primitive_begin_texture(primitive_type ,   texture_id) :- Used for beginning a 3D primitive of the given type with the specified texture

d3d_vertex_texture(x ,   y ,   z ,   x_texture ,   y_texture) :- Used for including the vertex   with the position (x ,   y,   z) to the primitive whose location in the texture is (x_texture ,   y_texture)

Note :- x_texture and y_texture must be in the range 0 to 1 ,   values > 1 are allowed but would lead to the repetition of the texture

Sometimes you have to specify a color for blending and an alpha value for blending this can be done by the function

d3d_vertex_texture_color(x ,   y ,   z ,   x_texture ,   y_texture ,   color ,   alpha_value)

Sometimes the other face of a shape is not visible in such case you can specify culling to avoid wastage of memory

d3d_set_culling (boolean value)

It is a must to learn the way to draw shapes in a game

Using Game Maker you can draw the following shapes

(Fig 534)

1)Block

2)Cone

3)Cylinder

4)Ellipsoid

5)Floor

6)Wall

Note :- In some cases the block may look like a rectangle (depending upon the co_ordinate values) but it is not true as a block has 3 dimensions

To draw a block

d3d_draw_block(x1 , y1 , z1 , x2 , y2 , z2 , texture_id , horizontal_repeat , vertical_repeat)

Note :- If you don't want to specify texture_id specify -1

2)horizontal_repeat means the number of times it must be repeated horizontally

3)vertical _repeat means the number of times it must be repeated vertically

To draw a cone

d3d_draw_cone(x1 , y1 , z1 , x2 , y2 , z2 , texture_id , horizontal_repeat , vertical_repeat , closed , steps)

Note :- closed is a Boolean value if true the cylinder is closed at the ends

steps :- I would recommend you try different values (experiment with different values) and select the one which suits your needs

To draw a cylinder

d3d_draw_cylinder(x1 , y1 , z1 , x2 , y2 , z2 , texture_id , horizontal_repeat , vertical_repeat , closed , steps)

To draw a ellipsoid

d3d_draw_ellipsoid(x1 , y1 , z1 , x2 , y2 , z2 , texture_id , horizontal_repeat , vertical_repeat , steps)

To draw a floor

d3d_draw_floor(x1 , y1 , z1 , x2 , y2 , z2 , texture_id , horizontal_repeat , vertical_repeat)

To draw a wall

d3d_draw_wall(x1 , y1 , z1 , x2 , y2 , z2 , texture_id , horizontal_repeat , vertical_repeat)

Projection

In a Game the way the world (terrain , creatures , other object , character) is shown is equally important (the figure 535 given below shows an isometric projection)

To set the position

d3d_set_projection(from_x , from_y , from_z , to_x , to_y , to_z , x_up , y_up , z_up)

There's a function which contains some extra parameters compared to this one d3d_set_projection_ext(from_x , from_y , from_z , to_x , to_y , to_z , x_up , y_up , z_up , angle_of_view , z_near_clipping , z_far_clipping)

Note :- To understand this completely you must possess some knowledge regarding vectors in 3-Dimensions and remember projection calculation can be complicated and you can use trigonometric functions sin(value) ,   cos(value) and others which are explained earlier

Sometimes you wish to return back to the projection used in 2-Dimensional Games ,   you can return to 2-Dimensional Games using the Function

Before beginning you must know that in Game Maker 2 types of projections are available for 2D

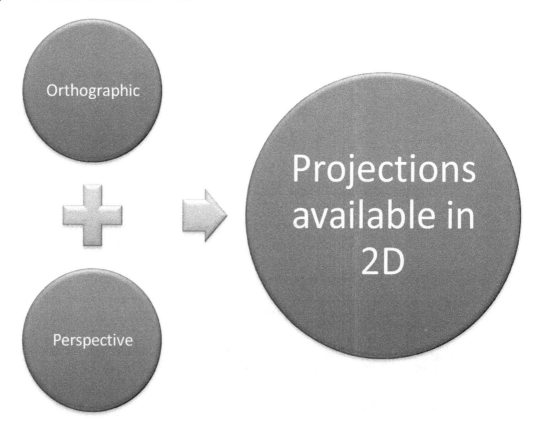

(Fig 536)

For setting orthographic projection

d3d_set_projection_ortho(x ,   y ,   width ,   height ,   angle)

For setting perspective projection

d3d_set_projection_perspective(x ,   y ,   width ,   height ,   angle)

Game Maker supports creation of fog in 3D mode

d3d_set_fog(enable ,   color ,   start ,   end)

enable :- This is a Boolean value

color :- color of the fog

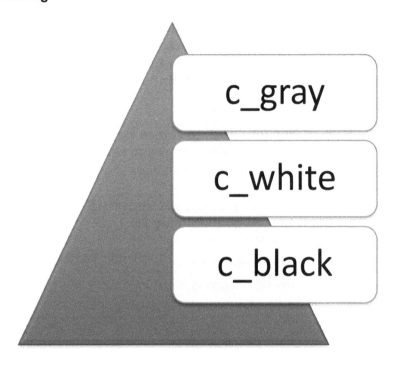

(Fig 537)

You must avoid trivial mistakes like yellow color fog etc

Sometimes in Games there's a need to rotate the world by an angle in such cases functions relating to Transformation are used

If you don't want transformation use the function

d3d_tranform_set_identitiy()

Sometimes there's a need to transform translation by a vector in such cases the function d3d_transform_set_translation(x , y , z)

You can even scale the translation

d3d_transform_set_scaling(x , y , z)

To rotate around the x-axis by a particular angle use the function

d3d_transform_set_rotation_x(angle)

Along the y axis

d3d_transform_set_rotation_y(angle)

Along the z axis

d3d_transform_set_rotation_z(angle)

To set transformation by a particular amount

d3d_transform_set_rotation_axis(x ,   y ,   z ,   angle)

To add translation

d3d_transform_add_translation(x ,   y ,   z)

To add scaling

d3d_transform_add_scaling(x ,   y ,   z)

To add rotation along x axis

d3d_transform_add_rotation_x(angle)

To add rotation along y axis

d3d_transform_add_rotation_y(angle)

To add rotation along z axis

d3d_transform_add_rotation_z(angle)

To add rotation by a particular amount

d3d_transform_add_rotation_axis(x ,   y ,   z ,   angle)

Note :- Transformations can be saved for later use to save transformation you have to push it in a stack ,   this can be done using the function

d3d_transform_stack_push()

Sometimes you want to clear the stack memory ,   in such cases you can use the function

d3d_transform_stack_clear()

Sometimes there's a need to check whether the stack is empty of filled ,   to check the stack you can use the function

d3d_transform_stack_empty()

Note :- This function would return a Boolean value depending upon whether the stack is empty or not

Using a transformation is also known as popping ,   can be done by the function

d3d_transform_stack_pop()

Stacks are like the arrangement of floors in a building

Suppose Fig 538 is the building

(Fig 538)

To make the top of the stack as your transformation use the code

d3d_transform_stack_top()

To remove the top transformation use the function

d3d_transform_stack_discard()

Lighting

Lighting is an important part of 3D effects ,   Game Make supports many functions dealing with lighting

1st thing you must enable the use of lighting using the function

d3d_set_lighting_enable(Boolean value)

Use 1 for enabling and 0 for disabling

Game Maker supports smooth shading ,   for activating smooth shading use the function

d3d_set_shading(Boolean value)

Let the value be 1

To define the direction for the light use the function

d3d_light_define_direction(index ,   x ,   y ,   z ,   color_of_the_light)

Note :- Index can be any real value , (x , y , z) is the direction.

Game Supports point light , to use point light call the function

d3d_light_define_point(index , x , y , z , range , color_of_the_light)

Note :- range means the distance the light can travel

Sometimes you don't want to end the effect put the light of a particular index , in hat case you can use the function

d3d_light_enable(index , Boolean value)

For disabling a particular index let the Boolean value be 0

Models

What are models ?

Models are shapes or figures

Game Maker supports the creation of model

Example

Fig 539 is a model

(Fig 539)

Note :- You must not expect the creation of such models , it's just an example , the meaning of model changes with every Game Programming software

2)Model may not necessarily be an animate object

To create a model

d3d_model_create() :- This function would create a new model and return it's index ,   this index should be used as a parameter value for other functions

Clearing a model

d3d_model_clear()

Deleting a model

d3d_model_destroy()

Drawing a model

d3d_model_draw(index ,   x ,   y ,   z ,   texture_id)

Note :- Id -1 means no texture

Saving a model

d3d_model_save(index_of_model ,   file_name)

Loading a saved model

d3d_model_load(index_of_model ,   file_name)

To use a model in 3D a primitive must be added

d3d_model_primitive_begin(index ,   type_of_primitive)

For the type_of_primitive observe Figure 525

Ending the primitive

d3d_model_primitive_end() // No parameters

To add a vertex to the model

d3d_model_vertex(index ,   x ,   y ,   z)

To add a colored a vertex

d3d_model_vertex_color(index ,   x ,   y ,   z ,   color ,   alpha)

Vertex with texture

d3d_model_vertex_texture(index ,   x ,   y ,   z ,   x_texture , y_texture)

Vertex with texture color

d3d_model_vertex_texture_color(index , x, y , z , x_texture ,
y_texture , color , alpha)

Normal Vertex

d3d_model_vertex_normal(index , x , y , z , vector_x , vector_y
, vector_z)

Normal colored vertex

d3d_model_vertex_normal_color(index , x , y , z , vector_x ,
vector_y , vector_z , color , alpha)

Normal texture

d3d_model_vertex_normal_texture(index , x , y , z , vector_x ,
vector_y , vector_z , x_texture , y_texture)

Normal colored texture

d3d_model_vertex_normal_texture_color(index , x , y , z ,
vector_x , vector_y , vector_z , x_texture , y_texture , color ,
alpha)

You can even add shapes to the primitives , by the code

d3d_model_model-name(index_of_the_model , other parameters)

For example

d3d_model_block(index , x1 , y1 , z1 , x2 , y2 , z2 ,
horizontal_repeat , vertical_repeat)

**Note :- You must not expect creating your own GTA , as these
functions are quite limited in their functionality , they look
complicated but are still the basic of programming 3D games , you
will have to learn much more than these for creating games like GTA ,
Empire Earth , NFS series etc**

Chapter 20 Creating the executable and selling your Game

When you distribute your Game you would not like others to make changes in your games and you would definitely like to distribute your game to those who don't own Game Maker , for distribution you can create an executable file (.exe) which can be executed on any computer (running any version of windows) irrespective of whether Game Maker is installed on it or not

Before proceeding Let us open Global Game Settings

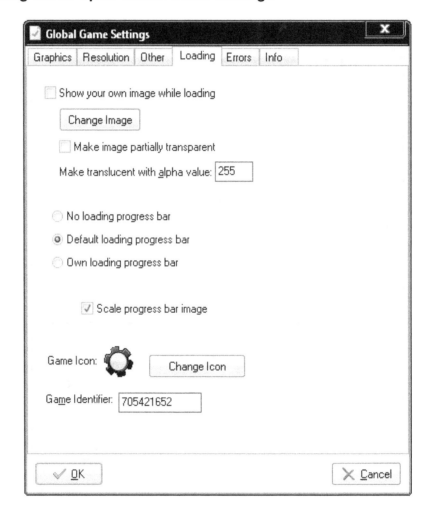

(Fig 540)

Change certain settings (For example Icon , Identifier , Image) etc .

Note :- If you create a new version of any Game it's not advisable to use the same identifier as they may create problems by overwriting high scores of each other or affecting each other in multiplayer games

Select Resolution and settings

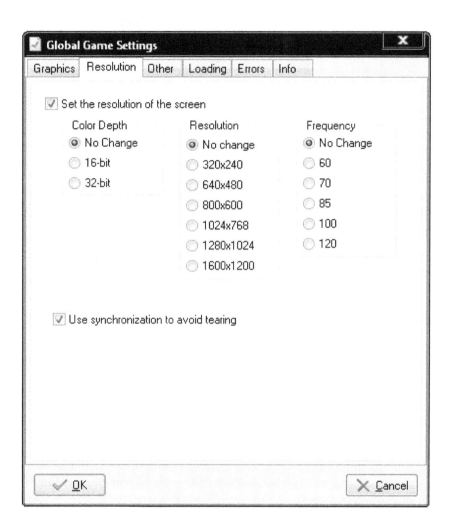

(Fig 541)

Note :- Do not use resolution of 1600x1200 or 1280x1024 as such resolutions consume a major part of the systems memory and also do not use frequencies of 100 mhz (Mega Hertz ,   100 frames per second) or more as few monitors may not support such high frequencies

Graphics

It is better to use of Full-Screen Mode

If you are using windowed mode allow the player to resize the

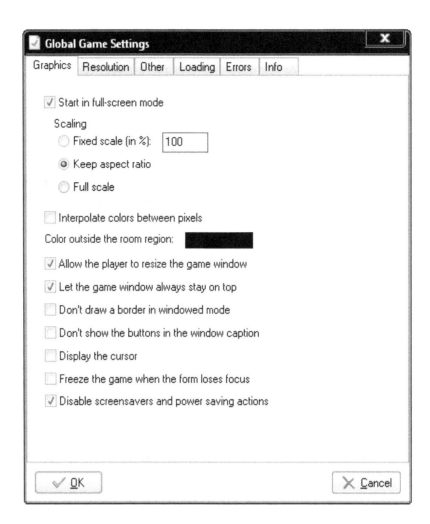

Fig 542)

window , let the window stay on top of the others , draw a border and show the buttons and don't display the cursor

Others

Here you can specify version , company and copyright info

You must copyright your Game so as to prevent others form copying it , copyrighting your game ensures the ownership of your game , to copyright your Game you can call or write to the trademark office of U.S.A (in the US copyright office is located in Washington DC)

The address is as follows

U.S.Department of Commerce ,

Patent and Trademark Office

Washington D.C 20231

(703)308-4357

Copyrighting a ame is a good way of protecting your Game but still there are possibilities of Piracy which cannot be avoided , In many countries across the globe , pirated softwares are available at a price which is approximately equal to 1/10th of the original price

The reasons for using pirated softwares are

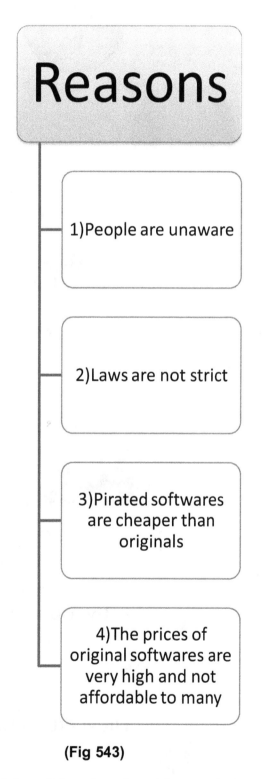

Reasons

1)People are unaware

2)Laws are not strict

3)Pirated softwares are cheaper than originals

4)The prices of original softwares are very high and not affordable to many

(Fig 543)

Even software giant Microsoft has faced problems relating to loss of revenues due to piracy

To recover lost revenues software firms increase the prices of their software and the result is more piracy due to increase in price , thus we are trapped in a vicious circle

(Fig 544)

Ways to stop piracy (Fig 545 given below)

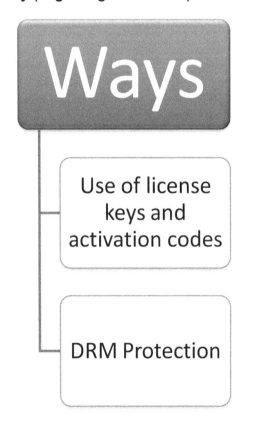

Use of License Keys and Activation codes

(Fig 546)

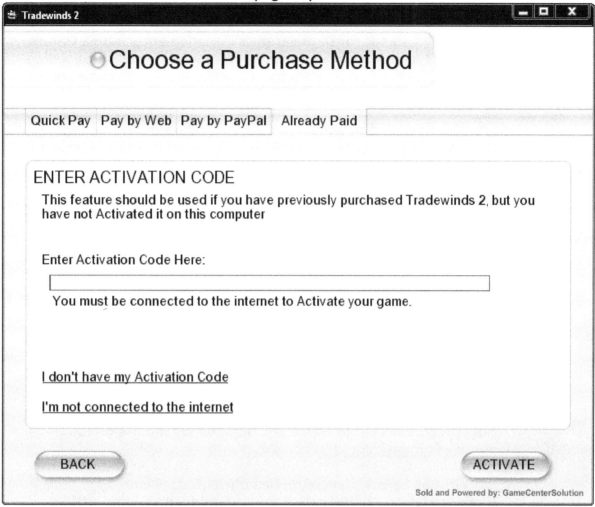

Note :- There is a difference between license key and activation code , license key is the one used during the installation process and activation code is used for activating an installed program or upgrading it (For example :- From Game Maker Lite to Game Maker Pro)

2)The license Key is usually provided in the pack

Tip :- It is not advised to use the same key for a particular ,   many companies provide unique license keys to all the Cd's of the same game

2)License Key is generally of the format

X86O-D3R5-KO94-FCX3

Note :- You must avoid the alphabet 'O' as the user may confuse between the alphabet 'Capital o' and zero

DRM Protection

DRM stands for Digital Rights Management, some Games don't start unless the user doesn't enter the original Compact disc into the CD/DVD drive, some of these games can be fooled by using virtual discs using (.iso) copy of the discs, Daemon Tools is one such software for creating virtual Discs, so some companies program in such a way that the Game would not install unless Daemon Tools is removed, this is not a proper remedial method as there are many more which allow the creation of virtual discs, if a Game is DRM protected that Game cannot be fooled by using a virtual disc this method is secure than the earlier one but not full proof as it can be cracked, but cracking a DRM protected disc requires a lot of manpower, time and programming skills

Once you program your Game you want others to buy and use your game, but for buying others must know your product, you can release the trial version of your Game on the internet.

Note :- Here Game Maker comes to your rescue

Game Maker Let us you publish your game online so that others can play your game

Note :- To publish your Game you must be logged in (on the website www.yoyogames.com)

and / or you can share your games through sites like RapidShare(www.rapidshare.com) or American-OnLine(AOL , www.aol.com), softwares shared through websites like these are known as sharewares

Note :- The success of your product depends upon the type of product , market demand, your efforts and your luck

You must know the principle 'If there's no need you must create it'

Note :- The Game must be tempting for the users to buy it

Advertising through the internet is the most powerful means of mass communication, If your Game is too good it would be advertised automatically, and if your game is too impressive, Gaming parlor owners may approach you for buying the rights of your game, one more method of advertising is to send your game sample to magazines on Gaming or Tech Games who review PC and / or Console Games, their team would play your game, and if they like it's obvious that the rating of your game would increase

Note :- Generally the highest point of rating is 5

You can even design your game in such a way that it stops working after a particular time period elapses for example 60 minutes

(Fig 547)

Or you may use the strategy used by the Creator of Game Maker , 'Disable some features of the softwares ,   enable them only when the user buys it'

Nowadays there are many ways of paying online ,   you can adopt any one or more of them or receiving payments

1)Paypal

Note :- You must possess a valid paypal account

2)Credit Cards

Note :- Some companies adopt a different strategy ,   they would invite you to visit their website and would ask you to review certain games of theirs and would equest you to provide feedback ,   after receiving your feedback they would grant you points depending upon the Game tested ,   your feedback and of course their wish and when you collect a particular number of points they would give you a game

2)In the above technique the company uses the person for testing their products and in return gives a game

But remember you have to provide 1000's of feedbacks after testing 1000's of Games for acquiring a game

Note :- The points earned may expire after a particular time , read the terms and conditions before use

You can adopt any of the above techniques.

If you distribute your Game as a shareware the user's are supposed to pay for continuing the use of your product , but there's no way a programmer can force them to pay , so you can adopt any of the following methods

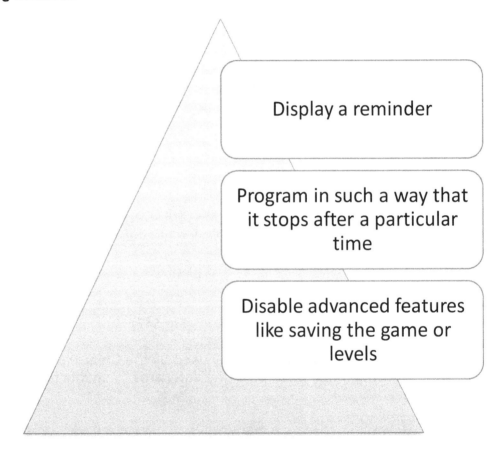

Display a reminder

Program in such a way that it stops after a particular time

Disable advanced features like saving the game or levels

(Fig 548)

You must encourage consumers to use original copy of your product by providing incentives like updates , patches , demos of new games , trailers of new releases , support and much more.

Support

Many types of systems are available in the market and new ones arrive each day , so a particular software runs differently on different machines , the world in which we are living is imperfect , sometimes the users unknowingly delete some files required for the game to run smoothly , so there is always a chance that someone has encountered an error , no matter how may times you have tested your game on how many machines , errors do exist , so you must provide appropriate support for your Game

You can adopt any of the following methods depending upon your volume of business, affordability , convenience of your as well as others etc

24x7 support by phone

Support through e-mail

Support through Fax

Toll Free number

Through Companies website

(Fig 549)

You may select any one of them or more depending upon your capacity and the quality of support you want to give, you must know how to handle aggrieved customers and you must try your best to ensure them that their problem would be solved.

When someone approaches you with a problem you must ask certain questions for analyzing the reason of the error , you must ask the following question

(Fig 550)

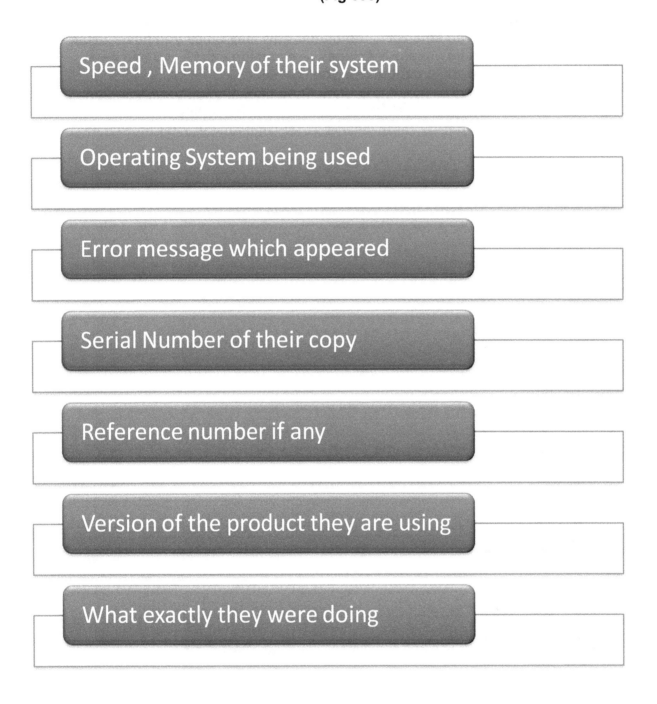

Speed , Memory of their system

Operating System being used

Error message which appeared

Serial Number of their copy

Reference number if any

Version of the product they are using

What exactly they were doing

Tip :- Operating system is the windows version being used by them

What is a reference number ?

Suppose you create a Game and distribute it , you allot different serial numbers for different copies of the Game , suppose a person uses the same serial number on many machines and distributes the serial number and the copy to his friends you would never know , in that case you can create a separate number known as the reference number , for that you have to program in a way that it generates an unique hardware key , the user has to provide you his serial number and hardware number , then you will provide him his reference number , the product must be designed in such a way that it would unlock itself only after the proper combination of the 3 keys , in this manner each system will generate different hardware keys and you would prevent someone from using the 3 key combination as it would be valid for only 1 system , this is also known as registering the application

Note :- This is a bit difficult to program in Game Maker

There's a possibility that someone using a pirated copy would call you up for support in such a case you have to decide whether you must take any legal action or refuse support

Types of Licenses

When you buy a disc you don't buy the software , you buy a single right to install it and run it on a single machine , buying the software means buying the rights , what you own is the right to use it on 1 system you don't possess any right to change/modify it and distribute it , these terms are specified in the license agreement of any software

Before understanding licenses let me tell you a story

In the earlier years computers ran the UNIX operating system , MS-Dos or Windows was not available at that time even Apple Macintosh was unavailable in those days , a professor at the Vrije Universiteit Amsterdam cloned Unix and created an operating system Minix , at that time the programming of GNU was in progress , GNU was the first attempt for creating a fully free software (here free doesn't mean the price it means the freedom to modify , share and sell) , the source code and derivative works were free to all , it's license was such that no one could every pirate it , as copying it and selling it was allowed , but due to technical problems this project was stopped , GNU was an unsuccessful attempt but the positive side of the coin is it's philosophy spread far and wide , then a programming student Linus Torvalds who was not satisfied with the operating system he was using , started creating drivers and finally created an operating system of his own today that operating system is known as Linux , he released his code under the License which was created for GNU , later on this license came to be known as the GNU/GPL license , as Linux is based on GNU/GPL license many distributions of Linux have been formed , such software which are free (freedom to modify , share) are now known as Open-Source Software

There are 3 Types of Licenses

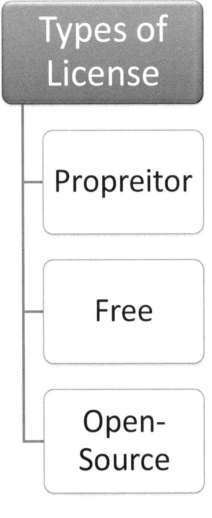

(Fig 551)

Note :- There is a major difference between free software and open-source software ,   the table given below explains everything about Free software license and opensource software license

Difference	Free Software	Open-source software
Price	Free	Free
Right to distribute	Yes	Yes
Right to change / upgrade / modify	No	Yes
Can charge for distributing	No	Yes , you can charge for the cost of disk and the cost of copying

Source available	No	Yes
Dialog box for donations	Yes	No
Anyone can contribute	No	Yes
Updates available	Depends on the creator	Yes
Right to decompile	No	Yes But there's no need as the source is provided with the software
Support Available	May be	There are open-source communities on the internet where discussions take place and problems are solved

Some of the Free softwares stop after a specified time and request for donations , but free softwares don't , from the above comparison we can conclude that Open-Source software License is more free than Free software license.

Note :- Even though Open-source softwares are free they are at par with their paid counterparts

Let us compare proprietor software license with open-source ones

Difference	Proprietor Software	Open-source software
Price	Depends upon the company	Free
Right to distribute	No	Yes
Right to change / upgrade / modify	No	Yes
Can charge for distributing	No , even distribution is not allowed	Yes , you can charge for the cost of disk and the cost of copying

Source available	No	Yes
Dialog box for donations or charges	No , provided that you are using the paid version	No
Anyone can contribute	No	Yes
Updates available	Yes	Yes
Right to decompile	No	Yes But there's no need as the source is provided with the software
Support Available	Yes	There are open-source communities on the internet where discussions take place and problems are solved

Now it's your choice , you can choose from any one of the above license.

Note :- Even Open-source softwares must be copyright protected , as someone may copyright the source and declare the code as his work.

Creating the standalone executable file

Reminder :- Before creating the executable check whether you have all the required rights to use the resources in your Game.

Note :- When you use a .lib (library) file or a .gex (extension package) or any other included file , that file is automatically merged with the executable , you don't have to provide them separately

Note :- INI files should not be listed in the included file

To create an executable , follow the procedure given below

1) Open the File Menu

2) Select Create Executable

A Browse window would appear on the screen

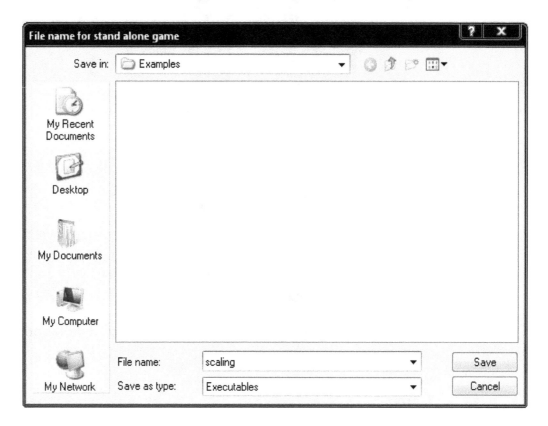

(Fig 552)

Save the executable at an appropriate location

Distributing the game

During the discussion of license keys we skipped on part which will be dealt with here,   license keys are of two types (Fig 553 given below)

License Keys

Incorporated in the setup :- Incorporated in the setup means the application would not be installed unless the proper key is provided

Incorporated in the game :- Incorporated in the game means the game would be installed but would not run unless proper license key is provided

My Recommendation :- Use the second one as you can add an option for using the demo / trial version of the game or can program hardware and system keys

Tip :- License Keys are also known as Serial Keys

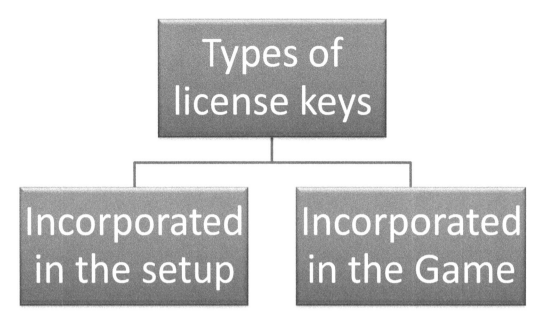

We are going to use CreateInstall Free for creating installations as

Is free

License is better than others

Many Features

Can be legally distributed

Setups work smoothly without any hassles

Supports 7 types of compression algorithms

Supports 36 Languages

(Fig 554)

Note :- CreateInstall Free doesn't allow you to incorporate serial keys in the setup , this feature may be available in the later versions (versions released after version 4.14.5.0 of create install Free

Note :- We will use version 4.14.5.0 of create install free in this book , you can use later version of the program if available or use any other setup creation program for creating setups for your game , I

personally have no objection but you must see to it that you are comfortable with it

Note :- When you distribute a game you must always distribute it in the form of setups , as setups look presentable , setups compress the size of the application and decompresses it during installation

Before Learning CreateInstall Free Let us install it , remember the steps carefully as you are going to learn how to create setups , the Installation procedure of the setups which you create would be similar to the installation process of CreateInstall Free

Note :- Create Install Free can be downloaded from www.createinstall.com

Execute the file cifree.exe

(Fig 555)

This is the main window even your setups should start with such an window , you don't have to type (Warning , Info etc)anything CreateInstall Free will handle almost everything for you. (Press Next >)

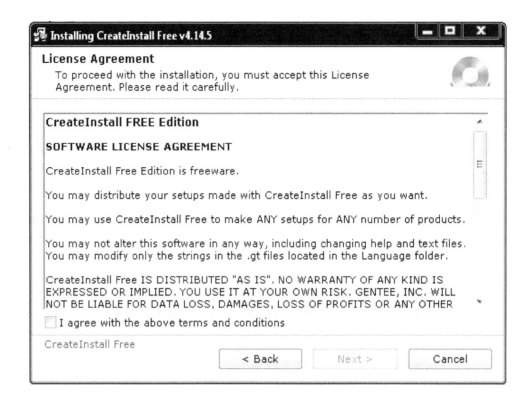

(Fig 556)

You must agree to all the terms or else the Next > button would not be enabled , this window is known as the License window , even your setups should have a License Window , to proceed select the checkbox 'I agree ....' as shown in Fig 557 given below

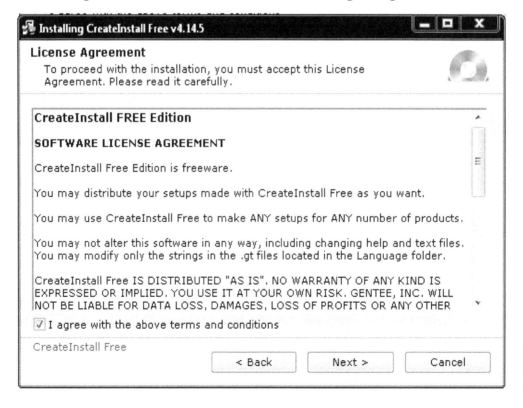

Press Next > , Fig 558 would appear

(Fig 558)

This the destination folder window , you can change the folder in which you want to save the Software (This setup shows the space available and the space required , this is like the cherry on top of the cake) Press Next >

Before Proceeding you must know the importance of a progress bar

A progress bar is a bar which is divided into 100 parts one for each percent , many a times it happen that the software is processing but the end user feels that it has stopped working and has hanged , this should never happen as this demotivates the end user from using your product , a progress bar displays the progress of the application and due to a progress bar the user knows that it's working and processing he even knows the progress of the softwares activity

Some examples of progress bars are given below

(Fig 559)   (Fig 560)

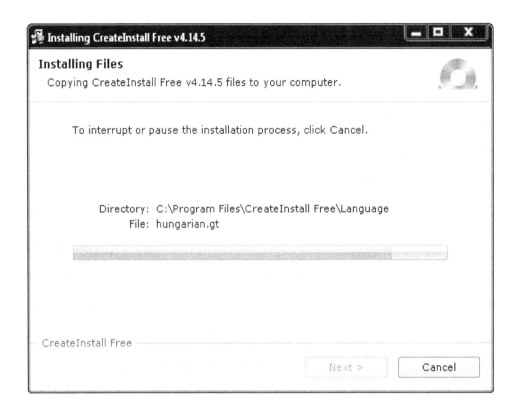

(Fig561 , the progress is being shown)

(Fig 562)

Note :- If your games requires a lot of registry entries it is better to program in such a way that the setup would request the user to restart the system

Create Install Free would now start

CreateInstall Free - C:\Program Files\CreateInstall Free\Projects\demo.ci*

Project Setup Options Tools Help

Demo

Output

General

Dialogs

Files

Registry

Shortcuts

To Register

Run

Uninstall

Advanced

Setup Output

Output Folder: * c:\setups

Setup Executable: * setup.exe

Setup Icon: Default

Volumes

☑ Create Self-Extracting Setup

Type: No Limit

Volume Size:

Volume Filename Pattern: disk%i.pak

(Fig 563)

Note :- The textboxes marked with red * are necessary to fill

The features of this application are divided into 10 parts

1)Output ,   2)General ,   3)Dialog,   ………………………, 10)Advanced

We will discuss each of them in the order in which they appear

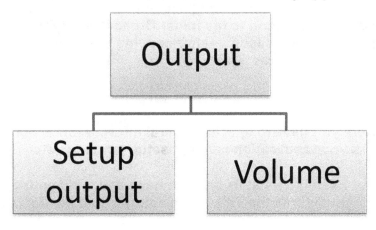

I) Setup Output

Sr No	Field (Textbox)	Use
1)	Output Folder	Here you have to specify the path where your generated setup file must be saved Note :- The default is 'C:\setups'
2)	Setup Executable	The name of the setup file Note :- It must end with the extension .exe
3)	Setup Icon	Here you can select any of the icon of your choice for your setup

(Fig 565)

Note :- If you want to add an icon of your own you can add one by copying your icon to the folder Create Install Free's path\Resources\Icon , after copying the icon you must start CreateInstall Free again

General

Here you have to specify general information about your application like your application name , setup language etc

For Example :- Let us say you have specified your application name as Adventures the Title of the setup would be ' Installing Adventures'

(Fig 566)

Sr No	Field	Uses
1)	Picture Theme	You can select any of the preinstalled themes for creating your setup
2)	Custom Logo Picture	This is the picture which would be shown in the top right corner of the window Observe the top-right corner of Fig 566
3)	Custom Left Picture	This is the picture shown on the left hand side of the window Observe the Left Hand Side of Figure 562

Note :- You don't have to check any of the runtime packages as you don't need them ,   only Visual Basic and MSData Access programmers require them

Header Text :- This is the text or bitmap which would be shown in the upper left corner   of the setup

Footer Text :- This is the text or bitmap which would be shown in the upper left corner   of the setup

Dialogs :- Here you specify settings for dialog boxes

Dialog Font :- Here you can change the size and font for the dialog (Fig 567) below

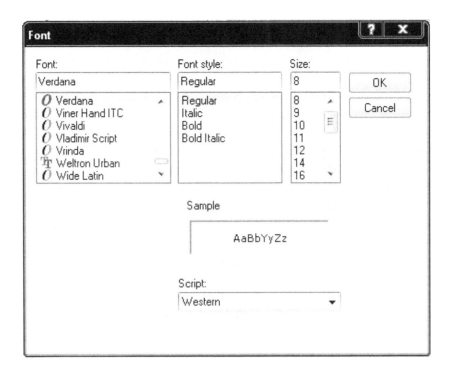

Show Dialog :-
If you check this box the introductory dialog is shown like Fig 568 below

Sr No	Field	Use
1)	Readme File	Here you have to specify the readme file Note :- CreateInstall Supports .txt and .rtf format Tip :- You should add a readme file and specify

		the type of game and the basic information
2)	License File	You can use GNU/GPL license or create your own. Note :- License must include the year of copyright and copyright holders name 2)If you don't specify the license the license window will not be shown
3)	Setup Path	Here you have to specify the default path for your setup Note :- Path must be in the format C:\Program Files\Your Company's name\Name of your Game\

Below these fields two checkboxes are provided

1)Enforce Path :- If the path is enforced the user will not be able to change the path for installation , It is best that the user decide the path for installation , don't enforce the path

2)Save path for subsequent Updates :- The path would be saved for updates , you may check this option

The later 2 checkboxes must always be checked for better setup files

Files

Here you can select additional files if any and the compression method

Note :- INI files must not be included here .

Tip :- A detailed comparison of speeds , file-size of the compression algorithms is provided on the next page

Note :- you may select any of the compression methods which suits your needs after studying the chart given below

Sr No	Name	Compression	Speed
1)	Default Fast	Less	Better than many
2)	Default Normal	Balanced by the program	Depending upon the balancing Note :- In this mode the program would select the

			ratio of compressed file:decompressed file itself
3)	Default Maximum	More than the previous ones	Slower than the previous ones
4)	PPMD Fast	Less	Slower than Default Fast
5)	PPMD Normal	Balanced by the program	Depends upon the balancing
6)	PPMD Maximum	Highest	Slowest
7)	Store	No compression	Fastest

From the above table you may have concluded that compression and speed are inversely proportional to each other

Source Folder :- Here you have to add files (Fig 569 below)

Note :- Here you can add only folder , all the folders and the subfolders would be copied as they were in the original folder

You can even add files from Additional Files

(Fig 570)

Path :- Here 5 options are available you can select any one of them.

Note :- Nor you nor the user has to tell the installer where the windows or the system path is it would automatically search for you

You can even specify what must happen if the file already exists

Sr No	Name	Meaning
1)	Ask	Would prompt a message and ask the user what must happen
2)	Ask if newer	It would ask the user only if the new file is created after the original file
3)	Overwrite	It would simply overwrite the old file with the new one
4)	Overwrite if newer	It would overwrite the original file only if it's newer else it would leave the original file as it is
5)	Skip	It wouldn't do anything , just skip that particular file and copy the others

Registry :- Here you can specify registry settings if any

Press the add a new item [Insert] button

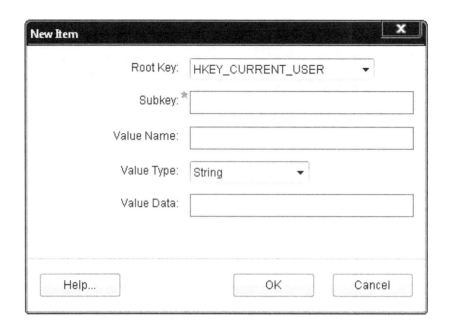

(Fig 571)

Shortcuts :- Here you can specify shortcuts if any

The target folder can be any one of the following 8

Sr No	Destination Folder	Meaning
1)	Common Desktop	The shortcut will be copied to the desktops of all the users irrespective of the user who has installed your game
2)	Common Program Group	The shortcut will be copied to the program group of all the users
3)	Common Startup	The shortcut will be copied to the startup of all the users Note :- If this is selected your program will start as soon as the system is powered on
4)	Custom Path	Avoid using this one as it is too complicated and is not required in majority of the cases
5)	Desktop	Shortcut is copied to the desktop of the user who has installed your game
6)	Program Group	Shortcut is copied to the program group of the user who has installed your game
7)	Quick Launch	Shortcut is copied to the quick launch folder
8)	Startup	Shortcut is copied to the startup folder of the user who has installed your game

Shortcut Name

You have to specify the shortcut name ,   example :- Adventurer

Note :- Don't write Adventurer.lnk

Tip :- .lnk extension stands for links (In this case Short Cut links)

Target File

This is the file whose shortcut is created , you can choose from any of the folder available

Note :- Filename is the name of the file whose executable is created , For example Adventurer.exe

Command Line Parameters

Used for giving commands through command line if any

Note :- With Game Maker you cannot create programs which can be accessed through command-line

To Register

Used for registering extensions

Note :- Game Maker doesn't support command line arguments so you don't need this one

Tip :- You don't have to register Fonts as they are incorporated in the .exe file

Run

You can specify any application which should be executed after the installation is complete

If you check 'Run installed Application' an option would be available to the player for running the game as soon as the installation is complete (Observe Fig 562)

Uninstall

Note :- You must never uncheck the checkbox 'Include Uninstaller' as an installer is a must at the same time you must not check the box 'Create Uninstall Shortcut'

Here you can also specify any application to be executed before the actual un-installation begins.

Note :- You don't need the above feature , the above feature is used by softwares which creates a large amount of temporary files , the application which is executed clears the temp folder

Tip :- The uninstaller would wait till the executed program stops

Note :- Don't uncheck the checkboxes in the dialogs part

Here you can add INI files which you would like to distribute with your Game

Tip :- If you want to reboot the user's machine select macros and type reboot = 1 ,   this will set reboot to true

Note :- Setups made by CreateInstall Free cannot force users for rebooting even if reboot = 1 ,   it would politely request the user to reboot ,   a message would be shown like Fig 573

(Fig 573)

It's obvious that if the user selects 'No' the system would not be restarted

Creating the setup

For creating the setup just press F5 a window would appear like Fig 574

(Fig 574)

This window shows the processing done.

Note :- If you use maximum compression then the time required for creating the setup is also more

> **Congratulations you have learned many concepts of Game Maker, Basic Animation and the ways of Packaging and Selling games , now you can call yourself a Basic Game Programmer (Even If you learn everything associated with Game Maker and become one of the masters of Game Maker , do not stop your journey over here as this was just one milestone , there are many more milestones and many more hurdles in the world of Game Programming so keep learning to be an Advanced Game Programmer one day or the other)**

HAPPY GAMING!!

This chapter ends over here

www.ingramcontent.com/pod-product-compliance
Lightning Source LLC
Chambersburg PA
CBHW080547060326
40689CB00021B/4770